T0305260

If I marry my housekeeper,
national income will decrease

(Phrase used by many economists
and attributed to as many)

The Economics of
the Family and
Family Policy

Francisco Cabrillo

Professor of Economics, Universidad Complutense, Madrid, Spain

Edward Elgar

Cheltenham, UK • Northampton, MA, USA

First published in Spanish as *Matrimonio, Familia y Economía*
by Minerva Ediciones, Madrid
© Francisco Cabrillo 1996

English Translation © Francisco Cabrillo 1999
Translated from the Spanish edition by Jennifer McDonald

Published by
Edward Elgar Publishing Limited
Glensanda House
Montpellier Parade
Cheltenham
Glos GL50 1UA
UK

Edward Elgar Publishing Company
6 Market Street
Northampton
Massachusetts 01060
USA

A catalogue record for this book is available from the British Library

Library of Congress Cataloguing in Publication Data
Cabrillo, Francisco, 1950–
    [Matrimonio, familia y economía. English]
    The economics of the family and family policy/Francisco Cabrillo
; [translated by Jennifer McDonald].
    Includes bibliographical references and index.
    1. Family—Economic aspects. 2. Family size—Economic aspects.
3. Family policy. 4. Marriage. I. Title.
HQ18.C313   1999
306.85—dc21   98–18611
                                                      CIP

ISBN 1 85898 828 4

Printed and bound in Great Britain by
MPG Books Ltd, Bodmin, Cornwall

Contents

List of figures

List of tables

Preface

Although much has been written on the economics of the family, very few works give a general overview of the subject and this has been my aim in this book. With such a broad field to cover, it has been necessary to drastically limit the topics broached. My purpose has been to analyse the family of today, that is, a family comprising a man and a woman who have married and who, in most cases, have children. Other types of family structure, such as the traditional extensive family or homosexual couples, are excluded not because economic analysis cannot be applied to such groups or partnerships, but because they carry less specific weight in present-day society. The reader will find some references to institutions that are of little relevance today such as polygamy or the bride price, but these are included by way of introduction to the analysis of certain problems or to assist in explaining the overall validity of certain forms of behaviour under different institutional conditions. Although the elderly do not form part of the nuclear family in the strict sense, a whole chapter is devoted to them and there are many references to the situation of the elderly in the chapter on inheritance. The reason for including such subjects is obviously their enormous relevance in the modern western world.

The family is studied in this book using the basic methodology of economic theory: the analysis of conduct for utility maximization in people whose aim is to achieve the greatest possible satisfaction with limited resources and imperfect information. This method of maximization under constraints has been seen to be very fruitful in the analysis of all types of economic behaviour and can also be usefully applied to the study of the family. In many cases, this approach is complemented with the use of game theory. Since the main objective of this theory is to analyse strategic types of conduct, it seems suitable for the study of certain short and long-term behaviour within the family. It also allows the emphasis to be placed on a matter that I consider to be of fundamental importance – the logical basis for cooperation in a small organization such as the family in which the incentives for altruistic conduct are greater than in any other social group.

With a view to reaching both economists and laypeople, I have written the book on two levels that can be perfectly distinguished within the text by the size of the type used. Most of the sections give economic reasoning, although without any type of formal or graphic elements, so they should be accessible to all readers. The texts printed in smaller type, however, do include some graphic and formal analysis of the sort that is commonly found in texts on economics. These mathematical and graphic tools, however, are very limited and I believe, and hope, that they can be understood by anyone who has studied the rudiments of microeconomics. I would recommend that these sections be read by all readers, even if they are not economists, not only because they might discover approaches or solutions that are likely to be new to them, but also because many of the most important ideas in the book can be best understood if the work is read in its entirety. I hope the glossary will help any non-economists to cope with the technical terms that crop up in the text and to understand the more specialized sections.

In the preparation of this book, I have received valuable assistance from several Spanish institutions which have helped to finance some of the research, especially that covered in the chapters on family policy. These are the Instituto de la Mujer, the Instituto de Estudios Fiscales, the Fundación para el Análisis y los Estudios Sociales and the Universidad Complutense de Madrid. I would also like to express my thanks to some of my colleagues in the Universidad Complutense and the Universidad de Cantabria who had the necessary patience to read the book intensively. Their comments were of great use in improving the text, completing the arguments and clarifying the ideas. Special mention should be made of Professors Antonio Bustos, Fernando Gómez, Carmen González de Aguilar and Pablo Vázquez. Cristina Castro has at all times been an efficient research assistant and she provided invaluable help in compiling the bibliography and the index. I am, however, most indebted to María Luisa Cachafeiro without whose help I could never have written the book. Some of the most important ideas covered in it are really more hers than mine and I only regret not having been able to present them with the brilliance they deserve.

1. Economists and the family

1 THE ECONOMICS OF NON-MERCANTILE CONDUCT

One of the most remarkable characteristics of economics towards the close of the twentieth century is its scope. Far from dealing only with strictly 'economic' problems – market and price analysis, money, banking or economic cycles – economists today do not think twice about studying matters that are far from their usual fields, such as the behaviour of politicians, the efficiency of law, family life or drug addiction. This is the 'imperialism of economists', welcomed by some as a first step towards a unified social science based on the theory of rational choice,[1] and rejected by others as unacceptable interference in the study of human conduct which, say the critics, has nothing to do with the rationality and maximization of utility that economists assume.

But there is nothing new in economists showing interest in human behaviour and the institutions that govern society. The origin of their interest goes back to the very birth of economics as a scientific discipline. To give one well-known example, Adam Smith, who was a Professor of moral philosophy and law, dealt fully with the role of the institutions in economic development both in *The Wealth of Nations* and in other works.[2] This trend continued with classic economics. And it is no surprise that John Stuart Mill, for example, should have devoted several pages of his *Principles of Political Economy* to subjects such as education, the legal protection of children or the ways in which property is transmitted within a family.[3] But, in the last decades of the nineteenth century, when economic science was becoming established as an independent discipline, separate from moral philosophy, economists gradually lost interest in the study of these problems and it was only in the second half of the twentieth century that they were to turn once more to such matters.

The variety of subjects now falling under the title of 'new political economy' leads to an important problem. What do all these studies have in common if they deal with such apparently unrelated topics such as criminality, the family, political life or the environment. The answer is simply that they apply the same methodology, that of economic analysis.

For a long time economists have studied human behaviour as a decision-making process under conditions of imperfect information. In economic life, every person or company tries to achieve the best possible results in their investments or business, and their attempts are made with limited resources in an environment that is often unfavourable and difficult. The method used by economists, which analyses the maximization of utility functions that are subject to restrictions, therefore, seems very appropriate for the reality of economic life.

But is it only suitable for economic activities? Why should a method that is valid for studying problems of wages or investments not also be useful for analysing other human activities? The economists who today specialize in the economics of politics, the family or law consider that their method can also serve to throw light on other aspects of human behaviour.

Such work, as was only to be expected, has been subject to much criticism. Is it possible, the critics say, to apply the techniques of economic analysis to the study of the behaviour of a criminal or to such strictly personal matters as the organization of family life? There is no doubt that at first sight some of the conclusions reached by the economists studying these matters may seem surprising. But if we look closer, this type of analysis can give a more coherent explanation of human behaviour than the traditional approach. And whereas the new theory offers a unified view of such behaviour in which people's conduct in all activities follows similar principles, the traditional approach implicitly presupposes that there is a dichotomy which is not easy to explain, namely that under certain circumstances man acts to maximize his selfish interests whereas under others his objectives may be different or he may even act irrationally.

However, the value of a theory should not be judged by its postulates. If this type of analysis can be used to predict human behaviour more accurately than other methods, the facts will show that such analysis is valid, even if its assumptions seem to some people to be debatable.

One of the most important characteristics of this economic analysis is its interest in the efficiency of institutions. By efficiency we refer here to the degree of optimization in the use of the society's productive resources that a specific institution allows. No consideration is given to the fairness or unfairness of a specific result obtained as a consequence of a specific custom or the application of a specific legal rule. What is considered is its effects on the allocation of resources. In other words, to study the efficiency of the system the only matter of interest is whether person A instead of person B will end up holding a certain right because the attribution of the right to one or the other may affect the optimum use of the society's resources.

The way in which economists use the term 'efficiency' is anything but uniform. It is difficult to affirm the superiority of a specific institution or norm substituting another when for some of those affected it may be beneficial and for others detrimental. So economists tend to use the Pareto principle according to which it is only possible to define the superiority of such a norm or institution over another when its effects result in an improved situation for everybody; or when at least some of those affected benefit from the change and it is not detrimental for anybody. This criterion thus avoids the problem of interpersonal comparisons of utility. The idea is that, since it is not possible to assess the degree of intensity of each person's preferences with respect to a specific good, there is no point in making interpersonal comparisons of utility for which we would have to know in advance what these preferences are to a degree of accuracy that is impossible to attain. This is why the Pareto principle is the only one that allows us to establish with certainty[4] the greater or lesser efficiency of an institution or norm regulating individual conduct.

But in the study of institutions we must remember that in many cases it will be impossible to find solutions meeting the strict conditions of the Pareto principle. Usually any norm or custom favouring a specific group will in some way be detrimental to another and society simply could not function if the Pareto principle were the only possible guide when drawing up legal rules or setting up institutions of any type. So the economists dealing with these matters generally use efficiency criteria that are less strict than the Pareto principle but that serve better to find practical solutions. The most usual of these criteria is the Kaldor–Hicks compensation principle according to which the norm or institution will be considered superior to an alternative, provided that those benefiting from it can compensate those for whom it is detrimental.[5]

2   THE NEW ECONOMICS OF THE FAMILY AND THE THEORY OF REGULATION

The application of microeconomics to the study of the family is fairly recent and only in the last 20 years or so has it been done regularly and systematically. This of course does not mean that there were no previous studies on certain aspects of family life from an economic point of view. In addition to the well-known work by Malthus on population theory, there were studies last century that never received much attention on inheritance or the structure of family property. But these works did not place the institution of the family at the centre of the economic analysis. This is precisely what present economic theory is doing in that it considers the institution of the family in close relation to the behaviour of such important economic magnitudes as the structure of consumption or the supply of labour in both the short and the long term. It also analyses changes in the family as a result of changing technology and changes in certain relative prices, mainly the shadow price of housework.

The work by Professor Gary Becker was of special importance in the development of these models. Becker started work in the 1950s but it was some years later that his model was to take the form it has today. In 1981 he published the first edition of *A Treatise on the Family*[6] in which he gave the results of many previous studies and which has become the most representative work on the new economics of the family. His starting-point is a neoclassical utility function and its arguments include, in addition to traditional consumer goods, other goods such as children, prestige and social esteem, altruism and, in general, all those goods that cannot be bought directly on the market but that are produced in homes. With this basis, he uses microeconomic tools to study the pairing of couples, types of marriage contract, divorce, demand for children, altruism amongst family members and trends in the family as an institution.

When studying the economics of the family we must remember from the start one important fact that, in spite of family relationships being strictly private, they have always been closely regulated by the society in which they existed. This regulation has adopted many different forms depending on circumstances or the specific time in history – religious precepts, legal rules or simple widely accepted customs. The specific solution chosen by each society in each historical period is not specially relevant for our purposes. What is important is that the reasoning behind individual behaviour within the family cannot be understood without bearing in mind the restrictions that its members are subject to. The question of the efficiency of such restrictions is a very complex matter to which we shall aim to give at least a partial answer in this book.

Some studies on the public regulation of family relations mention the idea that many of the regulations of the family institution increase the efficiency of the family and the welfare of its members.[7] The basic argument is the lack of maturity of children which generally makes it impossible for parents and children to reach efficient agreements on their mutual obligations both for the present and the future. They also add the idea that many of the regulations of all types which today affect families really only substitute the agreements that would be reached in free negotiation if the children were able to carry out such a negotiation. If we accept the principle whereby legal rules, having been refined over the years, tend to offer efficient solutions[8], it could be concluded that the survival of this type of regulation is due to its positive effects on the wellbeing of society.

But this problem of lack of capacity for negotiating efficient agreements does not exist to the same degree in all family relations. Let us now take the case of the relationship between married couples and the marriage contracts, both tacit and explicit, that their unions are based on. It seems reasonable to assume here that both parties act rationally and that neither of them will adopt a decision leaving them in a worse position than before the agreement. However, the data seem to show that, when distributing the benefits of the agreement, there are great differences in the advantages received by each group and women clearly get the worst deal. This can be seen in many ways but the relative impoverishment of some groups of women indicates the type of problem.

If we assume that the satisfaction of personal interest is one of the most important factors in the determination of human conduct, we must accept that both women and men adopt decisions allowing them to obtain maximum benefit at the minimum cost. The fact that their decisions are so different can be explained to a large extent as a consequence of the legal, social and biological restrictions that each group has traditionally been subject to. Limited access to important, well-paid jobs in the labour market has, practically throughout history, led to an artificial reduction in the shadow price of the time devoted to housework and child care. And this helps to explain the reasons for the specialization of women in these activities, the type of many forms of marriage contract and the various degrees of stability in marriage, irrespective of the existence of legal possibilities for divorce.

Reforms of family regulations and the gradual closing of the gap between men and women in the labour market are now reducing the legal and social barriers to activity by women. This explains why there has been such a change in the relative prices of women's activities that well-established patterns of behaviour are now having to change. The removal, although only partial, of discriminatory norms and customs has led to efficient results with respect to both the maximization of income and the utilization of the comparative advantages.

If the problem of discrimination against women seems to be on the way to a solution in the western world, a new matter is now arising in these countries which, until recently, was of little importance but is now greatly relevant and which is linked to the changes mentioned in the above paragraph – the fall in birth rates. This reduction can be explained perfectly in terms of individual rationality. It does, however, pose serious problems of social efficiency in that the supply of children seems to be lower than the desired level as a result of the non-remuneration of most of the external economies that the production of children and the corresponding creation of human capital generate in these countries.

There is also another type of legal rule for individual conduct for which the objective seems to be to protect the interests of minors who cannot look after themselves, but which is difficult to explain from the point of view of economic efficiency, namely the laws covering such topical matters as the purchase of newborn babies or surrogate mothers. These regulations, strangely enough, do not prohibit adoptions or the use of a volunteer's body to help an infertile couple to have a child. What is prohibited is the formalization of a contract involving payment. And the actual effects are that it is thus impossible to reach agreement which would be beneficial for all the interested parties – mother, adoptive parents and the child – and the activity of women as mothers is undervalued. Some of the most striking contributions of the economic analysis of family law have been those focusing on the study of this type of rule, some of which lead to conclusions that are quite the opposite of what widespread public opinion would prefer.[9]

3   THE ECONOMICS OF THE FAMILY AND BIOLOGY

When analysing certain aspects of human conduct, biology becomes a very interesting aid for economics and, in the economics of the family, it may play a very important role. Family behaviour undoubtedly involves a large cultural component. But it would be a mistake to forget that it also involves a significant biological element whereby certain family behaviour such as marriage strategies are easier to understand if we look at the behaviour of certain animal species that have shown their efficiency in successful natural selection.

In economic jargon we could say that animals – both male and female – pair up in line with well-defined strategies that maximize some sort of 'utility function'. The degree to which the genetic structure of the animal determines its strategy may vary greatly.[10] An insect may live for just a few days and behave almost like a robot whose actions reflect no active intelligence in order to achieve the reproduction of its genes. The restrictions imposed by the environment and the short duration of its life – what economists would call its 'nature' – force it to follow a strict pattern of genetically established behaviour.

The more highly developed the animal, the greater its degree of freedom of conduct and the less its behaviour is determined by its genetic structure. A mosquito has approximately one hundred thousand nerve cells. A man has about ten thousand million neurons and his genetic structure allows him a much greater range of possible reactions to external stimuli. But this does not mean that his behaviour will be 100 per cent cultural. The idea of a radical difference between men and animals, according to which the latter are guided only by biological instinct and the former follow the guidelines of the society and culture in which they live, is difficult to accept. It should first be stated that any conduct, whether cultural or genetic and on the part of man or animal, will contribute to the reproductive success of that individual and consequently also to the survival and evolution of that species or its society but only if it follows economic criteria – that is, criteria of the efficient use of the available resources – or, at least, is compensated by other conduct following these criteria.

If we are looking for the most basic form of behaviour of any living being, there can be little doubt that the main argument of what could be called, taking certain terminological liberties, the 'utility function' of any living creature, seems to be its own reproduction. According to Dawkins' theory[11], the main objective of any living being is to reproduce its own genes. Many strategies for mating and reproduction can only be understood from this point of view.

This general idea, however, does not involve the identification of strategies in all animals nor in both sexes. On the contrary, although newborns receive the same number of genes from their father and their mother, in view of the biological differences between the sexes, the optimum reproductive strategy of the males and females of the same species may be substantially different. In principle, the strategies of both sexes must once have been identical as we can still see in the simplest of animals: each sex transmits the same number of genes and makes the same investment in reproduction. But over the course of evolution, those females making a greater investment had the greatest reproductive success. So in the most highly developed animals, although the females continue to transmit the same number of genes as the males, their reproduction strategies are 'intensive', being based on high levels of investment on a relatively small number of descendants. A female in a higher species, following a high-investment strategy from the time of ovule formation to the time when the offspring reaches adulthood, invests such a great proportion of its life and so much effort in the process that the number of opportunities it has to reproduce its genes is much smaller than in the case of the male. It is constantly running the risk of losing its investment and that leads it to invest even more.

The male strategy, meanwhile, tends to be 'extensive'. Fertilization of the eggs does not require much investment. And the greater the number of eggs a specific male fertilizes, the greater the probability that his genes will be transmitted to the future generation of its species. The male can be fairly sure that the female who has taken charge of his genes will do everything possible to produce an adult individual. Promiscuity is therefore an efficient form of reproductive strategy for males.

To what extent does biological conditioning affect the behaviour of the human species? It does not seem possible to give a definite and general answer to this question. On the one hand, not all human activities are determined in the same way by genetic structure and, on the other, the debate on the importance of genetics as against the conditioning imposed by the social environment is far from reaching a widely accepted conclusion. But, without attempting to define man as a simple animal whose behaviour is determined by biology, it is impossible to deny that social and cultural elements have a biological basis without which many aspects of human behaviour cannot be understood; and family structure has always reflected this biological conditioning in different societies and historical periods.

4   THE ECONOMICS, ANTHROPOLOGY AND SOCIOLOGY OF THE FAMILY

The economists, anthropologists and sociologists devoted to the study of the organization and functions of the family have not always been on speaking terms. The main discrepancy between them has been the existence of the figure that has been vaguely and imprecisely named *homo oeconomicus*, this term being used to designate the universal characteristic of the rational behaviour of man.

The origin of the debate on the existence of *homo oeconomicus* is almost as old as economic science itself. One of the basic postulates on which economic theory has been built comes directly from a famous text in *The Wealth of Nations* in which Adam Smith spoke of the human propensity to trade and exchange certain things for others[12]. This has led economists to draw up a model of behaviour that is applicable to any period or society. Differences in levels of development or values would therefore imply not the rejection of this basic model for universal behaviour, but the existence of various circumstances relating to the physical environment or the institutional framework that act as restrictions for the model and produce different results.

The classic economic model by which theories are deduced from certain basic, universal postulates has been criticized by those who consider that human societies all have very different characteristics and that it is not possible to build up a science of human behaviour by deduction. Such a science, they say, should be based rather on detailed study of the different ways, both present and past, of organizing the economy and society. Social anthropology was to adopt this alternative view of the study of behaviour by attempting to search for general principles using the induction method and comparative study of societies and institutions.

Apart from these methological implications, the debate centres above all on determining what is understood by 'natural propensity' or, in more general terms, 'human nature'. The functionalist anthropology of Malinowsky, for example, considers the fact that man must meet basic needs such as eating, sleeping, reproduction and so forth to be part of human nature. Specific forms of social organization, tools, arts, beliefs and customs are considered part of 'culture'. Culture is, in the opinion of Malinowsky, conditioned by human nature but goes further and is actually what differentiates man from other living beings. The problem is therefore similar to what happened when the biological conditioning of human conduct or the borderline between nature and culture were considered. Basically the aim is to know whether Smith's statement that a propensity for commerce forms part of human nature. Whereas economists would almost unanimously answer in the affirmative, the anthropological literature gives a wide range of opinions, from those close to the principles of economic rationality in early Malinowsky to the anti-economist culturalism of Marcel Mauss, for example.[13]

It is not difficult to apply these general ideas directly to the specific case of the family. Throughout this book it will be shown that the economics of the family is based on the existence of certain general principles governing human behaviour within the institution of the family. This allows us to apply the model to all types of family – from the modern, western family to the extensive family of a traditional agricultural society, from monogamous marriage, as we know it, to the poligamous African or Islamic societies. Human beings are not considered as essentially different. Their various customs and institutions are understood rather as responses to a varying environment.

The predominant anthropological approach, however, is different. The emphasis on the idea of different cultures, and on their being studied individually, has led anthropologists to a long series of field studies and comparative studies which have not resulted in a theory that can explain the phenomena systematically. Anthropological studies therefore constitute a very useful source of information for economists interested in the family but cannot offer either the systematic reasoning nor the predictive capacity of economic theory.

At this stage two important points should be clarified concerning the model behind the economics of the family. The first is that the emphasis on economic behaviour and on the importance of the environment as a restriction to such behaviour has little to do with Marxist analysis in which it is production relations that determine a specific social structure, and the position occupied by each person in the latter determines their behaviour. But in economic analysis of the family, man acts rationally, searching for maximum satisfaction from limited natural resources in whatever type of family institution or historical time he finds himself in.

The second clarification refers to the actual definition of human nature that is present in the model. For economists the propensity to trade is not the only one in human nature, nor is *homo oeconomicus* by definition selfish or antisocial. In *The Theory of Moral Sentiments,* Adam Smith stated that, however selfish a person may be, there are in his nature certain principles that make him concerned about the fate of others and by which the happiness of others may make him happy.[14] In other words, the economic model also allows for altruistic behaviour, as will be seen in greater detail in a later section of this chapter. The utility function arguments that each person tries to maximize may include not only material goods but also all types of psychological satisfaction involving the wellbeing of others, especially those who are most closely related. So economic analysis of the family is not exclusively a study of the material conditions of family life but offers a much wider and richer view of human behaviour.

The postulate referred to above of rational behaviour on the part of the economic agents has, however, given rise to debates not only in economics but in general in the whole field of social science. This postulate will be interpreted in this book based on what in modern economics is called bounded rationality which, even if it leaves aside some of the principles of the theory of strict rationality (such as the existence of a series of given alternatives or a distribution of probability that is previously known for each of them), conserves the basic principles of rational action. So, even when we continue to use the traditional terminology of the models that maximize utility, what is really assumed is that the economic subject adopts decisions to attain his objectives with limited information; and that the result, rather than a strict 'optimum of utility', in many cases will become a 'satisficing strategy' to use the term coined by H. Simon.

This is why, within the framework of family economics, game theory can be useful in analysing the effects of these strategies. It can help us to see how each player should act to achieve the best possible result at the end of the game, which may be a representation in terms of strategies for a marriage contract, a divorce procedure or the relations between spouses or siblings within a family. This is what we mean when we define individual strategies as rational.

On the other hand, the principle of rationality in human action allows us to establish a close link between the economics of the family and the sociology of rational choice. The economics of the family and this sociological approach move away from the vision of Durkheim and his followers, according to which joint or collective action cannot be reduced to individual actions or be considered the sum of individual actions but rather is something different and separate which determines individual behaviour. Against this way of seeing society, both the economics of human behaviour and the rational choice school base their theories on methodological individualism – which postulates that any collective phenomenon can be explained in terms of individual behaviour – and try to build up a theory of action to analyse the role of the agents in the social system. This sociological approach creates very interesting bridges between this discipline and economic theory and constitutes a remarkable step along the path towards a unified study of man's behaviour in society.[15]

5   THE ECONOMICS OF COOPERATION AND ALTRUISM

Economic behaviour is often linked to selfish and non-cooperative attitudes. But this approach is excessively simplistic and reality shows us many cases of altruistic behaviour and cooperation without which social life would be incomprehensible. It is therefore logical that economists should now be devoting special attention to the analysis of this type of behaviour.

Altruism is usually defined as a feeling or rule of conduct that leads us to strive for the benefit of others, even to our own cost. But the search for the benefit of others may take many different forms and be based on many different motivations. For sociobiology, altruism may be conscious or unconscious. Unconscious altruism is impulsive and those practising it expect no type of reward. It is a mechanism that responds to the genetic legacy of the species, which was developed during evolution and that aims to protect the group rather than the individual. For this reason it is a characteristic of animals that live in society. Bees that die when they use their sting, or the adoption of orphaned young amongst superior animals could be good examples.[16]

Conscious altruism, however, is exclusive to man. Obviously man may also show impulsive or unconscious altruistic conduct and it is easy to find examples of this type of conduct in real life (the person who dives into the water to save a drowning man, or who braves the burning house to save a child and so on). But human behaviour reflecting an altruistic attitude over a fairly long period is usually based on the existence of some type of compensation, either material or psychological. This therefore is rational and conscious altruism.[17]

Conscious altruism, which is the product of our culture, developed gradually as the processes of civilization advanced. It is a fact that superior animals abandon their decrepit or sick members and get rid of weak offspring. And probably the same occurred amongst primitive tribes and peoples living in a subsistence economy in which apparently infanticide and the abandonment of the elderly were not unusual.[18] However, during the process of civilization and the development of more advanced economies and societies, mechanisms were created that aimed to enhance the value of the least productive members, lowering the high costs they represented by means of incentives of a spiritual or psychological type which would act as a reward for the individual who took charge of them. In this way, protection was afforded for the most vulnerable beings who thus avoided the laws of natural selection of the species that probably would have condemned them to death, a fate which, according to our present system of values, would be considered untimely and cruel.

This conduct can be interpreted as an insurance taken out by a person against the uncertainty of his own future. An individual behaves altruistically in the hope that, when the time comes, people will behave in the same way towards him. It is an exchange of altruistic conduct, or reciprocal altruism. Since conscious altruism is a cultural product, it may develop out of observation of altruistic conduct and from learning within the family or social group, and it varies depending on the type of society and its values. An invalid old man is not valued in the same way by a Chinese or Jewish family whose tradition and religion promotes the veneration of the elderly as by a modern family in a large city. In the same way, the cost and productivity of each member varies greatly depending on their lifestyle. It would be risky to think that a traditional, farming family is more altruistic than a post-industrial revolution family because the latter has much higher costs when its weakest members lose their economic value and become a burden.

Altruistic conduct is often governed by complicated social requirements and rules which are internalized by education and moral pressure, and rejection of them is penalized with moral and even legal sanctions. Traitors, cowards, 'unnatural' mothers, and any person deviating from the attitude of collaboration towards the group are universally condemned.

Conscious altruism is efficient in economic life because it reduces the transaction costs that are implicit in any activity. Let us think, for example, of long-term contracts or agreements in which an attitude of collaboration and promise-keeping substantially reduces the need for establishing assurances. In consequence, a society with a high degree of altruism will reach a higher number of agreements and greater cooperation.

From the point of view of economic theory, it may be considered that an altruistic individual behaves rationally and aims to maximize his benefits through his conduct in exactly the same way as any other economic agent. What differentiates an altruistic person from a non-altruistic person is basically that for the former his wellbeing depends partially on the wellbeing of others. So altruism means that the utility of other people is included in one's own utility function. If the utility of person A is defined as:

$$U_A = U_A (x_1, x_2 \ldots x_n, U_B \ldots U_Z)$$

it can be said that this person is altruistic, because his utility function includes as arguments not only the goods he consumes $(x_1, x_2 \ldots x_n)$ but also the utility of the persons (B . . . Z), whose welfare interests him.[19]

In the analysis of social institutions, it is usual to put on one side those in which the members are guided by the selfish principle of searching for their individual benefit and on the other those that are governed by the principle of social cooperation. The market would be a good example of the former and the family the prototype of the latter. However, the reality is more complex than this. It is not unusual to find cooperative behaviour in 'selfish' institutions and non-cooperative behaviour in apparently 'altruistic' institutions. In addition, there may be apparently altruistic behaviour whose main aim is to achieve individual wellbeing but for which it is necessary to help or cooperate with people whose wellbeing is of no interest or whom we actually detest. Collaboration with the group may be the best way of improving our own situation.

Although it is possible that the wellbeing of a person we do not know may form part of our own utility function, normally our degree of altruism towards another person will be a direct function of the degree of our proximity to that person. We can therefore expect greater altruism towards a son or daughter than towards an outside person; and we are more likely to give our 'disinterested' collaboration to a small institution of which we form part, such as a residents' association in a small town, than to a large institution in which we are little more than a number, such as the town council of a large city or the State.

This selective behaviour can be clearly explained from the points of view of both biology and economics. With respect to biology – and in line with section 1 of this chapter – if the objective of any living being is to maximize the transmission of its genes to other creatures, then the optimimum strategy must be for the individual to give priority to those who form part of its most immediate group and share its genes.

This preference for the individuals that are closest to us and for our family can also be explained from the point of view of economic theory. There are two basic reasons. The first is that it is in our closest group and especially within our family that we make our greatest investments. It is therefore logical that the intensive investment of women in their children should make them more altruistic towards their children than men are with respect to their descendants. And secondly, it is in the framework of the closest group, and especially within the family, where we can expect to receive reciprocal cooperative behaviour because the relationship amongst the various people is regular and long-standing.

The idea that, in the long term, 'honesty is the best policy' and that frequent contact is the most important factor in explaining why in some circumstances men relinquish maximum satisfaction in the short term, has very early precedents in economic and political thought. One of the most characteristic examples is the old debate on the link between national character and honesty in mercantile operations. The idea that honesty and integrity in business exist to varying degrees in the various countries has traditionally found a lot of support. And it is probably true. But this does not mean that national character is the only reason for such varying types of behaviour. It may also be due to frequency of contact. When a trader carries out a large number of contracts or operations every day, his objective is not to achieve maximum benefit in one of them but in all of them. As a result, it would be against his interests to be deceitful or false because his honesty has an important commercial value which will mean he may prefer to lose money in a specific operation rather than allow people to suspect him of being dishonest. But when there is no frequent, regular contact, the incentives for dishonest behaviour are much greater.[20]

If we apply this idea to family relationships, which are characterized precisely by the fact that family members live in close proximity and have frequent contact, this preference for cooperative behaviour within the family as opposed to other social groups can be better understood. Along the same lines, there have been studies in the modern literature on rationality and the effects of altruism on the wellbeing of both individuals and the family as a group. One of the most relevant of the various models that have been formulated is Gary Becker's 'theorem of the rotten kid' which has given rise to much debate on the nature of cooperative behaviour in social groups.[21]

This theorem basically establishes that, in the case of a family in which the father's conduct is in the interests of his two children Ch_1 and Ch_2, the selfish child – let us take Ch_2 – will not behave selfishly if, by doing so, the family income would decrease. His objective will be to maximize the income because the father's reaction might harm the situation of Ch_2 if the family income were to decrease. In other words, any member benefiting from belonging to the family group will try to maximize the income of the persons favouring him and will internalize the effect of their positive actions. A striking corollary of the theorem establishes that, even for the envious child, in this case it will be efficient to adopt a cooperative attitude to allow the family income to increase, even though in this way he will be favouring those of his siblings that he would prefer to harm.

Cooperative behaviour is thus imposed by the interests of each member of the family. However, no generalization can be made concluding that a family relationship will necessarily create incentives for cooperation or that in a family altruistic behaviour will always predominate over egoistic behaviour. The phenomenon is much more complex than this and the result will depend on the effect on the person's own interests of being cooperative towards others.[22]

As a general rule, it is possible to assert that altruism is most efficient in a group when put into practice equally by all the members.[23] The problem arises when one individual is egoistic and tries to benefit from the conduct of the altruistic group. If altruism is not equal on both sides, inefficient situations may be reached. And in a family in which not all the members have the same ethical principles, it may happen that the altruistic conduct is not efficient, from the point of view not only of individual interest but also of the group interest. In a family group in which all the members behave spontaneously in a cooperative way, the mutual altruism reduces the need to establish methods of defence by each of the members against the others. Bilateral or multilateral altruism thus becomes a valuable asset because it means that the mutually beneficial links become tighter and their cost decreases. But the situation may change substantially when the altruism is no longer mutual. If an altruistic person observes that other members of the family are not altruistic, this person will adopt defence measures to avoid being exploited and will reduce to a minimum his links with those members of the family from whom reciprocal cooperative conduct cannot be expected. The result will be a reduction in the number of cooperative actions within the family leading to an inferior situation from the point of view of collective wellbeing.[24]

6   ALTRUISM, GAMES AND STRATEGIES FOR COOPERATION

Several chapters of this book use elementary game theory as an auxiliary tool because it is very useful in throwing light on strategic behaviour in the framework of family economics. As a first approach to this type of analysis, let us take the case of two siblings who have to decide what behaviour would be best to obtain maximum satisfaction in their family life. Each of them will consider the advantages and disadvantages of adopting an attitude of cooperation and help towards the other or an attitude of non-cooperation trying to obtain the maximum advantages for himself without concerning himself about the benefits to be obtained by the sibling.

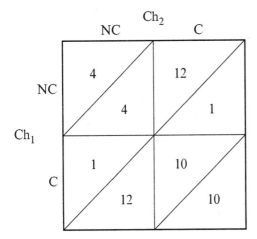

Figure 1.1   Strategies in a prisoner's dilemma

Let us set up a matrix of payments as shown in Figure 1.1 in which each of the siblings (Ch_1 and Ch_2) may choose the strategy of cooperation (C) or non-cooperation (NC), and in which the first of the figures in each of the boxes shows the level of utility to be reached by Ch_1 and the second the utility of Ch_2.

There is no doubt that the optimum result for both is to reach the lower right box in which both adopt the attitude of cooperation and each obtains a benefit valued at 10. But the optimum individual strategy for each of them is NC, that of non-cooperation. So, if one of them is not sure that the other is going to cooperate, he will choose the strategy NC because it offers an expected result (4.12) which is higher than that of strategy C, for which the expected value is (1.10); and if both choose NC, the result will have a value for each of 4, much lower than what could have been achieved. So, in this game which follows the pattern of the well-known prisoner's dilemma, the strategy of individual maximization seems to lead the children to non-optimum behaviour.[25]

Reality shows, however, that cooperation strategies are often used to obtain maximum individual benefit. This cooperative behaviour for reasons of personal interest can be explained in two basic ways.

Firstly, if the cost of non-cooperation is so high that for each sibling, however selfish and distrustful of the other, it is in his interests to behave in an altruistic way, then this is what he will do. An example of this case would be Gary Becker's 'rotten kid theorem' referred to above.

This theorem can be simply reformulated in terms of game theory. We would need to assume that the added value to be shared out amongst the two siblings depends to such an extent on the strategy adopted that the expected value of the cooperation strategy is greater than that of non-cooperation. A first approach to the subject is by simply restructuring the previous game as shown in Figure 1.2 in which the values of the benefit to be achieved are presented as percentages of the different total benefits for each possible combination of strategies.

In Figure 1.2, the values that can be obtained by each of the siblings are not presented in absolute terms but as percentages of the possible total revenue (R) that can be

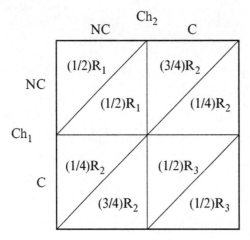

Figure 1.2   Strategies with increasing revenue from cooperation

achieved which, in turn, is a function of the chosen strategies. For all the values of R_1, R_2 and R_3 in which the results of the strategies are such that

$$(1/4\ R_2,\ 1/2\ R_3) > (1/2\ R_1,\ 3/4\ R_2)$$

it would suit each of the siblings to adopt a cooperation strategy irrespective of the strategy adopted by the other.

It would, however, be more interesting to pose the problem in terms of a repetitive game in which the aim is not to maximize the benefit in a single action because it might be more profitable to collaborate in a process of cooperation in which the benefit to be reached increases with the various stages, on condition that the process finishes as soon as one of the parties deviates from the cooperation strategy. This type of game is especially relevant in the study of family relationships and is used on several occasions in subsequent chapters of this book.

What distinguishes this repetitive game substantially from the case described in Figure 1.1 is the possibility the siblings have of maximizing their revenue not in a single move but throughout a long process during which they are repeatedly offered the possibility of adopting a cooperative or non-cooperative approach. Now each of the siblings is aware that if they cooperate, the total revenue will increase for both of them and this creates clear incentives for them to try to sustain the joint activity and trust in each other. As shown in Figure 1.3, the total benefits gradually increase in each of the phases of the game and, the longer the game, the greater the total benefit expected. Either of them can opt at a specific stage for the NC strategy which would give him a better position than if he were to cooperate and the other were not. But it seems reasonable that expectations of a future benefit will lead them both to cooperate, even though there is a risk that the other might, at a given time, adopt the NC strategy. This result basically coincides with the efficient strategies that have been described as 'tit for tat' in which cooperative behaviour can be expected from a person as long as the other party acts in the same way, but a strategy of reprisals is adopted as soon as the other party stops cooperating.[26]

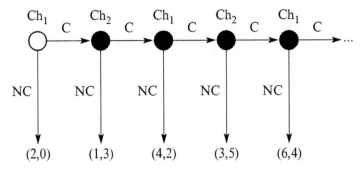

Ch_1 $\quad$ C $\quad$ Ch_2 $\quad$ C $\quad$ Ch_1 $\quad$ C $\quad$ Ch_2 $\quad$ C $\quad$ Ch_1 $\quad$ C $\quad$ ...

NC $\quad\quad$ NC $\quad\quad$ NC $\quad\quad$ NC $\quad\quad$ NC

(2,0) $\quad\quad$ (1,3) $\quad\quad$ (4,2) $\quad\quad$ (3,5) $\quad\quad$ (6,4)

Figure 1.3   Strategies in a repetitive game

It is also possible that cooperation may be a type of behaviour that is reinforced by the habit of cooperation. When in a family one of the children has grown up with cooperative attitudes and has received incentives to act in the same way, he may acquire a habit which will lead him to behave cooperatively with his family throughout his life, at least while he is not forced to adopt reprisals because of non-cooperative behaviour by other family members.

The problems mentioned in the above section concerning unilateral altruism can also be seen in this game approach. Let us go back to the matrix of results in Figure 1.1, but now let us assume that the expected benefits refer to a specific activity that the siblings may carry out or not and that their decision will depend on the comparison of these benefits with a prior level of utility which we can arbitrarily set at 6. Let us also assume that Ch_1 will always adopt a cooperative approach whereas Ch_2 is above all interested in his own personal benefit. In this case, since the position of Ch_1 is known in advance, the choice by Ch_2 will depend on his knowing his possible benefits, 12 if he is not cooperative and 10 if he is cooperative. Given the postulates of the problem, he will always choose the NC strategy. But, in this case, Ch_1 will prefer not to play, that is, not to undertake the joint activity planned. Only if we admit the possibility of redesigning the strategies and that the threat of withdrawing from the game will have an effect on Ch_2, will the latter be forced to adopt a cooperative attitude.

NOTES

1. See Coleman, J.S. (1986).
2. Smith, A. [1776] (1976), (1978a).
3. Mill, J.S. [1848] (1909). See especially Book II on problems of income distribution.
4. Although utility is subjective and interpersonal comparisons are impossible, a person may feel that his situation has worsened, even if it has improved in material terms, if that of another person has improved to a greater extent.
5. Application of the Kaldor–Hicks compensation principle is, however, not problem-free and may give rise to incoherence. But it is still considered one of the most interesting methods in the analysis of the efficiency of institutions. On the logical incoherence of the principle of compensation, see Scitovsky, T. (1941) and Coleman, J.L. (1982).
6. Becker, G.S. (1991) (2nd ed.).

7. For instance, Becker, G.S. and Murphy, K.M. (1988).
8. See, for instance, Posner, R. (1992a), pp. 23–4.
9. Many examples could be given here and some are mentioned in this book. But probably the greatest stir was caused by the article by Landes and Posner on the supply and demand of babies for adoption. See Landes, E.M. and Posner, R. (1978).
10. Wilson, E.O. (1978), Ch. 3.
11. Dawkins, R. (1989).
12. Smith, A. [1776] (1976), p. 25.
13. See Mirowski, P. (1994).
14. Smith, A. [1759] (1978b), p. 9.
15. On the sociology of rational choice, in addition to the work by J.S. Coleman referred to in note 1, see Swedberg, R. (1990).
16. Wilson, E.O. (1978), Ch. 7, and Dawkins, R. (1989), Chs 1 and 10.
17. This altruism may acquire a special value in certain social organizations in which heroic acts in the public interest are praised and guarantee that those responsible will receive their reward in the other world. The Japanese kamikazes who crashed their planes against American ships believed that to die for the Emperor was to live eternally. This was also the expected reward of the followers of Islam who died in the Holy War. Catholic martyrs, saints, heroes, etc. were all praised, venerated and elevated above the ranks of ordinary mortals. For this type of conscious altruistic conduct to appear, the right circumstances must first be created by ritual, emotion and gratification. The altruistic individual is valued as an example for the rest of the group and this value is essential for the purpose of proselytism because conscious altruism is based on learnt rules.
18. On the behaviour of families towards their elderly and young members, see, for example, de Beauvoir, S. (1970), Ch. 2, and Minois, G. (1987), Ch. 1.
19. On the economic theory of altruism, see Becker, G. (1991), Ch. 8; Collard, D. (1978), and Stark, O. (1995).
20. Smith, A. (1978a), pp. 538–9.
21. Becker, G.S. (1991), pp. 288–95.
22. Note that the benefit need not be exclusively personal. The wellbeing of another person or other people may form part of one's own benefit if the person is altruistic towards the others; that is, if his own utility function includes the utility functions of these other people.
23. The idea that multilateral altruism is efficient in most cases does not imply, however, that it always gives rise to social harmony. See Stark, O. (1995), p. 25.
24. On the problems of unilateral altruism, see Stark, O. (1989), pp. 86–90; and Bernheim, B.B. and Stark, O. (1988), pp. 1034–45.
25. Note that, in order to simplify the reasoning, this pattern excludes the possibility of drawing up a new contract and using the strategy of non-cooperation as a tool for forcing the other party to cooperate.
26. This is the well-known conclusion of the experiments on cooperative behaviour by Robert Axelrod. See Axelrod, R. (1984).

2. The family as an economic unit

1 ECONOMIC ORGANIZATION AND THE FAMILY

At the close of the twentieth century, family structure and the changes that have recently been taking place in the family in the western world have become very relevant for understanding developments in contemporary economic market systems. This statement may seem surprising because modern social organization has meant that the family is no longer carrying out many of its traditional activities. But it is precisely this new, more limited social role that has given the family its protagonism.

The economic system in which we live is based on a specific family organization which, when altered, casts doubts on many of our longstanding assumptions. Many studies have been carried out on the adaptation of the family institution to the new methods of social organization for production. But not much attention has yet been paid to the reverse influence. And this is also very important because if family structure changes, the economic system will necessarily be affected.

A simple example should clarify these ideas. Let us think of the effects of a high rate of unemployment over a long period, a well-known phenomenon in many European economies. In a family in which only the father works in the market and in which the wife and children have no independent income, if the father were to be unemployed for a long period this would be likely to have serious effects. But in crisis situations there may be collaboration from the rest of the family who may provide social support for the unemployed person.

If the traditional family disappears and we move to a situation in which both the husband and wife obtain income from the market, have small numbers of children and there are a large number of unmarried people and divorcé(e)s living alone, then unemployment will be less serious and may cause less social conflict. But, on the other hand, that buffer of security offered by the family will also disappear.

Moreover, a person's family situation determines his habits of work, leisure, spending and saving. A person with no family responsibilities will tend to have a less stable labour situation than a person who is married with children, a fact that personnel managers are well aware of. Also, the type of consumer goods required by one another varies, and business must take population structure into account and duly adapt its supply of all types of commodity, from housing to cars, clothing or holidays.

2   PRODUCTION AND CONSUMPTION

Over history, humanity has conceived a wide variety of methods of cooperation for its production and consumption activities. And the institution of the family has always played a relevant role in both of these. When a husband works in a company and his wife looks after the home and the children, both are sharing production and consumption activities. There is joint consumption when, for example, a meal prepared by the wife is a commodity that provides utility to both husband and wife. There is productive activity on the part of both of them because both the wife and the husband produce goods for the family. The goods are either consumed directly by the family or they are goods or services that are used in the market to obtain money which can be transformed into consumer goods for the family. So, in this example, each of the spouses carries out a different type of production but both types of good are equally necessary. The husband's activity has an opportunity cost in exchange for which he obtains monetary resources that go to the family. The wife produces goods and services – which also have their opportunity cost – some of which could be purchased in the market if she did not produce them herself.

The national accounts, however, do not consider activities such as the preparation of meals or child care when these are carried out within the family with no explicit remuneration. But the value of these activities would be included if they were to be carried out by people taken on by the family at a price; or if the family were to resort to businesses such as restaurants or private nurseries offering substitute services in exchange for payment.

One of the most important changes in modern economic theory of consumption is precisely that it takes into account this type of domestic producer goods in the microeconomic analysis of human behaviour. The traditional theory is based on a simpler model whereby a person only has two options when deciding how to spend his time. The first is to work for a company or to sell his own products or services in the market in order to receive a monetary income, which can then be spent on purchasing goods and services providing utility. The second is to devote his time to leisure. What we have called the traditional theory includes under the heading of 'leisure' any type of pleasurable activity that directly provides the person with utility. One of the basic economic problems of a person who tries to organize his life to obtain maximum utility is, therefore, how to determine the number of hours that should be devoted to each of the two groups of activity. Time spent on work may be not especially pleasurable but it brings in money. Time spent on leisure is undoubtedly more pleasurable but, if the person were to spend all his time on leisure activities, he would obtain no money at all to purchase the goods he needs to live and to carry out such activities.

So in our example, economists consider that the opportunity cost of leisure is determined by wages. This means that the cost, measured in monetary terms, of every hour devoted to leisure is precisely the income we would have obtained if those hours had been spent working for a company or in a private market activity. So, an increase in the hourly wage that a person obtains in a company can be interpreted as an increase in the price that this person will have to pay for one hour of leisure. And it can be expected that, if other circumstances remain the same, people earning a higher hourly wage will devote more time to work in the company and less on leisure.

The facts seem to confirm this. But there are two important considerations that may substantially modify our conclusions. The first is that not everybody has the same preferences. There are people who value money more than others; and not everybody is prepared to give up one hour of leisure time for the same amount of money, even if all other circumstances were the same. The second is that this assumption that the other circumstances remain the same is not very realistic. People's needs vary greatly. And here the family undoubtedly plays an important role. For a father with a large number of children and limited funds, a specific amount of money will probably be much more useful than for a bachelor with no family responsibilities. In other words, the utility provided by money varies from person to person, so this different subjective consideration of the value of money will necessarily be behind any decisions taken on the number of hours to be devoted to paid work or to leisure.

If activities such as housework that involve neither production for the market nor consumption are included in the model, our basic outline becomes more complicated but is also enriched. At the same time it enables us to find a more realistic explanation for the division of labour within the family. Now the problem is not just to choose between paid work and leisure, but also to find the most efficient way of satisfying basic needs, either through work in the home or through goods and services acquired on the market. Let us take the case of a person who lives alone and consider what would be the most efficient way for him to deal with the problem of food. Suppose that there are two basic alternatives – either he prepares his own meals or he eats out. Let us also suppose that in principle he has no preferred alternative and that the time he devotes to leisure activities should remain the same, whatever the solution chosen.

Given these conditions, it is easy to see that the time devoted to travelling to the shops, buying food, preparing it at home and washing the dishes can be measured in terms of opportunity cost as explained above. The final decision will depend on the earnings he does not receive as a result of devoting less time to work in his company and more time to work at home. A person earning a high salary will probably find that the decrease in income caused by eating at home is greater than the extra cost of paying the restaurant bill and therefore will prefer to eat out. If we consider people with lower earnings, we find that the difference between the opportunity cost of working fewer hours and the extra cost of eating out decreases. And, as from a specific level of earnings, it will be more efficient to reduce the numbers of hours spent on paid work and eat at home.

3   PRODUCTION AND CONSUMPTION: A FORMAL ANALYSIS

The economics of the family has allowed us to reformulate some of the basic principles of the model for maximizing utility to include domestic activities and labour division within the family. This section gives a simplified formal model which constitutes the analytical basis for this chapter and those that follow.

The starting-point for the neoclassical theory of consumption is the idea that everybody tries to achieve the higher possible level of satisfaction by maximizing a utility function that is subject to restrictions, the most important of which is income. If we call the goods that offer utility $x_1, x_2 \ldots x_n$, the problem can be formulated as follows:

$$\text{Max } U = U\left(x_1, x_2 \ldots x_n\right)$$

with the budget constraint:

$$Y = x_1 p_1 + x_2 p_2 + \ldots + x_n p_n = \sum_{i=1}^{n} x_i p_i$$

where Y is the consumer's income and $p_1 \ldots p_n$ are the prices of each of the goods.

The condition for equilibrium is that marginal utility divided by price must be the same for all commodities and this means that the last unit of income spent on each of the goods should offer the consumer the same utility.

If we define

$$MU_i = \frac{\partial U}{\partial x_i}$$

then equilibrium will be obtained when

$$\frac{MU_1}{p_1} = \frac{MU_2}{p_2} = \ldots = \frac{MU_n}{p_n}$$

According to consumer theory, it is easy to deduce the fundamental law of demand according to which the demand-price curve decreases reflecting an inverse relationship between price variations and changes in the amount consumed.

If the demand for a good x_i is defined as

$$D_i = D_i \, (p_i)$$

$$\text{then } \frac{dx_i}{dp_i} < 0$$

Since income is a constraint for maximization of the utility function, we can also analyse the demand for a specific good in terms of the consumer's income. We can generally expect a direct relationship between a rise in income and an increase in the amount demanded although for some goods it is also possible to find an inverse relationship. This is the case of the so-called inferior goods for which consumption decreases with increased income because the consumer can now acquire goods of better quality and so

$$\frac{dx_i}{dy} > 0 \text{ in the case of normal goods}$$

$$\text{and } \frac{dx_i}{dy} < 0 \text{ in the case of inferior goods}$$

One of the most important contributions of the microeconomics that developed during the 1960s was that it attributed a fundamental role to time and the time spent on domestic activities in the analysis of consumer equilibrium. Many of the activities offering most satisfaction are very time-consuming. Relaxing, reading a novel or watching a football match on television are activities that have a very low monetary cost but are very time-consuming. And since, by definition, time is a scarce commodity, optimum usage of time should respond to the same criteria as those traditionally applied in microeconomic studies to the consumption of goods.

The explicit consideration of time as a scarce commodity makes it easy for us to reformulate the utility function given at the start of this section so it now becomes

$$U = U \, (x_1 \ldots x_n, t_{c1}, t_{c2} \ldots t_{cm})$$

where t_{cj} represents the time devoted to domestic consumption activities.

And we now have two constraints – the income constraint as mentioned above, and the time constraint.

$$Y = \sum_{i=1}^{n} x_i p_i$$

$$t = \sum_{j=i}^{m} t_{cj} + t_w$$

where t represents all the time the person has available and t_w is the time devoted to market activities allowing him to obtain monetary income. So the two constraints are not separate because

$$Y = Y(w, t_w, Z)$$

where w represents the wages the person can obtain in the market and Z the wealth that provides non-earned income for him.

The conditions for equilibrium also change. Firstly, we need to determine the cost of t_{cj}. Since these goods are not purchased in the market, they have no monetary price; but their 'price' can be calculated as the opportunity cost of devoting time to reading novels or watching the television, that is, in terms of what a person does not earn in the market because he is spending his time on these pleasurable activities. Since this shadow price is determined by wages (w), it is the same for all the t_{cj}; and the equilibrium condition on the use of domestic time can be written as

$$MU_{tc1} = MU_{tc2} = \ldots = MU_{tcm}$$

The same principle, now applied to all market goods (X) and the time spent on domestic activities (tc) will be

$$\frac{MU_{tc}}{w} = \frac{MU_X}{P_X} \text{ and therefore } \frac{MU_{tc}}{MU_X} = \frac{w}{P_X}$$

where P_X represents the price level and w/P_X the real wage.

The conclusion, therefore, is that the real wage is the criterion that determines whether more or less time is spent on market activities. If the price level (P_X) and the utility of the market goods (MU_X) remain constant and if w increases, equality will only be maintained if MU_{tc} increases and this, because of the principle of decreasing marginal utility, will require a reduction in t_c and an increase in t_w.

So far, however, we have only considered the substitution effect caused by a change in wages. But the wealth producing non-earned income (Z) will also affect the decision on the number of hours to be devoted to work and to leisure. An increase in Z will lead to a reduction in the utility of the earned income (because of the principle of decreasing marginal utility). It can therefore be expected that the greater the growth in non-earned income for a family, the higher the t_c and lower the t_w.

So if

$$t_c = t_c(w, Z) \text{ and}$$

$$t_w = t_w(w, Z)$$

then

$$\frac{\partial t_c}{\partial w} < 0 \text{ and } \frac{\partial t_c}{\partial Z} > 0 \text{ and}$$

$$\frac{\partial t_w}{\partial w} > 0 \text{ and } \frac{\partial t_w}{\partial Z} < 0$$

The time that the members of a family spend at home, however, is not solely spent on pleasurable activities that directly provide utility. Much of the time at home is spent on productive activities such as preparing meals, washing and ironing and so on, for which there are substitutory goods offered on the market (catering services, laundries and so forth). If we call each of these activities s_i and the time devoted to them t_s, if there is to be equilibrium there must be two conditions: equality of the marginal productivity of the time devoted to each of them, and equality between the marginal productivity of the time devoted to the market and the time devoted to the activities s. That is

$$MP_{ts1} = MP_{ts2} = MP_{tsn} \text{ and}$$

$$MP_{ts} = Mp_{tw}$$

Since $w = MP_{tw}$, equilibrium will also require that $w = MP_{ts}$. This means that any increase in w will make it necessary to raise MP_{ts}, and this, *ceteris paribus*, will require a reduction in t_s and that more time be spent on market activities (t_w).

4 DIVISION OF LABOUR WITHIN THE FAMILY

It is not difficult to see, firstly, that the introduction of a second person enriches the model in that it allows for division of labour between the couple and, secondly, that the model can be extended to a larger number of people within the framework of a more extensive family. One of the basic principles of economics establishes that division of labour is efficient because it allows for specialization which leads to increased productivity and in turn to greater income. As with any human organization, over the years the family has set up complex systems of specialization. Although the specific models for specialization vary from culture to culture, we shall see below that the general principle of specialization prevails in all of them.

According to the basic principles of economics, specialization will be based on the criterion of comparative advantage. This means that each member of the family will specialize in and carry out those activities that he can do with greater relative efficiency than the others. And the theorem of comparative advantage shows that, even where one of the members has the absolute advantage when carrying out every one of the activities, everyone will benefit if specialization is in those areas in which this advantage is relatively greatest. For example, if in a married couple one of the two is better than the other both at obtaining income from the market and housework, it will suit both if that person specializes in the activity in which his (or her) advantage is relatively greater.

So what is it that determines within a family which of the two spouses has the comparative advantage in a specific activity? Clearly their capacity for carrying it out. And since in modern society physical strength is of little importance, we have to conclude that what is really relevant is training and the precise technical knowledge necessary for carrying out the activity. In economic jargon, it is the human capital of each of the family members that is the criterion for determining specialization.

In our urban western culture, men have until recently traditionally carried out market activities and have therefore generally received broader technical and cultural training for such activities than women. The latter meanwhile have devoted themselves to the home and their children and not only have they received less technical training than men but their education has been orientated mostly to preparing them for their roles as mothers and housewives. These facts comply with the theory of comparative advantage. But they do not explain why education has historically shown this sex bias. Why have investments traditionally been made on the professional education of men and not of women?[1]

The neoclassical approach to the economics of the family locates the origin of the traditional division of labour between men and women in the biological differences between the sexes. The exclusive role of women in giving birth to children gives them a comparative disadvantage in activities involving moving away from the home and means that men have the advantage for work in the market. Starting from this initial difference, a process is then set up by which these biological differences, however small they may seem, give rise to investments in human capital of a different type for men and women and this in turn reinforces the process. The basic theory of comparative advantage shows that a small difference in production costs may lead to a very marked division of labour.[2]

This argument may explain the differences between men and women considered as groups. As a result of the biological differences and the theory of comparative advantage, most men can be expected to specialize in the labour market and most women in domestic activities. But this model cannot explain certain special situations such as why it is so rare for men with a low level of human capital to specialize in domestic activities, or to marry women with a high level of training, allowing them to obtain high earnings in the market.

A second explanation for the specific forms of division of labour within the family can be found in the models, which are based on the existence of restrictions of a social or cultural type, that to a great extent predetermine the behaviour of men and women. What can be used to represent this approach is what has been called the model of 'male superiority'. This term is used for a social construction which, irrespective of any natural or acquired characteristics or any objective reason, aims to preserve the superior status of men as a group over women.[3] According to this model, belonging to one sex or the other is what determines differences in status. Thus matters such as discrimination between boys and girls in education, wage differences between men and women carrying out similar activities, or segmentation of the labour market in which there are (important) jobs for men and (subordinate) jobs for women can be understood as manifestations of the characteristic prejudices of the principle of male superiority.

The male superiority model could be used to explain the paradox mentioned earlier that women with a high degree of human capital rarely marry men with a lower cultural level so that the latter can carry out domestic work. A marriage like this would be unlikely to take place because it would be violating the principle of male superiority. However, this answer would be insufficient because the model cannot explain the origin of the actual principle of male superiority as a social objective which seems to be assumed. So here, too, it is possible to use biological arguments. It could be argued, for example, that since the principle of male superiority has been a force in practically all societies throughout history, its origin must lie in the physiological differences between men and women and it is therefore intrinsic to human social organization.[4] Another possible explanation, which doubtless will be more acceptable to many of the people who agree with this model, attributes male superiority to cultural forms which, although dominant in a great majority of human societies, do not necessarily need to remain constant over time and could be modified by social developments. But the question still remains. What was the origin of this principle and how can we explain its widespread application if we exclude biology as the basic reason?

5   A THEORY ON THE BASIS OF THE PRINCIPLE OF 'MALE SUPERIORITY'

In order to bring the debate back to economic terms, we need to start from the basic principle of family economics – the utility functions of men and women. According to the idea given in Chapter 1,[5] transmission of one's genes seems to be the main argument of the 'utility function' of all living beings. But to come closer to man, let us think of a group of primates in which the extensive reproduction strategy of the males means that each of them has to adopt a strategy of domination which, if successful, will allow them to mate with all the females in the group for a certain time and prevent the other males from passing on their genes. We can then define utility functions (U_M and U_F) for males and females, according to which

$$U_M = U_M (G_M)$$
$$U_F = U_F (G_F)$$

where G represents the transmission of genes to the following generation.

Because of the different reproductive strategies of males and females – extensive for the former and intensive for the latter – the production function of G will, however, be substantially different for each. If we focus only on the main argument of the function

$$G_M = G_M (D_M)$$
$$G_F = G_F (T_F)$$

where D_M represents the dominant position of the male and T_F represents the time and resources devoted by the female to the care of its young.

A model of this type, when applied to the closest relations of the human species, could allow us to explain both the origins of the principle of male superiority in terms of reproductive strategy and some of the behavioural differences between males and females. If we take the step up to the human species, we can explain in terms of reproduction strategy why women devote much more time to their children than men and show much greater altruism towards them as this behaviour conforms to their intensive reproduction strategy. And the principles of male superiority and female inferiority can be interpreted as characteristic elements of different reproduction strategies in a primitive social environment. This biological legacy can therefore perhaps explain why men place such importance on not feeling subordinate to their marriage partners. And why women accept what has been called 'consented domination'[6] if this will increase the welfare of their children.

6   THE DIVISION OF LABOUR IN PRACTICE

As previously stated, the division of labour is a characteristic phenomenon of practically all human societies but this does not mean it follows the same pattern in all cultures. It would be unrealistic to say there is a universal model for division of labour whereby it is the man who obtains the resources to feed and meet the basic needs of his wife and children because, in many cultures, it is the women who carry out most of the agricultural activities and who guarantee the survival of the social group. This is the case, for example, in almost all the cultures in sub-Saharan Africa in which the role of men in food production is often limited to forest-clearing and land preparation on the one hand and hunting on the other, although the latter often involves much more ritual than efficacy.

The differences between the various patterns for division of labour between the sexes make it very difficult to carry out a study that will be universally valid. Table 2.1 summarizes the studies carried out by G.P. Murdock on allocation of activities according to sex in 224 traditional cultures. If anything can be deduced from this large number of observations, it is that there are few productive activities than can be considered the exclusive domain of either men or women. Male activities include certain types of work that require special physical strength or are particularly arduous such as wood-cutting, mining and quarrying or forest-clearing. But there are others that are equally gruelling such as transporting water or carrying heavy objects that are predominantly carried out by women. Amongst the typically masculine activities there are some, such as the production of weapons, which have nothing to do with strength or skill but rather are related to their final purpose – hunting or warfare – which are always male occupations. And the predominantly male nature of other activities such as fishing, grazing or hunting and, to some extent, trade can be explained as being

Table 2.1   Allocation of activities according to sex in 224 cultures

| Task | Number of cultures in which the task is | | |
	feminine	shared	masculine
Lumbering	6	8	104
Mining and quarrying	1	2	35
Land clearance	13	44	73
Building of dwellings	36	73	100
Hunting	0	13	166
Fishing	4	56	98
Herding	5	12	38
Trade	7	56	51
Gathering of vegetable products, etc.	137	50	20
Water-carrying	119	12	7
Cooking	158	38	5
Manufacture and repair of clothing	95	20	12
Boat-building	1	8	91
Weapon-making	0	1	121
Basketry	82	19	25
Mat-making	61	12	16
Pottery	77	16	13
Burdenbearing	57	59	12
Agriculture: soil preparation	37	76	31
Agriculture: cultivation and tending of crops	44	89	10

Source: Murdock, G.P. 'Comparative data on the division of labour by sex', *Social Forces* (1937), pp. 551–3.

occupations that are incompatible with child care because they require moving away from the home or village for long periods of time.

Amongst the basically female occupations there are some, such as cooking or the manufacture and repair of clothing, which respond to the usual pattern of division of labour. But there are many others, such as burdenbearing, soil preparation and cultivation and tending of crops, or activities related to handcrafts or domestic industry, such as mat-making or pottery, which are also mostly undertaken by women.

In brief, if we observe these traditional cultures from the point of view of a modern economy, we will see that there are very few basic sectors which are under the control of men. We would have to look to relatively advanced societies and cultures to find women shut away at home and devoted to domestic activities and, even in such cases, such specialization is often limited to the upper classes of society.

But a phenomenon that does seem to be widespread in both traditional and modern cultures is the 'prestige' of the mainly masculine activities, as opposed to the lack of prestige of most women's occupations. Many examples can be given to support this idea and they are further reinforced by another phenomenon that is well-known to those studying racial discrimination, the phenomenon of 'tipping'. This occurs when, in societies in which racial discrimination exists, those forming part of the ethnic group, who are considered inferior, gain access to certain jobs which then become discredited, or set up home in certain areas in which the prices of housing then start to drop.[7] And in this case, when it comes to social esteem, what often seems to be important is not the activity in itself so much as who carries it out, whether men or women. A simple example is the prestige that cooking acquires when in the hands of renowned chefs although it is generally an underestimated skill when carried out by women.

Sometimes this curious combination between prestige and activities has given rise to paradoxical situations. A specific case can serve as an example. As previously stated, in sub-Saharan Africa, agricultural activities were always carried out by women whereas the basically male activity of hunting, though unproductive and inefficient, enjoyed great prestige. When the European settlers considered introducing new agricultural techniques, their training efforts were not directed to the women who were responsible for the crops but to the men who had hitherto taken no interest in such activities. The new crops and machinery thus acquired a prestige that traditional agriculture had never had, and the women continued to use the traditional, much less productive cultivation methods.[8]

Western societies in recent decades have been in the midst of a process in which women are increasingly working outside the home. But their starting-point is different to that of the traditional cultures studied by anthropologists. Unlike the situation in other continents, the ideal western family used to be one in which, unless there was a personal fortune, the husband would obtain the resources that were necessary to maintain the family in the market while the wife stayed at home to look after the house and children. This ideal was not restricted to the well-to-do classes but extended throughout society, or urban society at least Trade unions used to insist that each male worker should obtain a sufficient wage to be able to keep a family of a normal size.[9]

The changes in western families in recent decades have arisen out of a more or less open rejection of this situation. But, unlike other cultures in which the division of labour persists – although it does not follow a uniform pattern – what people seem to be seeking in the western world is that there should be no division of work for reasons of sex and that men and women should both carry out all the tasks, both in the labour world and in the home, simultaneously and on an equal footing, even though this has never occurred in any known society. To what extent has western society advanced in achieving this objective?

To judge the results of developments leading towards the convergence of activities, we can consult two basic sources of data – statistics on the participation of women in the working population and surveys on division of labour in domestic activities.

The statistics show that throughout the western world there has been very significant growth in women's participation in the working population. According to OECD data, the women who formed part of the working population in 1960 amounted to 46 per cent of all women aged between 15 and 64, and in 1989 the percentage had risen to 59 per cent. And these figures possibly do not reflect the real situation as many women find employment in the informal or underground economy. But the figure is still far from reaching the 83 per cent of men who were classified as the working population in 1989.[10]

Table 2.2 shows participation by women in the labour market, measured as the percentage of women of working age forming part of the working population and as the percentage of women in the total working population.

Table 2.2   Male and female working population in percentage of the total of men and women aged between 15 and 64 (1989)

	Men	Women	% working women/ total working population
Sweden	85.0	80.7	48
Denmark	89.5	77.3	46
United States	86	68.1	45
United Kingdom	86.8	65.4	43
Portugal	84.8	59.7	43
Japan	87.3	59.3	41
France	75.1	56.2	43
Germany	82.8	54.8	40
Italy	78.5	44.3	37
Greece	75.7	43.5	37
Spain	77.4	39.9	35
Ireland	82.7	37.5	31

Source: OECD and ILO (quoted in Jacobsen, J. (1994), p. 375).

Surveys on domestic activities (as shown in Tables 2.3 and 2.4) show that the distribution of activities in the home is much further from a situation of equality than participation in the labour market. And the two variables are not independent

Table 2.3   Distribution of household tasks in Spain amongst men and women (in percentages) (1990)

Tasks	Mostly by women	Mostly by men	Both equally
Preparing breakfast on weekdays	59	3	33
Washing dishes and/or clearing up the kitchen	77/74	1	18/21
Household repairs	50	23	22
Feeding the children	63	1	21
Cleaning	80	1	15

Source: J. Iglesias Ussel (1994), p. 468.

Table 2.4   Hours devoted per week to household tasks in the United States by men and women (1985)

	Men	Women
Employed	8.1	14.7
Non-employed	14.7	23.6
Married	11.1	22.4
Unmarried	7.9	14.9
All	9.8	19.5

Source: J.P. Robinson (quoted in Jacobsen, J. (1994), p. 131).

but are necessarily related because the lower the participation of women in the labour market, the greater the number of hours devoted to the home. But the comparison of both types of data allows us to reach another important and evident conclusion. Work outside the home does not mean that women do not still have to deal with most of the household activities, and this confirms that employment for women often goes alongside work at home.

So why have these changes taken place which, although far from achieving the desired equality, have in fact led to an important alteration in the traditional structure of division of labour? There are two basic reasons. The first refers to the greater potential of women for obtaining good jobs and the second to the reduction in work for the housewife.

The improved situation of women in the labour market is due both to the disappearance of all types of legal discrimination, with the possibility of access to higher-level and better-paid jobs, and to the substantial growth in investment in the human capital of women. These two factors have raised the opportunity cost of domestic work and have directed women towards the labour market.

The second factor also has two basic causes – the reduction in the number of children and the technological advances facilitating housework. The role of children in the modern family is analysed in Chapter 5 so all that needs to be stated here is that there is an inverse correlation between employment for women and the number of children. Technical progress has reduced the number of hours required to carry out domestic tasks and may have a dual effect – the quality and quantity of domestic services may increase because the housewife has more free time, or that free time may be used in the labour market. The first effect does not seem to prosper because, once women have reached the level they consider sufficient in their household chores, they do not usually devote more time to perfecting them, because of the clear decreasing returns of such work. It is generally much more efficient for them to devote such hours to the labour market, especially in countries where the market is sufficiently flexible for them to be able to find part-time employment.

The housewife substitutes that are offered by the market seem to be less important. Such substitutes have always existed in the form of domestic service but one of the characteristics of all the western economies has been the reduction in the number of people doing this type of work alongside the increase in opportunities for better-paid work. This has meant that the costs of domestic help for housewives have risen sharply with the consequent drop in demand. But, at the same time, the market has created other substitutes at lower prices so that people in the labour market can gain access to child care services, laundry or ready-to-eat meals without having to spend time on such tasks themselves. It is not therefore clear to what degree the net effect of the reduction in domestic service on the one hand and the development of substitution services on the other facilitate the entry of women with children into the labour market.

7   EFFECTS OF HIGHER REMUNERATION AND IMPROVED TECHNOLOGY ON WOMEN'S PARTICIPATION IN THE LABOUR MARKET AND ON THEIR WELLBEING

In order to analyse the effects on employment for women of higher remuneration and the technical progress that facilitates housework, let us start with a production potential curve indicating that a woman can produce two types of good, called L and S. L represents the monetary resources earned on the market that can be used to purchase goods that are on sale on the market (X), so that, with savings at zero

$$L = XP_X = \sum_{i=1}^{n} x_i p_i$$

S represents the domestic, or non-market, goods that a woman produces for her own use or for her family, so

$$S = \sum_{j=1}^{m} s_j$$

The line AB on Figure 2.1 represents the initial production possibility line of the woman whose behaviour we are analysing. For the purpose of simplification, this is represented by a straight line, and implies constant costs. The slope of this line, defined by the angle α, reflects the marginal rate of transformation between L and S and, therefore, the opportunity cost of devoting time to the production of S in terms of L, or of obtaining L in terms of S. This line also represents the limit of the possibilities of consumption of the person in question. The optimum will be reached at E_1, where the production potential line is at a tangent to the indifference curve with the highest index that can be reached, in this case I_1.

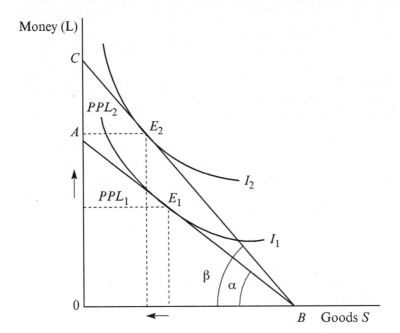

Figure 2.1   Effects of a pay rise on women's participation in the labour market

7.1   Effects of a Pay Rise

If the wages a woman can receive from the market rise, the marginal rate of transformation changes and is now defined by the angle β, and the production possibility line becomes CB. The pay rise means that the woman will devote less time to producing goods S and more time to obtaining L, so the point of equilibrium will move from E_1 to E_2. This change will have a positive effect on the woman's welfare because, while with the first production possibility line she could only reach the indifference curve I_1, with the second she will be able to reach a higher indifference curve, in this case I_2.

7.2   Effects of Improved Technology on the Production of Goods S

A technological improvement that saves time on the production of goods S will also give rise to a change in the production possibility line by changing the marginal rate of transformation. The case represented in Figure 2.2 involves a move from line AB to line AD. However, the effect on the number of hours devoted to the labour market and to the production of domestic goods is not clear. Greater efficiency in domestic production could mean that the woman is devoting more time to domestic activities. But the available data seem to indicate that what happens is actually the opposite, because technological improvements for housework usually go together with increased market activity. This trend could be explained by the fact that technical progress in housework is not isolated but takes place in parallel to general advances in technology, which bring with them higher wages and produce results of the type described above. But it may also happen that in the utility functions of women, while it is difficult to determine a limit for the obtention of L, the production of S may reach the desired point at a certain level and this means that by going further than this point there would be no marked increase in utility. This is the case shown in Figure 2.2. Here the indifference curves show that this point is reached for a level of S that is equivalent to $0F$ and indicate that the gain produced by technical

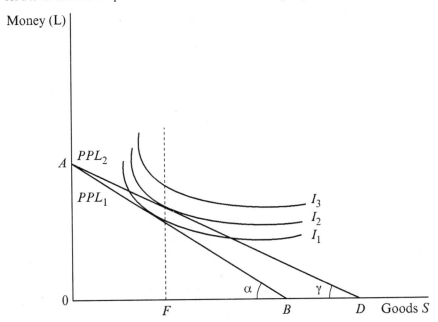

Figure 2.2   Effects of technical progress on the production of goods S and working activity of women

progress will result in a greater number of hours being devoted to market activities. At the same time, as in the above example, there is an increase in wellbeing because the woman moves from the indifference curve I_1 to I_2.

8   THE BENEFITS OF FAMILY DIVISION OF LABOUR

In order to analyse the advantages for the family of specialization and the division of labour, let us assume that the two spouses (M) and (F) are able to produce the two types of good, *L* and *S*, referred to above. Let us now suppose that M and F have a different relative efficiency in the production of *L* and *S* so that, with his greater human capital for the labour market, M is relatively more productive in the obtention of *L,* and F is relatively more productive in the production of *S*. This is the most common situation in today's world; but the analysis would be no different if F had a comparative advantage with *L* and M with *S*.

Figures 2.3 and 2.4 represent the production possibility lines under conditions of constant costs for F (*BC*) and M (*KT*) respectively.

As in the above section, the slopes of the production possibility lines, as defined by the angles α and β, represent the opportunity costs of devoting time to producing *S* or *L* for F and M respectively. Since these lines also represent the limits of consumption possibilities, while unmarried, neither of these two people could move their point of consumption to the right of their lines. In our model, the initial points of equilibrium will

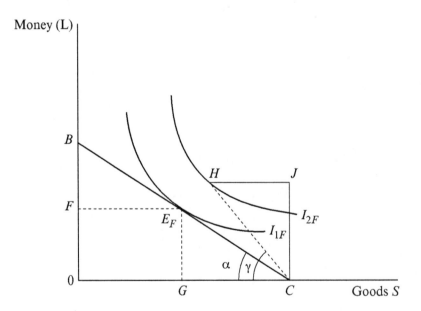

Figure 2.3   Improved welfare for the wife resulting from division of labour amongst the spouses

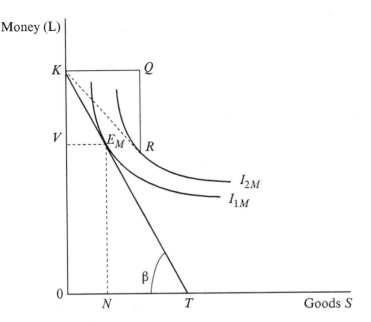

Figure 2.4   Improved welfare for the husband resulting from division of labour amongst the spouses

be determined by E_F and E_M, with a production of $0F$ for L and $0G$ for S, in the case of F, and of $0V$ and $0N$ for the same goods in the case of M.

If F and M marry, it will be possible for each of them to specialize in the production of those goods for which each has a comparative advantage: S in the case of F, and L in the case of M. Assuming that costs are constant, there will be full specialization: F will specialize in the production of S and will produce $0C$ of this good, while M will specialize in the obtention of L and will achieve the amount $0K$.

Both spouses will proceed to exchange the goods produced by each of them at a price varying between the opportunity cost defined by α and that defined by β. The closer the new terms of trade to the initial opportunity cost of F, the greater the advantages obtained by M, and vice versa. If the new terms of trade are those defined by the angle γ, with $\alpha < \gamma < \beta$, the exchange will be as follows: F will supply M with an amount of $HJ = KQ$ of goods S, and will receive in exchange an amount of $JC = QR$ to buy goods X. The points indicating the consumption of each of the spouses will now be H for F and R for M.

What is most relevant about this analysis is that each of these points of consumption is located to the right of the production possibility line for each of the spouses. This means that both now enjoy a potential for consumption that they lacked previously, and that they can reach indifference curves of a higher index than the initial curves, I_{2F} and I_{2M} respectively. So the situation defined by specialization and exchange is therefore higher in terms of welfare for both M and F.

9   COSTS OF FAMILY DIVISION OF LABOUR

The above section explained the basic principles of the economics of division of labour and its advantages. But the division of labour within the family may also give rise to costs.

Firstly, it is possible that the utility functions of each of the spouses may include more than just material goods – market and domestic goods – produced by the family. For example, the husband may find satisfaction in dealing with his children, and the wife may maximize her utility by working outside the home, although in terms of strict productivity this may not be the most efficient thing to do.

Problems arising with division of labour may take various forms, and one of the most significant is doubtless the poor social integration of a housewife in a society which, for a variety of reasons, does not show much esteem for housework or grant social rank or standing to women who carry it out.

Another argument against full specialization is based on the fact that spouses try to maximize their utility in the long term under conditions of uncertainty. The model for specialization and exchange described in the above sections is based on at least one of the following implicit assumptions: (a) the exchange will continue permanently under the same conditions; (b) once full specialization is reached, it is possible to return without any transaction costs to the situation before the marriage and the exchange. In other words, assumption (b) implies that the production potential of each spouse, both in the home and in the market, will not alter after an undetermined period of full specialization.

Both assumptions have little to do with reality and this helps to explain why, in practice, women no longer consider complete specialization in the production of domestic goods as their optimum strategy for utility maximization in the long term. The possibility of divorce or widowhood and the cost of finding a new spouse, who will accept the exchange under the same conditions, make fulfilment of the first assumption very unlikely. And the second is untenable. The formation of human capital for domestic activities and lack of use for long periods of any market training acquired earlier implies a comparative disadvantage in market activities which is difficult to overcome. In addition, full specialization in domestic work necessarily implies a high degree of dependence for the woman because, unless she obtains income from capital or a pension or generous aid from the social security, it is impossible to live without obtaining monetary income.

It is therefore efficient for a risk-averse woman to maximize a long-term utility function and not to choose full specialization, even at the cost of reducing her short-term utility.

10 THE ROLE OF THE STATE IN FAMILY DIVISION OF LABOUR

As in most of its actions, public authority is not and never has been neutral in the organization of family division of labour. One of the most important aspects of State intervention has undoubtedly been the application of laws preventing women from undertaking several types of work. Prohibition of this type amounted to arbitrary alteration of the opportunity cost of a woman's domestic work, so that, if she was prevented from obtaining a high wage in the market, the incentives for remaining at home were much greater.

Today legal discrimination by the State has disappeared from practically all the western nations,[11] and this has made it easier for women to reach jobs with responsibility. However, although legal discrimination has disappeared, there can be little doubt that, in practice, the position of women in the working world is still far from reaching that of men. With a view to changing this situation, governments are bringing out laws making it compulsory for companies to pay equal wages to men and women and even to apply affirmative action in favour of women.

Are such measures significant for greater integration of women in the labour market? The effects of this type of policy are the subject of debate. Some people consider that only by applying measures of this type will it be possible to progress towards more egalitarian integration of women in the labour market. But others think the effect of these policies will be to segment the market and make companies take on fewer women. In a market in which there is wage discrimination and much higher unemployment at the lower wage levels, to force a rise in women's wages could result in a drop in employment for women.

In more general terms, it is debatable whether a more tightly regulated labour market will benefit women. Deregulation, on the other hand, could benefit them by allowing types of contract that are of interest both to companies and job-seekers. The clearest case is that of part-time work, which is of such great importance for the integration of married women into the labour market. In Spain, in which such employment has never been widespread, in 1991 only 11.9 per cent of employed women worked part time whereas the figures were above 40 per cent in Great Britain and the north European countries.[12] Such figures indicate that few measures would facilitate job-seeking for married women as efficiently as deregulation of types of employment.

Furthermore, it would seem that measures designed to protect mothers – maternity leave, time off for breastfeeding and so on – do not encourage employment for women because part of the cost has to be taken on directly by the company.[13] And the present method of establishing social security contributions, whereby a company has to pay a proportionally greater sum for the lowest-paid jobs, seems hardly beneficial for female workers. Since on average women receive lower wages than men, this places them at a disadvantage when job hunting.

In summary, a labour market that is tightly controlled and often protectionist and inflexible with regard to anything but an eight-hour working day may create, and in some countries is creating, serious restrictions to employment outside the home for married women.

One last important method the State can use to influence family division of labour is the tax system. There has been much debate on the effects of income tax on the supply of labour, because the income effect and the substitution effect here work in opposite directions. Because of the substitution effect, that is, the effect of the variation in the opportunity cost of leisure when wages change, income tax tends to make people less willing to work, because the net wage is lower and therefore the opportunity cost of leisure falls. But, because of the income effect, that is, the effect of the variation in income caused by the change in wages, the tax creates incentives for people to work more because, by reducing the net wage, workers feel poorer and are prepared to devote less time to leisure. The final result will depend on which of the two effects predominates. If the substitution effect predominates, people will work less (or will enter the black economy) and, if the income effect predominates, people will work more.

For our purposes what is relevant is not, however, which effect will predominate for the whole of the working population but whether the reaction to the tax will be the same for both men and women. And here economists generally agree that, because the woman's wage tends to be treated as a complementary income for many families, the supply of labour for women will show a greater negative response than that for men when taxes are imposed. In other words, the higher the rate of income tax the woman has to pay, the greater incentive she will have to leave her job and save money by personally carrying out a greater number of domestic tasks.

The matter of taxation becomes even more relevant if we take into account the fact that, in progressive taxes, the tax rate that determines whether a women will work more or less is not the average rate but the marginal rate, that is, the tax paid on the last units of income earned. So the income tax treatment given to the family may determine whether a married woman will work or not.

NOTES

1. The comparative advantage model was initially devised by the economists of the classical school to explain why it is efficient for international trade to exist and for countries not to close their frontiers to trade. However, the model is more general than this and can be used with good results to explain most of the situations in which there is a process of division of labour, such as in this case of the family.

2. The classic description of the neoclassical theory of the division of labour within the family is given in Becker, G. (1991), Ch. 2. But this chapter may be difficult to understand for readers without some knowledge of economics. Simpler versions of the theory can be found in Papps, I. (1980), and Lemmenicier, B. (1988). For a criticism of this theory, see Jacobsen, J.P. (1994), especially Ch. 3.
3. For the development of the 'male superiority' model from the point of view of economics, see Boserup, E. (1989), and (1987).
4. This is the thesis defended, for example, by Goldberg, S. (1994).
5. See section III of Chapter 1 entitled 'The economics of the family and biology'.
6. Bozon, M. (1990).
7. Boserup, E. (1989), pp. 216–17. On this effect in connection with racial discrimination, see Becker, G.S. (1971), pp. 58–62.
8. Boserup, E. (1989), pp. 53–68. The results of this policy were, as might be expected, very bad for the economy of many African countries.
9. E. Rathbone stated in 1917 that in England it was the male trade unions that had the greatest support amongst the population because it was widely accepted that men had to maintain a family whereas women had no such obligations. Rathbone, E. (1917), pp. 55–68.
10. OECD (1991).
11. But not from other institutions such as the Catholic Church.
12. OECD (1991).
13. This problem is covered in greater depth in Chs 9 and 10 on the effects of policies for the family.

3. Marriage (I)

1 THE MARRIAGE CONTRACT

The term 'contract' is, no doubt, the best way to define the legal relationship between two people who decide to live together and form a family. However, we are not talking here about a contract reached on the basis of complete freedom of agreement between the parties. On the contrary, the marriage contract is a strongly regulated one in which the law substantially limits the freedom of the parties in reaching an agreement.

Why does the law interfere with freedom of agreement in some contracts, particularly in the marriage contract? Two different reasons are usually given to explain this interference. First, reasons of efficiency. According to this point of view, the existence of rules that regulate marriage contracts can reduce transaction costs in the negotiation of clauses, and can act as a reference if queries appear at a later date in the resolution of issues not previously agreed upon specifically by the parties. In practice, people getting married do not normally sign a specific agreement but just comply with the general conditions established by civil law. The few marital agreements that are reached before getting married generally refer to the future economic functioning of the marital partnership.

The second reason why the law strictly regulates the marriage contract is equity. In pursuit of equity, the law often tries to favour the supposedly weaker party, as opposed to the better placed party who could use this dominant position to obtain unfair advantages. In principle, nothing could be more laudable than this attitude of the law-maker. The problem arises, however, when undesired effects occur as a result of the strategies of each of the conflicting parties. Let us take a simple example. It is generally believed that joint property ownership, by which all property acquired by either of the partners during the marriage belongs in equal shares to both parties, is an institution that favours women. The reasoning is that, since women in the majority of cases devote less time to employment in the work force and more time to domestic chores, they earn less money and, therefore, the equal share of earnings benefits them. But, in the long run, this institution may well have been detrimental for women if the expectations raised were high enough to make them think that with joint property ownership their future was guaranteed in the case of a divorce. A law establishing the separation of property during marriage as a general rule, in the absence of any other agreement to the contrary, would possibly produce the effect of giving women the incentive to obtain training that would allow them to earn sufficient income in the job market on their own, or to negotiate advantageous conditions in the case of a divorce.

An important characteristic of the relationship between marriage partners is that the marriage contract has always been conceived as an agreement destined to last a long time. Quite apart from whether we believe or not that the objective of marriage is the commitment to live together 'for life', the marriage contract is not conceived as a fixed term agreement, at the end of which the parties know that their rights and obligations are those specified at the time of signing. In other words, although in practice the contract may last only a short time, it is drawn up without previously determining the time of duration. The marriage contract also has several other interesting characteristics. Firstly, not all the conditions are going to remain constant during the time it is in force; secondly, the parties do not have precise information on the possible nature of such changes; and, lastly, it is possible to redraft the contract or add new conditions at any time while it is in force.

These characteristics affect the nature of the contract in an important way, specifically with respect to the possibility of bilateral or unilateral breaking of the marital contract, which the law in western countries allows today. Although marriage is a long-term contract, its implicit conditions may be the object of a new contract at any time within the general framework of family law. This means that the marriage contract, in this sense, shares the characteristics of adaptability and flexibility of recurrent short-term contracts. In the economic literature on contracts, it is usual to insist on the superiority of recurrent short-term contracts over those covering a long term in a single agreement.[1] This is because, rather than having to make allowances for all the changes in the original circumstances and their effects on the conditions initially agreed upon, it is possible to adapt the clauses to the new circumstances each time the short-term contract expires. As will be seen in the next section, this form of contract is useful for the efficient organization of marital relationships.

All these characteristics mean that the 'informal' elements of the contract take on special importance. Trust, cooperation and willingness to accept change are thus efficient attitudes in a marriage in that they reduce the transaction costs which any process of adaptation and new contract implies. Furthermore, both marriage partners have incentives to behave in a more cooperative way if they want the contractual relationship to continue over subsequent periods.

2   MARRIAGE AS A SUCCESSION OF SHORT-TERM CONTRACTS

The idea that marriage, considered as a succession of short-term contracts, reinforces the incentives for the partners to maintain a cooperative attitude can be explained as an infinitely repeated game.

Figure 3.1 shows this type of game in which each partner (M and F) is offered the chance of bringing the game to an end with whatever strategy best suits him or her at that particular moment, or of handing responsibility for the decision to the other partner, knowing that if the other partner decides to end the game, then the first player will be in a worse position than that which he or she would have gained if only the decision to end the game had been taken in the previous move.

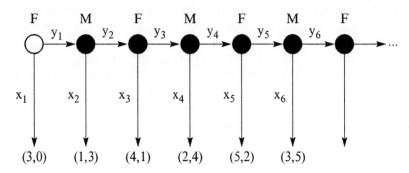

Figure 3.1   Marriage as an infinitely repeated game

The 'x' strategies represent the options for maximizing individual utility in the short term; the 'y' strategies represent cooperative strategies based on sufficient trust in the other partner to assume that, although the other partner could decide to end the game to his or her own benefit, he or she will also adopt a 'y' strategy allowing higher utility levels to be reached by both partners.

Finally, two conditions should be established for the game to take place. The first is that the number of recurrent short-term contracts is indefinite and neither partner really knows when the marriage will come to an end. The second condition assumes information on the utility levels they may be able to reach, although for the model to function it is sufficient that the utility level increases with the number of contracts, as can be seen in the figure. The benefits sought by each partner do not have to be symmetrical and the utility level each aspires to can be obtained from very different sources (for example, one partner may seek benefits from material consumption and the other psychological satisfaction).

Which strategy will each player adopt? In the first move, F may choose x_1 and attain a value of 3, or risk leaving the decision to M, who may choose x_2 and attain the same value of 3, while F's utility is reduced to 1. And so on. Will the partners trust one another, or will they try to maximize their utility in the short term? There is no clear answer to this question since it would seem that by using an appropriate parameter to calculate the discounted values to be obtained in the future, that there is no optimal strategy for F or M independent of that adopted by the other partner.

There are good reasons, however, to think that the incentives are great enough for each partner to cooperate and adopt 'y' strategies, which will allow them to maximize the updated utility values that can be attained throughout their married life and that, therefore, an initial 'y' strategy will result in the same strategy being adopted by the other partner.[2]

The key assumption to obtain this result is the indeterminate number of short-term contracts the married couple will face throughout their marriage. If a predetermined limit is placed on the number of contracts, a completely different result could arise in which the optimal strategy would be non-collaboration from the very beginning.

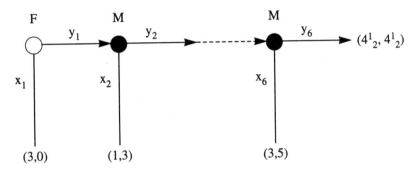

Figure 3.2   A repeated game with a finite number of contracts

This case is shown in Figure 3.2. This game is the same as the one shown in the previous figure, with the only exception being that the number of times a strategy can be adopted is limited and the game finishes when M reaches either y_6 or x_6. In this case, the result of an x_6 strategy clearly favours the partner who makes this decision (M) and hurts the other partner. Faced with this decision, M is bound to choose x_6 which is the most satisfactory strategy. However, it will not be easy to get the opportunity to make this choice. The reason is that F, foreseeing this result, will not choose y_5 in the previous move but x_5. Based on the same reasoning, M will not play y_4, F will not play y_3 and so forth and in the first move F will choose to make the most of her short-term utility and will choose x_1, which will result in the non-existence of the marriage from the very beginning. The very nature of the marriage contract as defined in the previous section will, however, allow this problem to be avoided and explains the predominance of sustained relations of cooperation throughout the life of a married couple.

3   COORDINATION: WHERE SHALL WE SPEND OUR HOLIDAYS?

The model which presents marriage as an infinitely repeated game made up of recurrent short-term contracts brings us to the conclusion that cooperative strategies allow both partners to reach the highest levels of satisfaction and a long-lasting marriage. But, within the framework of this type of strategy, there may be a wide range of possible solutions. In other words, the husband and wife can act in coordination, following the lead taken by the other partner.

The case of coordinated activities and of several possible equilibrium points is usually analysed by economists in game theory using the so-called game of the battle of the sexes. Let us assume the following situation. When deciding where to spend their holidays, F likes to go to the beach but M prefers to spend the time in the mountains. However, while F and M may disagree, they still agree that they want to spend their holidays together, and for each partner it is better to be together than to be alone in the preferred destination. The satisfaction levels each partner attains with each choice are shown in Figure 3.3, where the upper numbers in each box represent F's satisfaction levels and the lower numbers in each box represent the M's satisfaction levels.

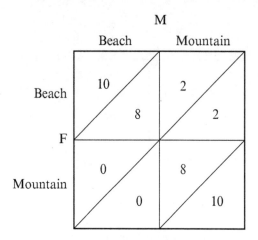

Figure 3.3   Where shall we spend our holidays? The game of the battle of the sexes

The assumption of a strong preference for spending the holidays together implies the exclusion of the upper right and the lower left boxes as good solutions. The final result will no doubt be one of the two boxes offering values of 8 and 10. But which of the two?

Both the upper left-hand box and the lower right-hand box represent Nash equilibria and, from an efficiency point of view, it is impossible to choose one over the other. The outcome is indeterminate and the choice one way or the other, therefore, will have to be based on other criteria. If both partners are equal and if their preferences are equally strong, the choice to go to the beach one year and to the mountains the following year would be the way to reinforce cooperative behaviour in the marriage partnership. But other solutions are also possible. If one of the partners has some sort of superiority over the other (for example, by bringing more money into the household), then it is more likely his or her choice will win and, in this case, he or she will benefit more from the holiday.

4   THE CHOICE OF A MARRIAGE PARTNER

The first step in forming a family is the choice of the marriage partner. In some cultures, the partner is selected by the parents of the couple but, with time, the idea has gained ground in most of the world that it should be the couple themselves who should make the choice. What are the criteria guiding them in their choice? As we have already seen, the family is as much a consumption unit as a production unit and both these aspects are taken into account when making the selection. Since the family is a consumption unit, the best results are obtained when the tastes and preferences of the husband and wife are similar. Therefore, based on this first criterion, it is to be expected that marriages between people who belong to the same class, religion and social group will be more successful in that normally their tastes, interests and behaviour coincide at least to a certain extent.

But the family is also a production unit. A partner is therefore sought to complement the comparative advantages of the other partner and allow for specialization and division of work. In this case, the criteria for selecting a partner are based more on the differences than on the similarities in aspects such as human capital or personal income. Traditionally, in these cases, the dominant position is taken by the husband, giving rise to the phenomenon of female hypergamy which will be studied in detail in a later section of this chapter.

The search for the ideal partner is always a complex matter requiring time and resources, as we shall see in the following section. But these costs are necessary if one wishes to reduce to a minimum the probability of a marriage breakup, which would imply even higher costs. Engagements and living together before marriage are aimed at acquiring the necessary information on the future partner before legally formalizing the marriage.

Marriage involves a large investment by both partners, especially by the woman since she takes on most of the burden of raising the children and generally her chances of promotion in the job market are limited. Therefore it is logical that each should look for information that gives a certain guarantee of how the other partner will behave once they are married. In this sense, the behaviour of the woman is not substantially different from that of females of other species in the animal world which demand that their future partners carry out certain activities (construction of nests, for example, in the case of some birds) to show they are willing to establish a relationship stable enough to guarantee the survival of their offspring.

At the same time this information is limited by the costs of obtaining it. In a society in which, for example, great value is placed on the unmarried woman's virginity, so that the possibility of finding a suitable husband is substantially reduced if she has previously had sexual relations with another man, sex before marriage will not be accepted as a general practice. In these societies it is not that people do not think that sex before marriage allows the future couple to get to know one another better, but that the costs for the woman are too high if the relationship does not end in marriage.[3]

The length of the engagement may be determined by many factors (social custom, the couple's economic situation, the families' acceptance or rejection and so forth). But, in addition to these conditions of a social nature, the expected cost of making a mistake in marriage is also one of the factors that helps to determine the time devoted to obtaining information on the potential partner.

Thus a couple who decide not to have children will face lower costs in the breakup of the marriage than a couple who have children, since children make up the main joint investment in the marriage. For this reason, it would be logical for the former couple to invest less in information than the latter and for their engagement to be shorter. The same can be said of those couples who regard marriage as a short-term agreement to live together, rather than considering the possibility of it lasting many years.

In general, the cost of ending a marriage may determine the optimal level of prior information in each social context. If the legal system does not allow divorce, or makes it difficult and expensive, the cost of selecting the wrong marriage partner will be much higher than in those systems in which divorce is simple and cheap. One can expect, therefore, that greater facilities in getting a divorce will mean not only a larger number of divorces but also shorter engagement periods.

5   THE MATING GAME

The complexity of the motives governing the selection of a marriage partner, as we have already seen, means that the choice of partner is not always based on similarities between the husband and wife. The following model tries to offer an explanation of this.

Let us assume a society made up of two women (F_1 and F_2) and two men (M_1 and M_2), in which M_1 and F_1 have characteristics which make them particularly desirable to the opposite sex, giving us

$$M_1 \succ M_2 \text{ for } F_1 \text{ and } F_2$$
$$F_1 \succ F_2 \text{ for } M_1 \text{ and } M_2$$

Let us also assume that being single is not considered an interesting option for either of these people and that any marriage is preferable to remaining single.

The combination M_1F_1, formed by the two people with the most valued characteristics is, logically, the one that offers the greater benefit; while the combination M_2F_2 is the one that gives the lowest result. How will each person involved in the selection process behave? If each partner in a marriage obtains half the benefits, then both M_1 and F_1 will prefer to marry one another, since in this way they will obtain the best result, not only in the partnership but individually ($19 > 7.5$). M_2 and F_2 would prefer to marry F_1 and M_1 respectively and obtain an individual benefit of 7.5 instead of 3. But these marriages will not be possible since M_1 and F_1 will always prefer to marry one another.

The situation changes, however, if we substitute the principle whereby the benefits from the marriage are divided equally among the partners and in its place we admit that the distribution of benefits may depend on a process of negotiation in which each party is going to obtain the largest possible individual benefit. It seems reasonable to assume in this situation that, whereas in the marriages M_1F_1 and M_2F_2 the balance in the relative position of the partners (the best with the best, the worst with the worst) will bring about an equal distribution of the benefits of the marriage as seen previously, in the marriages M_1F_2 and M_2F_1 the partners with the more highly valued characteristics would be in a stronger negotiating position and would obtain more than 50 per cent of the benefits.

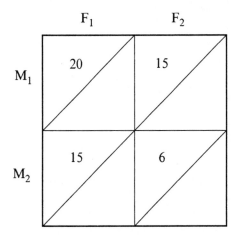

Figure 3.4 Benefits from possible partnerships

In this case, the best strategy for M_1 and F_1 could be not to marry one another but to marry someone with inferior characteristics. The only restriction they would have to respect in the distribution of benefits is that, their individual benefits now being higher than those achieved by marrying one another, the final result for M_2 and F_2 is better than the one these two people would get if they were to marry one another.

In the example shown in Figure 3.4, such negotiation would be possible since the benefits are distributed in such a way that, in the combinations M_1F_2 and M_2F_1, each person improves on the result they would have obtained in the marriages M_1F_1 and M_2F_2. Figure 3.5 shows this possible negotiated situation. In it the total benefit from each marriage

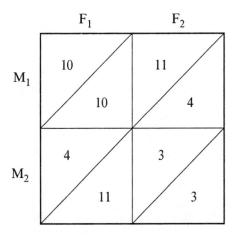

Figure 3.5 Benefits from negotiated partnerships

is divided, the first number showing the benefits to be gained by M and the second number the benefits to be gained by F.

In this case, M_1 and F_1 will choose to marry the person of the opposite sex with inferior characteristics as long as they gain a sufficiently large share of the benefits to exceed the individual result they would gain if they married the person with better characteristics. M_2 and F_2 will be willing to reduce their percentage share of the benefits of the marriage as long as the individual result for each of them is higher than they would get if they married one another.

6 ECONOMIC ANALYSIS OF THE SEARCH FOR A PARTNER

Economic theory can help not only to establish the characteristics of the most convenient marriage partner but also to determine the length of time to be devoted to looking for a partner and the investment to be made in the search. So the so-called search theory that is frequently used by economists to explain problems of disequilibrium in the economy, especially in the labour market, is also relevant in the analysis of the search for a partner.

Finding a potential marriage partner with satisfactory characteristics requires time and money. As in any other search process, the greater the effort made and the longer the time spent, the greater the probability of finding a suitable partner. But does this mean that the search process is more efficient the more intensive it is and the longer it lasts? Clearly, the answer is no. Because, on the one hand, the marginal returns of the investment decrease in the search for an ideal marriage partner and, on the other, the search incurs costs for the person undertaking it. These costs vary depending on the person and are not only financial. The most important element is the opportunity cost that a person has to pay for remaining single. For a person who is happy being single, the opportunity cost of the time used in the search will be much smaller than for a person who needs or strongly desires to stop living alone or to leave the family unit he or she has lived in until that time.

According to this model, the optimal search process should terminate when the return – in terms of 'quality' improvement of the possible partner – from the last unit invested in the process (marginal return) is equal to the cost of the unit.

Figure 3.6 shows this point of equilibrium. The optimal investment level in the search for a marriage partner will be determined by the quantity $0B_1$, the point at which the curve of marginal costs (*MC*) intersects that of the marginal returns of the investment (*MR*). At all points situated to the left of B_1 (the *P* area), $MR > MC$, so it will be efficient to increase the amount of investment in the search. But to the right of B_1 (the *N* area), since $MR < MC$, it will not be efficient to spend any more time or effort because the returns will be negative.

The process of searching for a partner, however, is more complex than is shown in Figure 3.6 because in this figure we are assuming that everyone has access

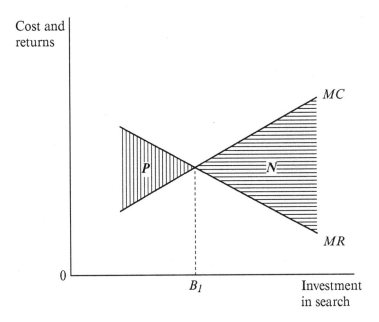

Figure 3.6   Costs and returns in the search for a partner

to fairly accurate information on what the costs and benefits will be of the resources invested in the search for a marriage partner. In reality people move in a context of uncertainty in which they do not know with any precision what the quality level of their future partner will be nor how people of the opposite sex value their own qualities. As a result, we can start from a more realistic assumption that each person has certain minimum expectations that are subjective and different in each case with regards to his or her future partner, and that he or she is prepared to marry any person who fulfils this minimum.

Figure 3.7 shows the role that this minimum quality level plays in the search for a partner by correlating the time and intensity of the search on the one side with the 'quality' of the partner on the other. Both variables have a positive correlation although from a certain point onwards one must expect decreasing quality improvements for each new unit invested in the search. Each person establishes minimum quality levels, below which he or she is not willing to marry. For example, a person who establishes a minimum level of Q_1 will be willing to interrupt the search process at B_1. Higher requirement levels will demand, *ceteris paribus*, the use of larger resources in the search. Thus, if a minimum quality of Q_2 is desired, a search investment of B_2 will be required.

Quality of
partner

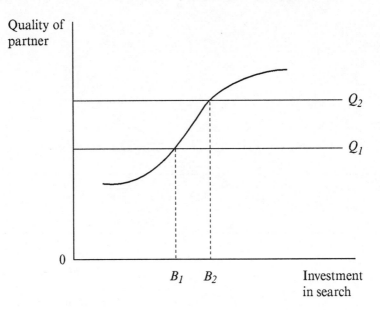

Figure 3.7   Minimum quality and investment levels in the search for a partner

This minimum level, however, does not have to remain always the same. A person could have made a very erroneous initial estimate of his or her possibilities in the marriage market and, after a long search period, not have reached the minimum level he or she had established at the outset. At this stage, the search process should be re-examined, introducing lower minimum quality levels for the possible marriage partner. In this way a process of exploring the market takes place in which each unit of time and resources invested in the search for a partner allows the person to improve the information he or she has regarding the real possibilities in the marriage market.

However, in this exploration of the market, as in many other searches for an equilibrium point, initial failure caused by placing one's expectations too high may not lead to successive reductions in the established level. Rather, the pendulum may swing the other way and the person may seriously underestimate his or her possibilities and accept a much lower quality level in the marriage partner than the one he or she could have attained by adapting expectations better to reality.

7   HYPERGAMY[4]

In the animal world, the difference in reproductive strategies between males and females seems to be one of the main reasons for the different behaviour they adopt in their relationships. From an economic point of view, the intensive reproductive strategy of females and the extensive reproductive strategy of males determine that females should be considered the scarce commodity in this mating 'market'. In other words, although the number of males and females born is approximately the same, the male demand for the reproductive services of females is much higher than the female demand for the reproductive services of males and, as a result, the males have to compete amongst themselves to mate with a female. In fact, it is usual in the animal world for a large number of males to be unable to father offspring in the course of their lives and, therefore, to transmit their genes to the next generation.

As a result, male behaviour in courtship is aimed at convincing the female that his genes are such that he merits the large investment she must make. It is a constant factor that the sex which does the courting always plans on a lesser investment. Once the males have shown what they are worth, the females will mate with those males which offer a better guarantee of survival for their offspring and, therefore, a greater probability of passing on their genetic inheritance into the future (female hypergamy).

The female of the human species is probably the animal who invests most in each of her offspring and, therefore, like the rest of superior females, should be the 'hard-to-get, scarce and demanding' sex, when compared with the male who should adopt the behaviour pattern and physical appearance typical of courtship, and not vice versa. This contradiction suggests the possibility that, in this peculiar characteristic of the human female as the sex which plays the active role in courtship, other very important cultural factors enter into play.

In this respect, the most important cultural peculiarity of the human species is that the market in which men and women get acquainted is subdivided into two different sub-markets. In the first, which we shall label 'informal', the relationships that are negotiated are non-matrimonial, whereas the second sub-market is the 'marital' one, taking this term in the broad sense of stable cohabitation, with the existence of reciprocal rights and obligations.

In the first of these sub-markets – the informal one – the cost paid by the woman is much higher than for the man. If the woman were to bear children without any commitment from the man who fathered them, she would have to make a further investment in bringing up and educating her offspring and, in all probability, the quality of her children would be inferior to that which they would have had if she had managed to get help from the father. In other words, she would be in the same situation as other female mammals who, only exceptionally and in very few species, receive help from the male. Furthermore, the human female would have to face the social sanctions which exist in almost all cultures and which tend to control the market between the sexes. Those members of the female sex who, throughout evolution, agreed to participate in this informal market did not have as much reproductive success as those who negotiated with the male sex to achieve some sort of help for their offspring. The result of following the most economic criterion has been that women have traditionally been reluctant to participate in the informal sub-market, a factor which has converted them into the 'scarce' sex in comparison with the large number of men who want to participate in it.[5]

The case of the matrimonial sub-market is different. In this market, the mutual advantages are the result of negotiation between the members of each sex. Here the man has to bear relatively high costs in comparison with the males of other superior species, since he is going to be required to use a large proportion of his material resources and efforts to maintain his home and his children. As a result, the number of men interested in taking part in this sub-market is likely to be smaller and here, therefore, the male is the scarce sex. What is peculiar to this matrimonial sub-market is that, contrary to what happens in the animal world and in the informal sub-market, it is not the scarce sex which, being in a position to choose, selects the most intelligent female companion, with the largest endowment of human capital. On the contrary, in this matrimonial sub-market too, it is the woman who adopts hypergamous behaviour.

8   THE ECONOMICS OF HUMAN HYPERGAMY

It is not difficult to find female hypergamous behaviour in both traditional cultures and modern societies. Hypergamy seems to be a constant in all human societies. However, there are important characteristics which differentiate traditional cultures from modern societies. In traditional cultures, the woman's position is usually notably inferior to that of the male, and this stratification based on sex is often associated with rigid social differences between the classes or castes. It is interesting to note that, even in very closed societies, hypergamous behaviour may violate the basic principles of social stratification and still be socially accepted. Hindu society, no doubt the most characteristic of caste societies, provides us with a good example. In spite of the existence of all types of barriers between castes in Hindu society, law and custom allow women of an inferior caste to marry men from a superior one. But the possibility does not usually exist for men to marry women from a higher caste.[6]

In modern societies, the difference in status which characterizes hypergamous behaviour is measured basically in terms of the relative endowments of human capital. In western societies, the principle has been maintained that women generally marry at a slightly earlier age than men. Apart from the biological or social reasons that could explain this custom, the implications for our analysis are very important. *Ceteris paribus*, to marry young means a lesser endowment of human capital. This inferior human capital is the result of a lesser investment in professional training – because of the lower age – both in years of academic

education as well as experience in the work force. A situation of inequality from
the very start, as will be seen further on, may give rise to important differences
not only in how work is distributed between the couple, but also in the advantages
that each partner obtains from the marriage.[7]

To raise one's social status by marrying a partner with a higher endowment
of human capital thus turns out to be a basically female characteristic. It is true
that in modern society it is also possible for men to improve their social
standing through marriage. But this rise in social standing is usually the result
of greater wealth and status inherited by the woman, and rarely through marriage
to a woman with a brilliant professional career. In fact, those women who
follow a professional career find their probability of marrying substantially
reduced, whereas exactly the opposite happens in the case of men. For instance,
French statistics in 1970 showed that the percentage of unmarried executives
aged between 35 and 52 was a mere 2.9 per cent for men, whereas in the case
of women it reached the high level of 24 per cent.[8] In Spain, the Fertility
Survey held in 1985 also showed that women with a higher education tended
to get married and to live with their husband to a much lesser extent than
women with lower professional qualifications. Amongst women with no formal
education, the percentage of women who lived with their husbands was over
85 per cent in 1985, whereas those who did not have a stable relationship
amounted to less than 15 per cent. However, these figures were considerably
different for women who had higher education: only 57.84 per cent were
married and lived with their husbands, whereas 39.32 per cent had no stable
relationship and 2.84 per cent had some sort of relationship other than a
matrimonial one.[9]

The statistics seem to show, therefore, that at least in some developed
countries, the chances of getting married or of maintaining a stable relationship
vary in the case of men and women according to their endowment of human
capital. *Ceteris paribus*, if we define the function that relates the probability of
getting married (P) with the endowment of human capital of the person in
question (C_H), for values of P between 0 and 1,

$$P = P (C_H)$$

data show that the function will increase in the case of men and will decrease
in the case of women. Figure 3.8 shows in graphic form the differences in the
probability of getting married as a function of human capital and sex.

Another example of these hypergamous practices in developed countries can
be found in the fact that men with a high endowment of human capital are
frequently willing to marry women from a lower status; but marriages are very
rare between high-level professional women and men of lower status. The
phenomenon can be seen nowadays even more often in the case of marriages

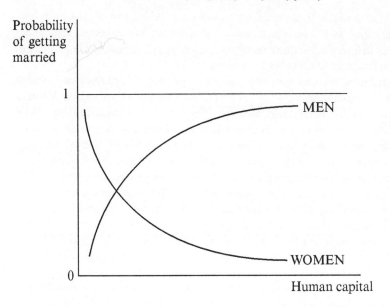

Figure 3.8   Probability of getting married and human capital

between citizens of developed countries and immigrants from Third World countries. These marriages take place relatively frequently between men from the host country and immigrant women, where the women devote their time mainly to the traditionally female household chores. Economic theory suggests that in these countries marriages could also take place between career women and immigrants of a lower status, where these men would look after the woman and the home. However, such relationships seem to be extremely rare.

What are the effects of hypergamy on the marriage relationship and on the distribution of gains resulting from the partnership? As will be seen later in more detail, above all, hypergamy allows the husband to gain a larger proportion than the wife of the benefits produced during the marriage. This does not imply that the wife is 'exploited' by the husband, since she seeks to improve her situation through the marriage and if she chooses a hypergamous marriage it is precisely because she hopes to gain from such a decision. But the difference in starting-points will limit her possibilities of developing strategies, once she is married, which would allow her to gain possession of the greater share of the benefits produced by the partnership. Therefore, one should expect that, *ceteris paribus*, the larger the degree of hypergamy, the larger the relative appropriation of matrimonial benefits by the husband.

Another important effect of hypergamy is that it reinforces the stability of the marriage institution by making a breakup more costly for women.[10] The reduction in the degree of hypergamy, due to the large endowment of human capital of women when going into marriage, can thus explain, at least partially, the rise in the divorce rate in western societies.

Thus, if time confirms the tendency for a reduction in the degree of hypergamy, we shall have to expect marriages to be on an ever more equal standing and, at the same time, increasingly unstable. It is not clear, however, how the level of hypergamy will evolve in the short term, since the effects of the rise in human capital endowment in women who marry may be partially balanced out by the consequences of the crisis existing today in the marriage institution in the western world. The substantial rise in the divorce rate and the generalization of successive marriages may, in effect, have reinforced the hypergamous behaviour of women. Studies carried out in various countries[11] show that the marriage rate for widowed and divorced men is substantially higher than that of widowed and divorced women. This difference shows that well-off widowed and divorced men are sought as marriage partners by all types of women, whereas widowed and divorced women do not find suitable husbands. The result is that a relatively large number of women compete for a relatively small number of well-off men, while many bachelors have difficulties in getting married and there is a substantial increase in the number of households made up exclusively of mothers and children. If this tendency which we are seeing now is confirmed in the future, there is likely to be a continuation – or even an increase – in the age differences between marriage partners and their capacity to generate income, these being the variables used above to define female hypergamy. The relative importance of each of these phenomena, with their contradictory effects, is not yet clear.

9 STRATEGIES AND DISTRIBUTION OF GAINS IN HYPERGAMOUS MARRIAGES

As seen in the previous section, hypergamy has serious effects on marital relationships. The following analysis uses elementary game theory to discuss the husband's and wife's strategies in the distribution of gains proceeding from their marriage and their respective attitudes when faced with the possible breakup of the partnership when one of them decides that reality does not live up to the expectations he or she had at the start of the marriage. The gains each person may obtain from a marriage vary greatly. Without going into the details of their nature or characteristics, we will simply assume that everyone who marries is capable of valuing these gains through a utility index, and can put his or her preferences in an order when faced with a list of possible situations, based on the utility to be gained in each situation.

The starting-point is the initial values of the husband's and wife's utility (U_M and U_F) before they were married. Let us assume, at first, starting-points of equal utility, with a value of 5, for example.

$$U_M = U_F = 5$$

Figure 3.9 gives us the extensive form of a game that shows the utility indexes that a husband (U'_M) and wife (U'_F) can reach in a marriage, given the above assumption.

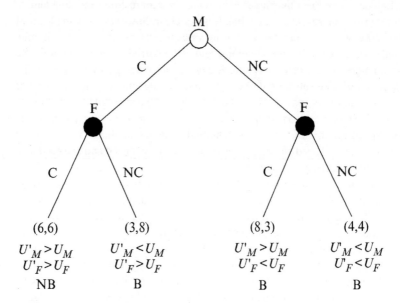

Figure 3.9   The game with equal starting values ($U_M = U_F = 5$)

In this marriage, each partner can choose between a strategy of cooperation (C), or a strategy of non-cooperation (NC) which consists of trying to make the other partner take on the burdens of everyday life. As the results of the strategies are symmetrical, it makes no difference which of the two is the first to adopt his or her strategy. In the model, it is assumed that the marriage is a contract that may be broken at any moment, that no transaction costs for entering or breaking the contract exist, and that each partner will be prepared to break up the marriage as soon as the utility index falls below the level that person had before entering the marriage. If we define U''_M and U''_F as the utilities that M and F each reach after the divorce, and if we assume that these utilities are the same as those that each partner had before entering the marriage,[12] it is possible to define two different situations: one of maintaining the marriage (NB) and the other of marital breakup (B):

$$\text{NB if, and only if, } U'_M \geq U_M$$
$$\text{and } U'_F \geq U_F$$
$$\text{B if } U'_M < U_M$$
$$\text{and/or } U'_F < U_F$$

In this case, mutual cooperation is the only strategy that allows the marriage to continue. As a result, if both M and F are aware of the matrix of possible results of the game, they know that the marriage will break up if they do not adopt the C strategy. Thus, the assumption of equal utility indexes determines the result of the game.

However, if we put a different restriction on the initial values, the optimal strategies vary. Let us, therefore, change the restriction by introducing into the model hypergamous behaviour, in the meaning given above, on the part of F. Hypergamy means, by definition, a difference in the starting-points and, specifically, $U_M > U_F$. This value difference before marriage may modify the strategies of both partners. Let us now take the case of a hypergamous marriage in which

$$UM = 5$$
$$UF = 2$$

and carry out the same game.

Figure 3.10 shows such a game. It can be seen how the optimal strategy of each partner changes substantially as a result of the reduction of the value of U_F. For the husband, the best strategy now is non-cooperation since the gains he can obtain from this strategy are greater than those he would obtain from cooperation. Since the initial restriction has changed, once the husband has adopted this strategy, the most efficient option for the wife is to cooperate. The reason is that, although the gain for her would be theoretically greater with a strategy of non-cooperation (4 < 3), such a strategy would lead to the breakup of the marriage and would reduce the value of her utility index to 2, which is the worst of all possible situations in the game, since $U_F < U'_F$ in all cases.[13]

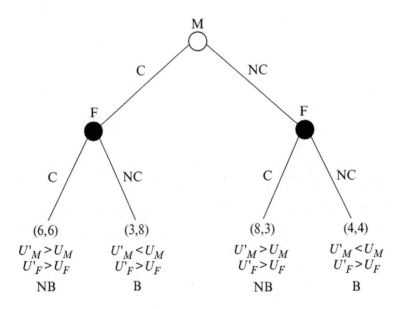

Figure 3.10 The game with different starting values ($U_M = 5$; $U_F = 2$)

NOTES

1. See, for example, Williamson, O. (1986), pp. 265–70.
2. Note that this is a similar result to the one Robert Axelrod attributes to tit-for-tat strategy in long-term relationships. Axelrod, R. (1984).
3. A different question is why so much value has traditionally been placed on a woman's virginity before marriage. One of the few existing explanations from an economic point of view is the one given by R. Posner who asserts that the reason could be that virginity before marriage is an indication of faithfulness after marriage. By marrying a virgin, the husband thus reduces the cost of watching over his wife's behaviour in the future. Posner, R. (1992b), p. 169. The relationship between virginity prior to marriage and faithfulness after, however, is very questionable. If the wife is a virgin at the time of marriage, the only thing the husband can be sure of is that she is not going into the marriage already pregnant by another man.
4. Previous versions of this section and the two following sections were included in Cabrillo F. and Cachafeiro, M.L. (1993) and in Cabrillo, F. (1995).
5. The growing tendency of women to participate in this sub-market in recent decades can be explained by the substantial reduction in costs which both technical progress and some important social changes have brought about for them, especially more effective contraception and the decrease in the social value of virginity and chastity. These changes in female behaviour, as a result of the lower cost of certain types of behaviour, fit perfectly into the model.
6. Boserup, E. (1989), p. 50.
7. The age difference at the time of marriage is quite a lot higher in traditional societies where the average difference may be nine or ten years, as in some peoples in Africa. Economic development and modernization, however, contribute to the reduction – although not the elimination – of these differences and to the fact that Third World countries pattern themselves closer on developed countries. In India, for example, the average age difference of eight years at the beginning of this century had fallen to five by 1970. See Lardinois, R. (1986), p. 292. In European countries, the average age difference between men and women who marry is 2–2.5 years.
8. Lemmenicier, B. (1988), p. 49.
9. Ministerio de Cultura-Instituto de la Mujer (1988), p. 14.
10. Note that the system of joint property ownership tends to weaken this effect in those cases in which the partners have acquired assets after marrying, since this reduces the break-up costs for women.
11. See references to Spain, France and Italy in Iglesias Ussel, J. (1994), vol. I, pp. 441–5. For a reference to England, see Wolf, M. (1994).
12. Such an assumption is clearly not a very realistic simplification of what usually happens in divorce cases. Precisely one of the problems faced by the courts when fixing the amount of alimony to be paid in a divorce by husbands to their ex-wives is that frequently $U''_F < U_F$ and, often, $U''_M > U_M$. But, for the purposes of the problem under discussion, it is possible to introduce this simplification without the conclusions being substantially affected.
13. Indeed, the possibility exists that the wife will use the strategy of non-cooperation and marital breakup as a threat, following the argument that the husband obtains a larger utility index in a situation of bilateral cooperation than in a divorce ($U'_M = 6 > U''_M = 5$). However, if this behaviour is carried to its ultimate consequences and no change in attitude is obtained from the husband, then it would bring a worsening in the situation of the wife who designed the strategy. Furthermore, if we change the assumption $U''_F = U_F$ to the surely more realistic one $U''_F < U_F$, as was indicated in note 12, there would be even less incentive for the wife to use the threat of marital breakup as a strategy.

4. Marriage (II)

1 FORMALIZATION OF THE CONTRACT: MARRIAGE OR COHABITATION

When establishing a relationship that involves life in common, that is, joint consumption and production, a man and a woman have two possible options – to legally formalize and register their relationship or simply to live together with no legal formalities. We shall call the first solution marriage and the second cohabitation.

Until fairly recently the choice of the second option meant that the couple relinquished, or were not eligible for, the compulsory provisions of family law with respect to the rights and duties of spouses and for the purposes of dissolving their relationship. Today the differences between marriage and cohabitation are much less important because cohabitation also produces legal effects, some of which are similar to those of formal marriage. But marriage still has greater implications and gives rise to a wider range of obligations and rights for the spouses. The transaction costs of enforcing rights are lower in the case of marriage than in the case of cohabitation because to claim certain rights as a result of cohabitation it is usually necessary to prove that the relationship existed and lasted for a specific period of time whereas these facts are proved in marriage by its mere existence.

Why should a couple prefer one alternative to the other? In a traditional society, in which cohabitation incurred serious social disapprobation, especially for women, it was unusual to find this type of cohabitation amongst people who placed a high value on their social status; and it was much more frequent amongst groups of workers living outside the social conventions of the upper classes. In today's society, the stigma of cohabitation has practically disappeared so these costs are no longer taken into account when couples consider the two alternatives. The variable that today determines the choice between marriage or cohabitation seems to be the degree of stability the couple wants or thinks they can achieve in their relationship. So there is a direct correlation between the volume of investment that the man and woman are prepared to make and the expected duration of their relationship. Since cohabitation implies less stability and lower costs for entry and exit, cohabiting couples can be expected to be less settled than those who marry formally. An example can be seen in the decision as to whether to have children or not. In western society today, not only is the percentage of married couples much greater than the number of cohabiting couples, but the households of cohabitants on average have fewer members than those of married couples.[1]

Since children generally constitute the most important investment made by a couple, it is reasonable that cohabiting couples should have fewer children and that many couples who have cohabited for some time decide to marry precisely when they are expecting a child. And this continues to be true in spite of the sharp increase in children born out of wedlock in proportion to those born to married couples and the fact that much of the aid offered to unmarried mothers in some countries may constitute an important incentive for them to not marry.[2]

So far we have assumed that the behaviour of the man and the woman are symmetrical or, more precisely, that their preferences for marriage or cohabitation are the same because no consideration has been given to the significant differences in the investment made by each partner in marriage. A more realistic assumption can now be adopted that takes into account the various levels of investment that are generally made by men and women. In earlier chapters, two facts have been mentioned that cause the woman to invest comparatively more in marriage than her partner. The first is her biological characteristic of intensive investment in her children as the most efficient means of guaranteeing the continuity of her genes. The second, her relative specialization in domestic activities as opposed to the relative specialization of the man in market activities.

According to these arguments, this greater investment by the woman will involve a greater preference on her part for marriage rather than cohabitation. The greater the influence of the woman in the couple, therefore, the greater the tendency towards marriage as against cohabitation. According to the relative position of the woman in terms of her income and wealth, the following correlations can be drawn up:

- A positive correlation between the wealth and non-earned income of the woman and the probability that the couple will consolidate their relationship through marriage.
- An uncertain correlation between the income earned by the woman in the labour market and the probability that the cohabiting couple will consolidate their relationship through marriage.

The first correlation is positive because the woman who is looking for matrimonial stability will have more chances of achieving it if she contributes greater resources. The second correlation is uncertain because it involves elements which both favour and deter stability. In favour of stability is the fact that the higher earned income will involve larger contributions from the woman to the couple so she will therefore have more possibility of demanding stability from her partner. But against stability is the fact, to be analysed in the following chapter, that the opportunity cost of having children is directly related to the woman's capacity for obtaining resources in the market. The greater opportunity cost means a smaller number of children, less dedication to domestic activities and therefore a smaller investment in the relationship of the couple.

This more intense preference on the part of women for marriage has been a constant throughout many historical periods. However modern social changes, which have led women to invest relatively less than before in marriage, imply a drop in women's concern for stability. A society with a low birth rate and a high level of participation by women in the labour market at all levels means the investment in children will be lower and there will be less investment in domestic human capital. This will therefore diminish women's preference for marriage as opposed to cohabitation.

2 PAYMENTS IN THE MARRIAGE CONTRACT: THE DOWRY AND THE BRIDE PRICE

Marriage contracts throughout history and in almost all societies have involved payments by the bride or her family, or by the groom or his family, as an essential condition for the marriage. Although such payments can take many forms, for the sake of simplicity they can be classified into two groups – the payments made by the bride or her family so that she contributes certain goods to the marriage, and those made by the groom or his family to the bride's family in compensation for their loss. We shall call the former 'dowries' and the latter the 'bride price'.

The existence of both types of payment is interesting because it points to structures for social and economic organization that are completely different in countries with similar per capital income levels. The fact that both types of payment may coexist in a single society and at the same period also shows the need for separating the economic behaviour of the different classes or castes within a given society.[3]

The western world has developed a specific type of urban society in which the man has worked outside the home whereas the woman, as soon as her husband attained a given economic status, dealt only with the care of her children and household tasks. It is no coincidence that in our culture the dowry used to be a most relevant institution whereas the price of the bride was used only exceptionally. When the woman does not obtain resources from outside the home or has no important role in agriculture, the husband requires her to provide goods to increase the productive assets of the new family.

However other societies are organized differently. In sub-Saharan Africa, for example, where traditional agriculture was based on the cultivation of lands which are abandoned once exhausted, most of the agricultural work was done by women. A man's wealth will depend on the number of women working for him, both wives and daughters. So husbands are prepared to pay the bride price to purchase a new wife and fathers will not hand over their daughters to another man unless they receive compensation. The bride price can then be used by the father to buy a new wife.

In the non-industrialized world, these two types of payment coexist. The bride price is an institution that is characteristic not only of the part of Africa just mentioned but also of several parts of south-east Asia and many tribal societies throughout the world. The dowry, however, predominates in the Arab world, China and India.[4] The prime example of the coexistence of the two institutions can be found in India and this can be explained as a consequence of the radical division of some Indian communities into castes and social classes. Since women in the higher groups do not work outside the home, the dowry prevails in marriages within their class. But when women work it is possible, although only in certain communities, to find payments to the bride's family.

So which of the two institutions is better for women? Apparently the 'purchase' of the bride is more degrading because the woman is purchased by the husband so that she will work the land and give him children, possibly in exchange for some heads of cattle given to her father. Moreover, it will be the woman who does all the work and in most cases she will have no right to inherit.[5] It is no surprise, therefore, that in those regions where the traditional cultures live alongside the Moslem culture, the young girls prefer Moslem husbands.[6]

But the analysis does not end here. The institution of the bride price has in its favour the greater freedom of movement and greater economic independence of women in the African tribal societies where husbands do not generally take much interest in the productive activities of their wives, whereas Moslem wives are subject to greater control. Moreover, the criteria for assessing women are different in both societies, with the Moslem woman being less valued. While the latter is basically considered as a bearer of children, the African is not only a bearer of children but also a worker. In other words, a sterile woman in Moslem society would suffer discredit where an African would not. One last argument that gives rise to doubts on the advantages of dowries for women can be found in those societies in which the payment of the dowry is often a real burden for parents with daughters. The best known case is that of India and there is no doubt that the relatively high number of infanticides in the case of girls reflects the cost that the payment of the dowry may represent for the parents.

It has often been stated[7] that the institution of the dowry is closely related to that of inheritance. There is in fact no substantial difference between the contribution made by the woman to her marriage at the time she marries (the dowry) and the goods she adds at the death of her father (her inheritance), especially in societies or historical times in which life expectancy is, or has been, much lower than in the modern western world. It is not surprising, therefore, that whereas women in traditional African cultures have no right to inherit, this right does exist in societies in which the institution of the dowry predominates, even in Moslem society in which women, in spite of their subjugation, receive their part of the family legacy on the death of their father, if it has not already been received on marriage in the form of a dowry.

3 POLYGAMY

Although polygamy is not common practice in western society, it has been the subject of much study in recent years and has received much attention in the framework of family economics.[8]

Sociobiology explains the frequent existence of polygamy in the animal world according to the Bateman effect. This effect takes its name from the experiments carried out during the 1940s by the biologist, A.J. Bateman, and establishes that variance in reproductive success is generally greater in males than in females. In other words, if reproductive success is measured by the number of copulations carried out in a specific species, it will be seen that, in many animal species, almost all the females mate and each a small number of times whereas there are many males that do not copulate and, amongst those that do mate, some do so many times[9].

For sociobiologists the basic reason for this trend towards polygamy is anisogamy, that is, the difference in size and mobility of the male and female sex cells, which determines the different reproductive strategies of the males and females referred to above. Monogamy and the existence of stable male or female couples in the human species could therefore be interpreted as the result of incomplete evolution in the human species in which polygamy continues to exist in many cultures. This evolution could be linked to the fact that the man is taking on the functions of caring for and feeding his children and these are forcing him to change his reproductive strategy to ensure the survival of his descendants.

The problem that arises with a hypothesis of this type is the one mentioned at the start of the book, namely the relative importance when interpreting man's behaviour of the biological inheritance of man as opposed to his cultural evolution. The polygamy thesis presented by sociobiologists has been criticized with the argument that it is very debatable whether, in peoples with a certain degree of cultural development, investments in reproductive success received priority in the allocation of resources. If it is accepted that cultural evolution brings with it a change in men's and women's preferences, it can be inferred that in their utility functions other arguments will gain priority over the reproduction of their genes, such as pleasure or the enjoyment of sex, for example.[10]

If a predominant role is played by the biological conditioning of the various reproductive strategies, it is not difficult to explain why in human societies polygamy generally adopts the form of polygyny (where the man has several wives) rather than polyandry (where the woman has several husbands). Whereas the former would fit in better with such conditioning, the latter would give rise to serious problems of coherence which could only be explained by the existence of especially difficult economic circumstances as a means of guaranteeing that several males contribute to the maintenance of the family and the children. One of the most serious problems of polyandry is the great difficulty of identifying exactly who is the father of each of the children of the common wife. Since the efforts of the man as provider are addressed mainly to the survival of his own children, polyandry reduces the incentives of each of the husbands to provide work and goods to the family. This fact could also explain why in some cases polyandry occurs amongst brothers so that the protection of any of the family's children amounts to a defence of a substantial part of the parents' own genetic legacy even if they do not know which of the children are actually their own.

However, the emphasis on social relationships and cultural structures invalidates this interpretation of polygamy. An alternative explanation could be the above-mentioned model of male superiority which allowed the maintenance of polygyny while the male exerted his dominating role. This model would also explain the diminished importance of polygamy in today's world as a result of the gradual reduction in this superiority.

In some primitive societies, the institution of polygamy is very relevant in the organization of productive activities. This is the case, for example, of societies in sub-Saharan Africa in which the existence of polygyny is closely linked to the marriage system based on the bride price as analysed above. In cultures in which women carry out most of the farming activities, the possession of several wives not only means the husband will have more children but also that he will gain greater wealth because a larger area of land can be farmed. As long as the marginal productivity of a new wife is greater than the cost of keeping her and the opportunity cost of the price paid for her, the purchase will be profitable for the husband.

The same reasons that allow us to explain the differences between the bride price and the dowry systems can also allow us to understand the varying role of polygamy in Moslem culture and the African world. In Moslem societies, polygamy is more closely related to the social status of the husband and his wish to have more children than to the economic advantages of having several wives. It is therefore no surprise, although the contrary is widely believed, that polygamy occurs amongst Moslems to a much lesser extent than it did amongst the traditional African cultures.

The most controversial aspect of polygamy is undoubtedly the status of the wives in this type of marriage. Whereas the traditional assumption is that the existence of several wives is necessarily degrading and detrimental for women, today economists consider polygamy to be a very complex phenomenon which, in some cases, may be preferred by the wives themselves. Anthropological studies show that in many cultures it is often the first wife who takes the initiative of suggesting that her husband take a second wife.[11] Economic theory explains this because polygamy may mean the wife receives more help in the home and achieves more efficient domestic organization.[12] In addition price theory suggests that polygamy involves a greater demand for women in the marriage market and this means, given a stable supply, that the price of women in the market will rise; and this should mean that women should have an improved situation in marriage if they are able to fully exercise their property rights over their own persons. From the point of view of a woman in a developed western country, the situation of a wife in a polygamous home in a Third World country seems very undesirable. But in cultures in which the main objective of a woman is to achieve her own basic subsistence and that of her offspring, in an environment of hunger and poverty, conduct and attitudes that are very different to ours become perfectly rational.

Under a system of polygamy the bride price can be expected to be higher and the dowry to be lower than in a monogamous system, and this should benefit the parents of potential wives. But those who get the worst deal from polygamy are the poorest men and those with the least human capital who will have greater difficulty in finding a wife and this will force many of them to postpone marriage or even abandon hope of ever marrying.

A different matter is the subjugation of women in most societies in which polygamous marriage is the norm. Is this subjugation caused by polygamy? The answer is not clear. There are arguments showing that the reason for male domination does not lie so much in the institution of polygamy itself as in the status of women in such societies and, more specifically, in the impossibility of their exercising property rights over their persons and the fruits of their work.[13]

This statement can be criticized with the argument that in those societies in which women do exercise full property rights over their persons and the fruits of their work – in western society – it is not usual to find voluntary agreements for cohabitation (the law would prohibit formal marriages) amongst several women and a common husband. But the reason why polygamous cohabitation has not become widespread in the western world can perhaps be explained – apart from social and religious prohibitions – by the fact that the economic capacity of women has pushed up their price in the marriage market. For a long time, the western world maintained a form of social organization in which it was not unusual to find cases of what we could call quasi-polygamy. This comprised the maintenance of relatively stable lovers in exchange for economic compensation paid by the men – usually from the well-to-do classes – who, together with quasi-matrimonial services, thus gained greater social prestige. And it has been the change in the economic and legal status of women, and not the legal rules on marriage, that has reduced the incidence of such situations.

4   POLYGAMY AND PARENTAL INVESTMENT: A BIOLOGICAL EXPLANATION

The different nature of male and female investments in their descendants may explain why polygamy exists in many animal species and why this polygamy usually means that a single male mates with several females. This explanation is based on a sociobiological model that does not aim to be deterministic but only reflects the result of a certain form of evolution.

Figure 4.1, which is based (with some modifications) on a graph by the biologists Trivers and Wilson[14], shows this phenomenon. If we start by assuming that the objective of both males and females is to maximize their net reproductive success, defined as the difference between reproductive success and the costs

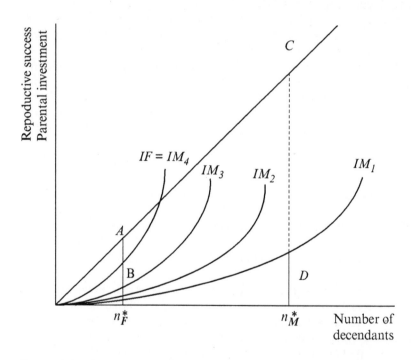

Figure 4.1   Optimum reproductive strategies and number of descendants

of investment, it will be the costs of investment for each of the sexes that will determine the optimum number of descendants for males and females.

Since the investment by the female is intensive, her curve of parental investment (*IF*) will reach a positive slope that is more than proportional as from a relatively small number of children. Her net reproductive success will be maximum (with a value of *AB*) for a number of children equal to n_f^*

But in the case of the male, his extensive reproduction strategy, represented by his curve of parental investment (IM_1) will mean that he will not reach maximum net reproductive success (with a value of *CD*) until n_m^*. This involves a much higher number of children and, to achieve this, he will have to mate with several wives.

But it is possible that in some species the male will play an important role in the care of the children so his strategies may be relatively more intensive for a relatively lower number of children. The graph represents this situation in which, when the successive curves for male investment (IM_2, IM_3 and so on) move to the left, in the case of IM_4 this eventually defines a reproduction strategy that is the same as that of the female and this would give rise to monogamous mating.

5   BREAKING OFF THE CONTRACT: DIVORCE

We have seen in a previous section how, taking the simplest approach to the problem, a decision to divorce depends on the level of wellbeing that the person expects to attain as a divorcé(e) in comparison with the wellbeing (or hardship) of remaining married. The costs and benefits involved obviously do not only include monetary or material considerations. Also to be taken into account are all the circumstances affecting the decision which may range from the psychological satisfaction or dissatisfaction of living alone or with the spouse, religious sentiment or the welfare of the children.

If marriage is interpreted according to the thesis of this book as a contract, then divorce must be considered as the breaking off of the contract. Economic analysis of such contracts has paid great attention to this matter and the compensation that laws and courts set in cases of breach of contract. The parties themselves may determine in their contract the effects of unilateral or bilateral failure to comply with it, or this can be left to the law and the courts of justice. In the case of the marriage contract, even if the parties are allowed to agree on the terms of their separation, the law sets certain conditions and gives the presiding judge a say in the approval of the conditions. There are two main reasons for the role played by legal regulations and judges in cases of marriage breakup. The first is the reduction of transaction costs made possible by the existence of laws which remove the need for agreeing prior to the settlement on each and every one of the possible contingencies. The second is based on the peculiarities of family law according to which the State takes on the mission of regulating and supervising marriage relationships.

As in any type of agreement, the continuation or breaking off of a marriage contract will depend on the costs and benefits of either option. It is thus possible to define an 'efficient' divorce as one in which there are fewer benefits to be gained from maintaining the marriage than from breaking up for each of the parties. However, the legal situation for breaking off the contract is a different matter. In principle, if both parties are not required to be in agreement over terminating the contract, then the termination will take place if one of the parties – or both – considers that the utility to be expected from the breakup is greater than its costs. The divorce will increase social wellbeing if both parties improve their situation; or, applying the Kaldor–Hicks compensation criterion[15], if the gains of one of the parties are sufficient to allow for the other party to be compensated so that it is not left in a worse situation than before.

Why at a specific time do couples decide to end their relationship when they had previously thought that it was best to be married? There are two possible explanations. The first is that when they decided to marry their decision was wrong because of lack of information about the future spouse. The second is that over the years the character of the spouse or spouses and the interests of the husband or wife (or both) have changed to such an extent that it is impossible to continue the marriage.

As explained in a previous section, finding the right partner requires a search process that may be costly in terms of both time and resources. It is therefore common for couples to marry thinking they have more information about the future spouse than they actually do. This type of marriage is quite likely to end in divorce in the early years because much fuller information will be obtained once they live together than was possible before.

From the point of view of family economics this problem of lack of information has been emphasized as the main cause of divorce because a very significant number of breakups take place during the early years of marriage. If changes in character or interests were the main reason, the divorce rate would rise with the years of marriage and this does not tie in with the statistics. But this does not mean that changes over the years are not relevant. They may in fact be very relevant indeed and yet have a relatively small effect on the total number of matrimonial breakdowns. The cause of this apparent contradiction is that the decision to divorce is adopted in terms of costs and benefits, and that, the longer the marriage, the more people are reluctant to divorce because they have invested more in the marriage and the costs of breaking up are therefore higher.[16]

6 MARRIAGE STABILITY, CHILDREN AND ALTRUISM

Does the presence of children in a marriage in any way affect the decision of either of the spouses when it comes to continuing or breaking up their relationship in certain circumstances? The answer is undoubtedly yes. And it is common for people in a difficult marriage situation to explicitly state that the welfare of their children is the reason for their continuing in a relationship which otherwise they would undoubtedly terminate.

The inclusion of the children in the model developed in the previous chapter means, first of all, that the utility functions of each of the spouses must be redefined and the utility function of the children included. Where there are no children, the utility functions of M and F in the marriage would be:

$$U_F' = U_F' (X_F, S_F)$$
$$U_M' = U_M' (X_M, S_M)$$

The reformulation of these utility functions because of the presence of children is determined by the altruistic behaviour of parents towards their children. Let us assume, for the sake of simplicity, that in the married couple made up of M and F there is a single child (Ch), whose utility function does not include his parents' wellbeing. The new utility functions will be:

$$U_F' = U_F' (X_F, S_F, U_{Ch})$$
$$U_M' = U_M' (X_M, S_M, U_{Ch})$$
$$U_{Ch} = U_{Ch} (X_{Ch}, S_{ch})$$

The parents' altruism requires that:

$$\frac{\partial U_F}{\partial U_{Ch}} > 0 \text{ and } \frac{\partial U_M}{\partial U_{Ch}} > 0$$

With this definition of utility functions, X_{Ch}, S_{Ch} and therefore also U_{Ch} are conditioned by the NB or B option chosen by the parents. Since the existence of the marriage is in principle efficient for the children, it can reasonably be expected that

$$(X_{Ch}, S_{Ch})\text{NB} > (X_{Ch}, S_{Ch})\text{B}$$

The decision on the future of the marriage will therefore be influenced by the child's wellbeing. The greater the degree of altruism of each of the spouses towards the child, the less the incentive to break up the marriage. Since women generally invest more than men in their children, if the wellbeing of Ch deteriorates, this will affect the mother's utility function more than the father's. That is, F will be more altruistic than M and will have fewer incentives to ask for a divorce. She will only want a divorce when the utility a divorce will give her personally is high enough to be able to compensate for the reduction she feels as a result of the reduced wellbeing of her child.

This means that F will be more prepared than M to give up goods *x* and *s* to preserve her marriage if this benefits the child. This attitude will reinforce the effects of hypergamy as studied in Chapter 3 in that it generally allows the man to keep most of the material benefits of the marriage.

7   STATE REGULATION OF DIVORCE

As in many other aspects of family law, the public authorities have traditionally restricted the autonomy of spouses when applying for and obtaining a divorce. In most legal systems a divorce is only granted under certain legally stipulated circumstances or if the couple have been living separately for a minimum period of time. And if the petition is made by one of the spouses with the opposition of the other, the conditions are even stricter.

Unilateral divorce and divorce with mutual consent can be said to be very recent phenomena in most of the western world. In France, for example, a very permissive divorce law was passed at the time of the Revolution which accepted mutual consent or incompatibility of characters amongst the causes for divorce. But, after several processes of legal reform, divorce by mutual consent with neither of the parties being blamed disappeared in 1816 and was only accepted again in 1975. In the United States, the various states gradually passed laws allowing no-fault divorce only in the 1970s and 1980s. If the aim of such constraints was to restrict divorce to cases in which one of the parties was clearly at fault, then undoubtedly they were very inefficient. When there was mutual consent, such regulations were of little effect since to get round them all that was required was for one of the spouses – usually the husband – to invent a story of adultery. This gave rise not only to a flourishing trade in fake lovers and specialist photographers but also to the birth of a minor literary genre.[17]

The problem becomes more complex when, in a legal system that only allows for divorce where there is fault, only one of the partners wants to break up the marriage – usually to remarry. The studies carried out in the United States in the years when some states allowed unilateral no-fault divorce and others did not seem to show that, contrary to what might be expected, this legal restriction did not substantially affect the number of divorces. The reason is probably that, when one of the parties wants a divorce and the other is able to prevent it, it is always possible to negotiate the conditions for the breakup. In other words, the prohibition of no-fault divorce creates incentives for rent-seeking strategies in which the refusal to accept the divorce may be used to achieve higher alimony or a larger share in the distribution of the family property. Comparison of the data for these two types of state show that, while the divorce rates were not very different, there was a significant difference in the alimony awarded to the women which was higher in the states in which unilateral no-fault divorce was not permitted. This can probably be explained by the fact that the women were more inclined than the men to maintain their marriages, so the non-existence of unilateral no-fault divorce forced the husbands to pay higher compensation in order to obtain their wives' consent.[18]

The restrictions placed on divorce by the State can be explained in several ways. The first is that divorce does not only involve the interests of the partners but also those of the children whom the State has a duty to protect by placing obstacles in the way of the dissolution of the parents' marriage. Irrespective of whether the artificial maintenance of a marriage can really benefit the children, this argument cannot be applied to childless marriages for which divorce should thus be available with no restrictions at all.

Therefore more weight is carried by the argument that the State considers family stability as a public good from which the whole of society benefits and that, in conditions of free contracts between the parties, would be supplied to an insufficient degree. If this were so, the public authorities could take on the function of promoting such stability to the benefit of the whole of society. But if this argument is accepted, attention must be drawn to the contradiction whereby the public sector tries to promote family stability by restricting divorce but, at the same time, applies social security programmes that create incentives for conduct leading to precisely the opposite result (unmarried mothers, single-parent households and so on). Such conduct is analysed in the last two chapters of this book.

8   DIVORCE SETTLEMENTS

From the point of view of contract theory, the alimony,[19] which one of the parties (usually the husband) must pay to the other party (usually the wife), can be understood as compensation for the loss of wellbeing caused by the termination of the agreement.[20] A different matter is the maintenance received by the spouse taking care of the children as the purpose of this is the wellbeing of the children and not of the divorced partner.

As compensation for breach of contract, alimony acts as a positive stimulus for people, especially women, to start a contractual relationship, that is, in our case, to marry and make specific investments in their marriage. Such investments, which are of great importance for the couple's life in common, range from obtaining domestic human capital to caring for the home, having children or helping the partner at the start of his or her professional career. If there were no compensation after divorce, a risk averse person would substantially reduce this type of investment.[21]

Since the economic evaluation of all the circumstances involved in a divorce is tremendously complex, the determination of the amount of alimony is one of the main problems faced by a judge dealing with a divorce case. There are many criteria that may help to determine the amount of the divorce settlement. The first is an argument of equity according to which it is considered fair that the party with the highest economic status should help the party with the lowest economic status. Although this may be socially acceptable and for many people the economic difference is sufficient cause to justify the payment of alimony, the argument is not very sound because the lack of material resources in one of the parties can hardly justify the payment of alimony if there are no other reasons for it. However, this is the criterion followed in many legal systems.

In order to determine the amount of alimony, legal systems usually take into account the woman's situation not so much before marriage as during the marriage, and this means that the compensation for breach of contract should be determined so that the damaged party is left in the same situation as if the contract had been maintained.[22] This criterion is not only debatable from the point of view of equity but it also gives rise to the same problem of moral hazard that would arise in any case in which total risk is insured, that is, that the insured party has no interest whatsoever in avoiding the risk. In the specific case of alimony, it could also lead to incentives for one of the spouses – usually the woman – to marry a person with a high income as the best way of guaranteeing that she will belong for life to a high social scale. And, if the problem is analysed from the point of view of the long term, it can be concluded that the woman's future may be linked more to her husband's expected income than to the opportunity costs she herself suffers as a result of the marriage. Such a formula for determining alimony seems very distant from the principles of economic efficiency.

From a second criterion, alimony is understood as being calculated in terms of the damage suffered by one of the parties as a result of the breach of contract. In this case, the economic reasoning behind the alimony would be the same as that of payment for non-fulfilment of contractual agreements, when the purpose of the compensation is that the damaged party should be left in the same situation as if there had been no contractual relationship.[23] This second criterion avoids the problems of moral hazard and inefficient incentives of compensation based on the loss of status for the woman, but it gives rise to an important practical problem, that of how to calculate the possible damages. These would have to include the opportunity costs of the damaged person which are practically impossible to calculate accurately. By way of example, let us take the case of an engineer who marries a young law graduate who never gets to exercise her profession because she devotes herself instead to her home and family. What was the opportunity cost of her marriage? She might have become a partner in a lucrative legal office, but she might also have just been one of the many law graduates that end up unemployed or working in a dull administrative job. It would therefore be very difficult to establish a fair amount of compensation.[24]

It should also be noted that the criterion of meeting the needs of whichever spouse is considered the weakest means that the alimony will terminate if the person receiving it remarries. It is thus assumed that, by remarrying, a woman will achieve a certain degree of economic stability that will allow her ex-husband to stop maintaining her.

Finally, there is a third criterion that is beginning to take hold in American courts that could be called alimony as reimbursement or restitution. A representative case is *In Re Marriage of Francis* that was tried by the Iowa State Supreme Court in 1989. In this case, a woman had maintained her husband by working while he studied medicine. When he finished his studies, the marriage broke up and the court had to determine what type of payment and how much should be paid by Mr Francis to his former wife. What was interesting here was that the court decided that the sum to be paid was of a different nature to the usual alimony because here it was a matter of the constitution of property that did not take the form of material goods but of a future capacity to obtain returns from the market. As a result, the financial provision order amounted to a share in the returns of an investment which the wife had helped to make and therefore she was entitled to a payment whether or not, and this is an important point, she was to remarry.[25]

From an economic point of view, this decision is of great interest because it introduces the theory of human capital into the reasoning of the judges and accepts the idea that an investment in education is not substantially different from an investment in physical assets. If it is accepted that, on divorce, the goods accumulated as a result of the work or the capital of both spouses are to be shared out, then according to the same criterion the returns of university studies, or the current value of the expected flow of such returns, should also be shared out. Such studies are considered as an asset, the returns of which should go not just to those holding the asset but also to the person who invested in it. It is more complex to determine how much the university qualification owes to the investment of capital and how much to the student's own efforts. But it is not difficult to quantify the investment made by the wife and apply to it a rate of returns in line with the risk of the investment.

In short, it can be concluded that there is an economic basis for divorce settlements and that there is therefore no need to justify them with arguments of fairness which are always debatable. In general, what the economics of the family suggest is that, not only does work carried out within the domestic sphere allow for a more comfortable life, but that there is also a correlation between market and non-market activities whereby the former cannot be carried out with the same degree of specialization and dedication if the person carrying them out also has to deal with domestic activities. Since the divorce settlement, as stated above, facilitates the division of labour within the family and investments in it, it should be understood not only in terms of fair distribution but also in terms of efficiency.

NOTES

1. Iglesias Ussel, J. (1994), p. 517.
2. In Great Britain, for example, the percentage of children born out of wedlock, which in 1978 was just over 10 per cent, in 1992 exceeded 30 per cent. See Morgan, P. (1995), p. 161. On the undesired effects of certain forms of family policy, see also Ch. 10 of this book.

3. The matter of the coexistence of the dowry and the bride price in societies such as India drew the attention of the first economists to publish studies on the economics of the family. See Bronfenbrenner (1971), pp. 1424–5.
4. Boserup, E. (1989), pp. 50–51.
5. Goody, J. (1976), p. 10.
6. Boserup, E. (1989), p. 47.
7. See, for example, Goody, J. (1976), p. 15; and Papps, I. (1980), Ch. 5c.
8. See, amongst others, Becker, G. (1991), pp. 80–107; Posner, R. (1992b.), pp. 253–60; Papps, I. (1980), Ch. 5d; Boserup, E. (1989), pp. 37–52, and Grossbard-Shechtman, S. (1993), pp. 214–39.
9. Wilson, E.O. (1975), Ch. 15.
10. For a representative work on this anthropological approach, see Harris, M. (1989).
11. Boserup, E. (1989), pp. 46–8.
12. Becker, G. (1991), pp. 90–91.
13. Papps, I. (1980), Ch. 5d.
14. Wilson, E.O. (1975), Fig. 15.6.
15. See the reference to the Kaldor–Hicks compensation principle in Ch. 1 of this book.
16. Becker, G. (1991), pp. 325–30. In support of the thesis of lack of information as the cause for divorce, Becker provides the fact that, in 1979, approximately 40 per cent of the divorces and annulments that took place in the United States took place before the fifth year of marriage. On investment in marriage and divorce costs, see Cohen, L. (1987).
17. A good history of divorce and divorce regulations is given in Phillips, R. (1991).
18. The fact that the divorce rates did not differ substantially between the two different types of state is not surprising from the point of view of an economist because it can be easily explained by applying the Coase theorem. According to the general principles of this theorem, attribution of rights to one of the parties is irrelevant for efficient allocation of resources with the condition that the property rights over these resources are well defined and the negotiation between the parties can be carried out with no transaction costs. When applied to the problem of divorce rates, the Coase theorem allows us to conclude that marriages will always be dissolved if it is efficient to do so. The different legal regulations will affect income distribution after the breakup but not the fact that more or fewer divorces will take place. See Peters, H.E. (1986), and the subsequent debate between him and Douglas W. Allen in Allen, D.W. (1992); also Peters, H.E. (1992). Similar conclusions to those of Peters had previously been reached by Becker, G., Landes, E. and Michael, R. (1997).
19. For the sake of clarity, the term 'alimony' is used in this text for the financial provisions stipulated by divorce settlements, in preference to the term 'maintenance' which is currently used in Great Britain and parts of the United States.
20. This is obviously not the only explanation for such alimony payments. I.M. Ellman, for example, explicitly rejects contract theory as a suitable tool for justifying this type of alimony and defends an alternative explanation based on a policy which aims to promote cooperative conduct by offering compensation for the losses suffered by one of the spouses in fulfilling his or her matrimonial obligations. See Ellman, I.M. (1989). But it is debatable whether this interpretation, which is right to a great extent, is incompatible with the breach of contract theory.
21. This idea is explained in Landes, E.M. (1978).
22. If this criterion is applied, the damaged party receives both the consequential damages and damages for loss of profit as a result of the breach of contract (expectation damages).
23. In this case the compensation would only cover reliance damages. For a clear description of the differences between both types of compensation and their economic effects, see Cooter, R. and Ulen, Th. (1988), pp. 296–303.
24. Though difficult, it is not impossible. The problem here is very similar to that faced by judges who have to determine an amount in damages in the case of injury leading to incapacity or death when the victim is, for example, a minor.
25. For a summary of this case and the court's arguments, see Pyle, R.C. (1994), pp. 304–7. See also Ellman, I.M. (1989), pp. 24–9.

5. Children

1 FAMILY AND CHILDREN

The family has always been and continues today to be the institution in which children are usually born, grow up and receive their initial education. From the economists' point of view, therefore, the family 'produces' children, not only in the sense of conceiving them, but also in that the family strives to improve the children's 'quality' through heavy investments in time and money.

Many different circumstances influence a person's development but they are often directly conditioned by the parents. It is the parents who transmit the genes to their children that will determine their physical appearance, intelligence and health. But biological characteristics are by no means all. Parents also offer their children the whole framework in which their intellectual, artistic and emotional qualities will develop. The family is an educating influence both for good and bad. It is no accident that several members of the Bach family were famous musicians or that the Bernouilli family gave the world excellent mathematicians. Neither is it unusual for the children of criminals to turn into criminals too.

Therefore children do not only receive a biological inheritance from their parents. They also receive an endowment of human capital which will condition to a large extent both their behaviour and their income levels in the future.

As for the children, they offer several types of compensation to their parents. These compensations have varied in nature and importance throughout the course of history and, in today's developed world, consist basically of psychological satisfaction, as we shall see in the following section.

2 WHY DO PEOPLE HAVE CHILDREN?

The reasons why couples decide to have children or not has become one of the most debated issues in the economics of the family. The question takes on more importance as the number of births becomes insufficient to maintain the population level or to allow for moderate growth in the long term. This circumstance can occur in two completely different cases. The first is the rapid population growth which still persists in certain Third World countries and which makes it very difficult to achieve a significant improvement in their inhabitants' standard of living. The second case can be seen in western countries which have such low birth rates that this is causing ageing of their populations and will result in a reduction in the number of their inhabitants.

The economics of the family distinguishes between two different functions that can be fulfilled by children. Children have played the role of production goods until fairly recently in the western world and still fulfil this role to a large extent in Third World countries. In a traditional agrarian society, children are an investment for their parents since they work the land and guarantee a means of support for their elders when the latter can no longer look after themselves. However this function has gradually become less important as the economy has been modernized and institutions have appeared, which allow people to continue living in an acceptable way when they are no longer productive and cannot earn an income in the work force. In a society which guarantees a pension on retirement, and which has an efficient financial system and a market allowing for the commercialization of real estate property, the idea of having children as an investment loses a lot of its meaning. Instead, children become consumer goods, in that they give – or at least their parents hope they will give – a variety of benefits and satisfaction. Without these benefits, which are largely psychological, it would not be possible to explain why people in modern-day societies continue to have children. In strictly financial terms, children are much more of a burden than a source of income, even making allowance for the possible help they can give their parents when they reach old age.

In spite of these benefits, statistics show that western societies today have very low birth rates. For the population to remain stable in the long term, it is necessary for each woman to have an average of 2.1 children, but the birth rate in European countries is much lower than this and Italy and Spain are currently at the very bottom of the worldwide scale, averaging 1.2 children per woman.

Why is the birth rate so low at present? The answer for economists is only too clear. If children are consumer goods and we apply the principle of diminishing marginal utility to them, the statistics show that for a large number of parents the estimated cost of a second or third child is higher than the benefits they can expect in return. The question, therefore, is why has there been this change in utility maximization behaviour on the part of parents? Let us look into some details.

When we say that children are very costly for a married couple, we are generally thinking of the financial expense of bringing them up and educating them. Among these expenses we would include their food, housing, clothing, education and so on, everything which is the result of acquiring in the market the goods and services required by the children. But these are not the only costs, since we should also take into consideration at least two other types of cost. The first one is the physical cost for the woman of pregnancy, labour and breastfeeding. The cost of this is difficult to quantify in monetary terms but in many cases it is very relevant. The second one is the opportunity cost for a person, mainly the mother, of having children. The opportunity cost is determined, as we have seen in a previous chapter, by what the mother fails to earn in paid employment because she has to look after her children. This cost will obviously rise in proportion to the possibilities the woman has of holding a well-paid job. For a woman with no professional qualifications, the opportunity cost of having children will be lower than for a woman with a high technical training. The low birth rate in the western world can be explained partially by the undeniable improvement in opportunities for women in the labour market.

It is interesting to point out here the asymmetry of this conclusion depending on the parent under consideration. As will be seen in a later section, a rise in the man's salary tends to have a positive, not a negative, correlation on the birth rate, since the fact that the father obtains an important, well-paid position not only does not reduce the likelihood of his having children but actually increases it. Therefore the relevant variable when explaining the drop in the birth rate in terms of the opportunity cost of having children appears to be the woman's salary.

Together with the increase in the opportunity costs of motherhood, the economics of the family has another argument which explains today's fall in the birth rate: the preference for 'quality' over the number or 'quantity' of children. The use of these terms, which may be rather shocking for a person seeing them in this context for the first time, refers to the human capital investment parents make in each of their children. Thus a child in whom a large amount of resources is invested by his parents can be said to be of better quality than another for whom the level of investment is low, with resources here being understood as not only the material means used in his education but also the time his parents spend on bringing him up.

Material resources are limited in most families, although some families do exist where wealth is virtually without limits when it comes to providing the best possible education for their children. But for all families, even the richest, time is a scarce commodity. As a result, there is an inverse relation between the number of children in a family and their quality, as measured in the sense explained above.

An exception to this general principle is that of only children, who receive larger amounts of time and resources, but often end up being of inferior quality to children who have a brother or sister. The reason, no doubt, is that living with other chidlren is a socializing factor that contributes positively to children's quality. If this is correct, the birth of a second child would not have a negative effect on quality. Rather, the positive effects of living with another child would overcome the negative effects of a lower investment up to a certain point (two or three children?), and only from this point on would the negative effects of a lower investment be greater than the positive ones of sociability.

The preference of modern parents for their children's quality is widespread and easy to see. Although there are still significant differences between various social groups, in all of them a concern for their children's professional training can be observed as has never been seen before. The question is to determine why this is happening. It could be argued that it is due to a simple change in preferences on the part of the parents. But it also seems possible to explain this change of preferences using economic analysis.

We have based our argument on the fact that parents are altruistic in that their children's wellbeing gives them a feeling of wellbeing too. Therefore they will strive for their children to achieve the greatest possible success in life. This makes it necessary for their children to adapt to the changes in modern society, in a world where skills play an ever more important part and which requires greater training than was needed in earlier times. Altruistic parents will invest in the human capital of each of their children more intensively than before. Given the limited resources already mentioned and the inverse correlation between quantity and quality, the need to invest more per child in human capital will mean that parents prefer to have fewer children in order to give them better quality.

On the other hand, longer life expectancy for today's children means that the returns from the investment in them are higher and, therefore, it is efficient to allocate higher levels of resources to such investment. The objection could be raised that, although life expectancy is longer, the length of people's working life has not increased – or at least it has not increased in the same proportion – because of the earlier retirement age in many cases. This objection is partially valid; but one must not forget that the investment in children's human capital has positive effects not only on the work force but also on almost all human activity. In this sense, investments in human capital continue to be profitable even after retirement.

Increased life expectancy has another effect on investments in human capital. This indirect effect is linked to inheritance expectations and can be applied, as a result, only to those cases where the children can reasonably hope to receive assets of some size on the death of their parents. Since life expectancy has grown more than the age at which parents have children has been delayed, children are now much older when they inherit than in previous generations. In this situation, children have less reason to expect that an inheritance will solve their economic problems while they are still relatively young. The result is that there is an increase in incentives to invest in children's human capital since there is a greater probability they will need to use it to obtain economic resources.

No mention has been made so far of one of the factors which is generally used to explain the fall in the birth rate: the development of contraceptive methods and the greater availability of abortion in today's society. Although public opinion usually attach great importance to these factors, economists do not consider them decisive. No doubt they have a certain importance in that they reduce the costs a woman has to pay for having an abortion, or for birth control and better contraceptive methods, and legal abortion certainly imply fewer unwanted pregnancies and births.

But some further observations should be made. First, in the case of unwanted pregnancies in unmarried women or women without a stable relationship (mainly teenagers), the greater security that contraceptives offer causes an increase in risk behaviour. As a result, the probability of getting pregnant is reduced less than it would have been if there had been greater aversion to risk. Secondly, the use of these contraceptives requires certain technical knowledge which is not available in all cases, especially where teenagers are concerned. The experience of some countries seems to show that better results are obtained in birth control through the use of contraceptives when the women who use them receive proper training, which does not exist today in many nations.[1]

Furthermore, it is wrong to assume that all the children not born because of the use of contraception or abortion means a reduction in the number of births. Rather it would seem that these methods are frequently used to plan the timing of births to coincide with the parents' interests. Therefore these methods not only help to control the number of wanted children through a reduction of costs but also allow these children to be born when it is most convenient for the parents. But the number of wanted children seems to be more a function of opportunity costs and quality preference, as has been seen above.[2]

2   THE DEMAND FOR CHILDREN: AN ECONOMIC ANALYSIS

If we consider children as consumer goods, then we may study the demand for them using conventional neoclassic economics. Let us define the parents' utility function, on the one hand, in terms of the goods the couple consume (X) which, for the sake of simplicity and to reduce the model to only two goods, include both market goods and domestic production goods and, on the other hand, in terms of their children (Ch)

$$U = U\,(X, Ch)$$

This function is maximized if we subject it to a budget constraint.

$$Y = XP_X + Ch\pi_{Ch}$$

where P_X represents the price of X goods and π_{Ch} the opportunity cost of bringing up and educating the children. The budget constraint is shown in Figure 5.1 as a conventional straight budget line, the slope of which is determined by the relative price of the two types of goods π_{Ch}/Px.

As in the basic model of consumption theory, the equilibrium point (E) is determined by the tangent point of the budget line and the indifference curve at its largest possible index. This point will give us the volume of goods (X) and the number of children (Ch) which parents with fixed preferences and income need to reach maximum satisfaction.

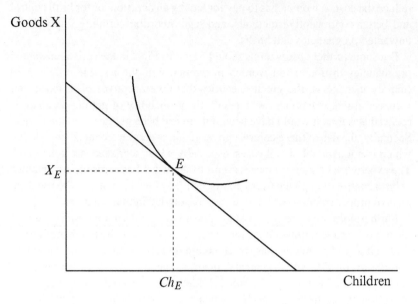

Figure 5.1   Consumer equilibrium point for parents

At this equilibrium point the equality condition will be met between the ratio of marginal utilities of such goods and the ratio of their relative prices.

$$\frac{\partial U}{\partial Ch} \bigg/ \frac{\partial U}{\partial X} = \frac{MU_{Ch}}{MU_X} = \frac{\pi_{Ch}}{P_X}$$

From here on, a demand-price function (shown in Figure 5.2) can be established that shows an inverse relationship between the number of wanted children and their price or opportunity cost. If we define the demand function as

$$D_{Ch} = D_{Ch}(\pi_{Ch}, P_X, Y, v)$$

where π_{Ch} represents the opportunity cost of having children, P_X the price of market consumer goods, Y the income and v other variables, and if we take all the variables apart from π_{Ch} as constants, the demand curve decreases since

$$\frac{\partial D_{Ch}}{\partial \pi_{Ch}} < 0$$

Variation in the relative price π_{Ch}/P_X gives rise to a substitution effect of the goods which have become more expensive in relative terms, as has been explained in a previous section.

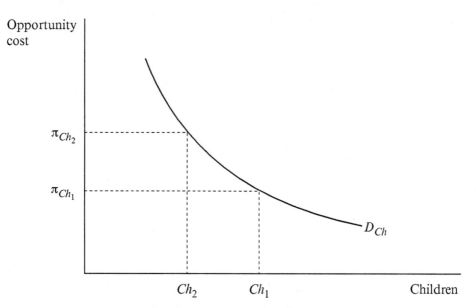

Figure 5.2   Demand curve for children as a function of their opportunity cost

However as soon as we admit the possibility that the income (Y) may increase, the problem becomes more complicated since the income and substitution effects may act in opposing directions. To be precise, an increase in the mother's salary (w_F) would have a double effect. On the one hand, an increase in income which would move the budget line of Figure 5.1 to the right; and, on the other hand, a substitution effect which would change the slope of this budget line. In Figure 5.2 the opportunity cost π_{Ch1} would rise to π_{Ch2} and the demand to have children would fall from Ch_1 to Ch_2.

It is fundamental, therefore, to know which of these two effects, income or substitution, is going to prevail in each case. If the income effect prevails, a rise in the parents' salaries will imply a larger demand for children. If the substitution effect prevails, however, the demand for children will fall.

At this point, the data force us to separate the father's behaviour from the mother's which, until now, we have considered jointly. The reason is that the available econometric estimates show substantially different values in the fertility elasticities with regard to the father's and mother's salaries. If we define these elasticities as

$$e_{\pi_{Ch}} = \frac{\pi_{Ch}}{Ch} \frac{\partial Ch}{\partial \pi_{Ch}}$$

and if we designate e_M and e_F for the respective elasticities of the father and the mother, the values we obtain for e_M and e_F are not only different, but they also have opposite signs:

$$e_M > 0 \text{ and } e_F < 0$$

Specifically, Butz and Ward's studies on North American data in the 1970s gave values of -1.73 for the variable we have denominated e_F and $+1.31$ for the variable e_M,[3] and the studies carried out in Europe do not differ much from these figures since Winegarden arrived at values between -0.76 and -1.34 for e_F and $+1.03$ and $+1.26$ for e_M.[4]

Another important question when analysing the demand for children is the link between the couple's income and the number of children they wish to have. Historical studies and contemporary statistics seem to indicate that the birth rate does not behave uniformly when variations occur in family's income.[5] But quite a regular tendency can be found in recent decades if a comparison is made between changes in income and the birth rate in any of the advanced countries.

An initial approximation to the problem could suggest that children behave as inferior goods, in the sense that people demand fewer children as their income increases. If we consider the relationship between income and demand for children, the children will be inferior goods if it can be shown that

$$\left(\frac{\partial D_{Ch}}{\partial Y}\right)_{\pi_{ch},P_X\text{constant}} < 0$$

Figure 5.3 shows an income demand function for children in which the children will behave as inferior goods once the income passes the level $0A$ and the demand for children will become stable from a certain level of income $0B$ onwards.

However we cannot deduce from this analysis and these statistics that children are inferior goods. Not only because empirical evidence is not determinant but because those

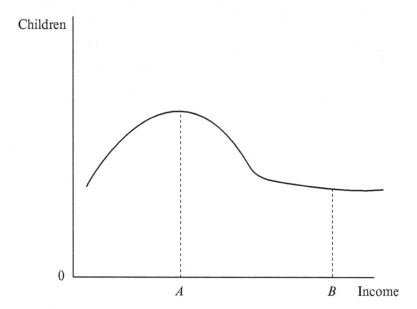

Figure 5.3   Children as inferior goods

who reach this conclusion may be making a basic mistake by confusing income effects and substitution effects. Even if it were absolutely true that a negative correlation exists between the income level and the number of children, this would not necessarily imply that children would be inferior goods. What could also happen – and it appears from the data that it does in fact happen – is that as women acquire better professional qualifications and, therefore, greater possibilities of earning a higher income in the job market, the opportunity cost will be greater so we would be facing a substitution effect and not an income effect.

From the point of view of family policy, the question is undoubtedly important since if the objective of the public sector were to increase the birth rate and children were inferior goods, a policy directed at raising available family income could have the effect of reducing the birth rate instead of increasing it.

4 THE VALUE OF CHILDREN

Human life has, without a doubt, very special characteristics which mean that, for many people, all human life has an incommensurate value of its own and there is no room for comparisons between the values of different lives. In practice, however, history has shown us how it has been accepted that not all lives have the same value when society has had to establish criteria for the penal code or for financial compensation in the case of loss of life.[6] In the case of evaluating children, this idea is extremely important because it allows us to reflect on certain types of family behaviour which would be inexplicable if we worked on the principle that there are no differences in the value that is placed on children's lives.

Various circumstances can bear an influence when placing a value on children; firstly, the number of children in the family. According to the principle of decreasing marginal utility – if we consider children as consumer goods or of decreasing marginal productivity, if we consider them as production goods – the value given to the loss of a child is not the same in the case of an only child, or if there is only one sibling, as in the case of a large family.[7]

The second factor is the age of the children. There are numerous statistics that show how during the course of history a child's value for the parents is related to his or her age, at least up to a certain age. In traditional societies it was usual for mothers to look on the development and wellbeing of children under two years old with a certain amount of indifference. In reality, until the infant death rate started to fall in the nineteenth century, it was so high that it was to a certain extent logical that mothers should invest little time, affection or human capital in their children when the investment was so frequently lost.[8] But when a child reached a certain age and had survived the period in which the probability of dying was very high, his or her value increased substantially and the parents could make a larger investment in their child in the confidence that this investment would turn out to be profitable.

When the Industrial Revolution concentrated the population in urban areas and the first studies on workers' living conditions were undertaken, there was great concern to reduce this waste of lives. Moralists, politicians and doctors tried to persuade women that they should show more maternal affection and fulfil their duty as mothers. This new attitude was encouraged by the reduction in the infant mortality rate and the slow but sustained growth in the standard of living of workers. As a result, behaviour gradually changed until we reach the current situation in which families devote special attention and effort to their smallest children. But we must be aware that this situation has not yet been reached all over the world, and the old patterns of behaviour on infant mortality are still present in many countries, as can be seen in recent experiences in countries of the Third World devastated by famine or civil war.[9]

A third differentiating factor when placing a value on children is their sex. This valuation may be purely subjective in the sense that some parents prefer sons and others prefer daughters. But it becomes a problem when the social value of a son is substantially different from that of a daughter. The cases of countries such as India, China and Korea are well-known, where the preference for sons has made many mothers abort when the fetus is female and wait until they give birth to a son.

These phenomena are not caused by simply irrational decisions since generally they have a basis which can be explained by economic analysis. In the case of India, it seems clear that the institution of the dowry, as discussed in the previous chapter, is the decisive factor in this discriminating behaviour. In the cases of China and Korea, together with certain types of family veneration of ancestors which is reserved for men, the unequal treatment no doubt originated in the greater usefulness of a son who worked the family's fields, remained in the family house after marriage and brought his wife home to work there. The problem was not very important in a traditional family in which the number of children was not limited except by nature or the economic possibilities of the family or the region. But in societies in which it is possible to determine the sex of the fetus and resort to abortion and in which, furthermore, the State itself encourages a reduction in the size of families, this differentiation between the children can lead to significant demographic imbalances, and a large number of men in the present generation can be expected to remain single through lack of women.

Economic theory predicts a balance in the long term in situations like these. The more men there are of marriageable age in comparison with women of the same generation, the lower their value will be and the greater the value will be of the women in the marriage market. This should lead to a reduction in dowries and a better consideration of women, which would raise their social position and bring it more in line with that of men. The problem is that this type of adjustment tends to be very slow since customs and social institutions are harder to modify than the economic circumstances in which they came into being.

5 EDUCATION AND INVESTMENT IN HUMAN CAPITAL

In the economics of the family, human capital, which is the productive capacity that a human being obtains through formal or informal education, takes on a particularly important role. Human capital may be generated in a variety of ways. Educational institutions are clearly very relevant but they do not stand alone. The business and the family are also key factors in forming a person's human capital. The business offers what is known as apprenticeship or learning in the workplace and this, for many businessmen, is more important than the training received in academic institutions. The family creates human capital in several ways. In a traditional society in which both the productive activity and daily life take place within the framework of the family, the latter is the source of all the human capital of its members in that they obtain from it both the basic knowledge and the occupational training they need.

Modern society, however, is characterized by great specialization in which the family has lost many of its traditional functions. It seems undeniable that one of the causes of the current crisis in the institution of the family is the appearance outside it of other institutions or markets that carry out functions that previously were the monopoly of the family. All the same, the family is still an important source for the creation of human capital because it is within the family that children receive their early education which is that which brings in the highest returns.

Figure 5.4 shows the process of formation of human capital and its effects on the person's capacity to obtain income. It shows that there are various factors that determine the eventual income level: intelligence, academic and non-academic education, wealth and the altruism of the parents. But what is of most interest for our purposes is the role played by the family in this process.

Parents exert their influence in two ways. Firstly, through genetics whereby they pass on certain biological characteristics to their offspring. Secondly, through the time, effort and resources devoted by them to the education of their children, which can be summarized as 'investment in the child'.

This investment is slightly different to the donations of goods which, depending on their wealth and altruism, parents give their children in the form of assets of all types thus allowing them to gain higher revenue. Here it is a question of investments in human capital which the parents make in two ways – by devoting time to their children and by spending part of their capital on them. The amount of resources parents devote to their children will in turn depend on

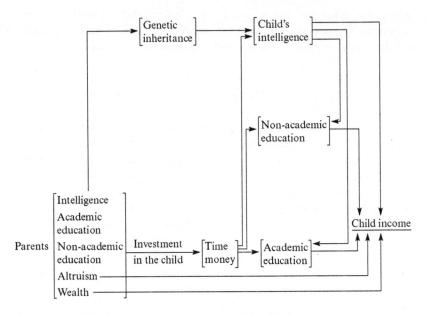

Figure 5.4   The formation of human capital in children

a wide range of factors: their intelligence and education which will allow them
to determine both what are their children's best interests and how they can obtain
the highest possible returns from the resources used; their wealth, which will
establish limits to the material resources available; their market income which
will determine the opportunity cost of the time devoted to their children; and,
finally, their altruism, which will determine the degree of sacrifice they are
prepared to make by foregoing the consumption of other goods.

The function of human capital creation is carried out by fathers and mothers
to an unequal extent, with the latter usually devoting more time and effort to
it. Dedication is reduced if the mothers work outside the home, but even in such
cases it is still they who carry out most of this activity. In other words, women
are not only the main producers of the good called 'children' but they also bear
the brunt of the early care and education of their children. So the creation of
human capital within the family is still basically a female activity.

This fact explains some of the results obtained in the analysis of the influence
of parents on the formation of the human capital of children. It has been noted,
when studying the intellectual coefficient of children, that the correlation
between their intellectual coefficients and those of their parents is similar in the
case of the father and the mother. But the correlation between the intellectual
coefficient of the child and the level of education of the mother is significantly

greater than that between the coefficient of the child and the level of education of the father.[10] If we also consider that there are studies that have shown that the capacity for obtaining income in the market is more closely related to the 'capacity' of a person – for whom the intellectual coefficient may be a suitable approximate measurement – than to the number of years of schooling, the economic value of maternal education becomes even clearer.

Here again it is necessary to apply the distinction between the 'quantity' and 'quality' of children and the idea that there is an inverse relation between them. It has also been shown that first-born children and those with few siblings tend to show a greater intellectual capacity than those belonging to large families and the reason seems to lie precisely in the difference in the time devoted to them individually.

It must also be borne in mind that the parents' investment in children also involves considerable risks, the greatest of which would be the death of a child to whom time, effort and resources had been devoted. So it can be said that the improvements in lifestyle, hygiene and medical knowledge that have substantially brought down rates of mortality and allow for a longer active life have also reduced the risk of losing the investment in human capital. As already stated, the obvious consequence of all this is a trend to increase expenditure on the training and education of children and young people.

But while this is the case for society as a whole, the changes taking place in the family in some countries are giving rise, to a limited but increasing extent, to an opposing phenomenon – a reduction in the investment by parents in their children as a result of family instability and the rising numbers of single-parent families. It is not just that single-parent families, especially if the head of the household is a woman, are on average poorer than ordinary families. It also happens that the increased probability of breakup and loss of the children means that the investment made by each of the partners in the marriage is smaller, whereas the investment in their own human capital, which is always conserved after divorce, tends to increase. This fact can be explained by the economics of the family. If there is a high probability that the children will not help to provide for their parents' old age and that, because of the divorce, they will hardly be enjoyed as consumer goods; if, in addition, the distance established as a result of the divorce weakens the altruism of the father who no longer lives with the children, then it is reasonable to expect a reduction in the investment in the children. The data available indicate obviously that it is the children who come out the worst. In the United States, for example, one of the countries where the family crisis is most obvious, a new phenomenon is beginning to be seen in that for the first time in the country's history, a generation is obtaining worse results than its parents' generation, both economically and in its social adaptation and psychological stability.[11]

Does this mean that there is to be a turn around in the trend towards increasing investment in children which still dominates in most countries? The answer is not clear because there are factors acting against it. But the appearance for the first time of a factor that makes the investment in the human capital of children decrease instead of grow shows that the trend towards increasing investment in the human capital of children by their parents is not irreversible.

6   THE FORMATION OF HUMAN CAPITAL IN THE FAMILY AND IN THE SCHOOL

The formation of human capital is a complex process involving a number of factors such as the education received at home, the education received at teaching institutions and the training received in the workplace. This section analyses the first two of these factors which are those that most directly affect parents' behaviour with respect to the formation of the human capital of their children, and the third is not considered. With this simplification in mind, we can define a function for human capital production as follows:

$$K_{Ch} = K_{Ch}(H,S)$$

where K_{Ch} represents the human capital of the child, H the education received in the home and S the education received in teaching institutions.

The marginal productivity of both factors is positive, so

$$\frac{\partial K_{Ch}}{\partial H} > 0 \text{ and } \frac{\partial K_{Ch}}{\partial S} > 0$$

Production is optimized by a restriction of costs that can be defined as:

$$C = H\pi_f + Ep_e$$

where p_s represents the price paid by the family (or by the State) for schooling and π_f represents the cost for parents of education within the family. The variables p_s and π_f differ in the way described in previous chapters. Whereas p_s is a price fixed by the market – or at least measurable in monetary terms if there is no market because of the existence of a state monopoly – the most important component of π_f is the opportunity cost for the parents of devoting their time and knowledge to the formation of their child's human capital. π_f can therefore be defined as a function of the parents' human capital (K_p) and of the time they devote to their children (t_p):

$$\pi_f = \pi_f(t_p, K_p)$$

The sign of $\partial \pi_H / \partial t_p$ is clearly positive. But the sign of $\partial \pi_H / \partial K_p$ is doubtful.

On the one hand, the effort required from parents for educating their children decreases the greater their own culture and knowledge, and therefore,

$$\frac{\partial \pi_H}{\partial K_P} < 0$$

But if we take into consideration that K_p is the most important factor in the determination of the salary that the parents might obtain, the result is different because $w_P = w_P(K_P)$, where w_P is the salary of the parents, and since

$$\frac{\partial w_P}{\partial K_P} > 0$$

and the salary is a basic component of π_f, $\partial \pi_H / \partial w_P > 0$, this would lead to

$$\frac{\partial \pi_H}{\partial K_P} > 0$$

In order to determine the combination of family and school education to optimize the formation of human capital, both factors (H and S) should be used so that at the break-even point their marginal products are equal to their prices. In our case

$$\frac{\dfrac{\partial K_{Ch}}{\partial H}}{\pi_H} = \frac{\dfrac{\partial K_{Ch}}{\partial S}}{P_e}$$

If the two factors of production (H and S) are substitutes, then any modification in the marginal productivity of one of the factors – with fixed prices – or any modification in its relative price π_f with fixed marginal productivities would give rise to the replacement of the factor that has risen in relative price or for which the marginal productivity has decreased relatively by the other factor. This is what has been happening in practice for a long time. Technological development and the complexity of today's world, on the one hand, and the increasing opportunity cost of family education on the other, have meant that school education has substantially increased its relative weight in the creation of human capital in advanced societies.

But although both types of education are substitutes, the experts consider that they are not perfect substitutes. If they were, it would be possible to centre education on just one of the factors (home or school) without affecting the final result, namely, the formation of the child's human capital. But today's family is not able to offer sufficient education in scientific subjects such as mathematics or physics or in interpersonal relationships with other children. Nor is the school able to develop certain feelings such as affection or certain types of behaviour that can only be acquired in the family. Therefore, optimization of the function of human capital production will require utilization of both factors to extents that will vary depending on the age of the child and the type of education desired.

7   OTHER WAYS OF HAVING CHILDREN (I): ADOPTION

Parents and children do not always have the blood relationship that we have been assuming so far. Adoption allows for the creation of a legal relationship of filiation between an adult and a minor between whom there was previously no natural link.

Until fairly recently, adoption was basically considered a matter of private law in which the role of the public sector was extremely limited. However, over the last few decades, there has been a continuous absorption of powers by the State to the extent that it is now not just the regulator but also has total control of the adoption market. The main reason for this has been to guarantee the rights of the children involved. But just a brief glance at the real situation will show that the results are far from what they should be.

The adoption market is very complex. There are currently two main characteristics – segmentation, and excessive demand for certain categories of children alongside a surplus of others. In most European countries there are long waiting-lists to adopt newborn children but, at the same time, the public institutions are full of older children. A deficient legal system prevented these children from being adopted when there were people interested in them and who would now be difficult to fit into a new family. Let us look into this in further detail.

The market segmentation is basically due to the existence of very varying children. This means that potential adoptive parents are not prepared to substitute one child for another. In addition to age, race or state of health, other differentiating factors may produce the above-mentioned excess demand or supply. The race factor may be especially relevant in multi-ethnical societies. The data show that, in such societies, adoptive parents have a clear preference for children of their own race. This is easy to explain. If what they are hoping to do is to create a family which will be as close as possible to the pattern of blood-related families, obviously such an image would be easier to attain with greater genetic similarities between the adoptive parents and the adopted child. In addition, since the existence of several races within a single country usually implies the coexistence of non-homogeneous cultural or family patterns, a child adopted by a family of a different race may face problems in knowing to which group he or she really belongs.

The situation is rather similar with respect to the preference for adopting very young children. The child's identification with the adoptive family group and the possibility of sharing its values and beliefs will depend to what extent the child's mind is already developed and how much experience it has had of its original family or an institution.

But in developed countries, the number of healthy, newborn children of the same race as the adoptive parents is very small in comparison with the number of potential adoptive families, and many children of different characteristics remain unadopted.[12] So why does this imbalance, until recently non-existent, persist?

Firstly, there have been technological, legal and social changes which has meant that the number of children offered for adoption has dropped. Technological changes have brought the development of birth control techniques, legal changes the regulations facilitating abortion, and social changes a more favourable attitude towards unmarried mothers which, in some countries, has gone together with generous economic aid to those who are prepared to keep their children.

But the problem does not only arise with supply, there is also a problem of demand. When in a market there is surplus demand we expect the price of the product in question to rise to increase the supply and reduce the demand to a new point of equilibrium. But this solution is not possible in this case because the public administration, when it allocates children to adoptive parents, in no way uses the price criterion but discriminates between the applicants according to other criteria such as family stability, age of the applicants, length of time on the waiting-list and so on.

Would it be possible to use price as an efficient criterion for allocation? Many economists believe this to be true and reject the arguments that consider such a criterion would be unfair or degrading.[13] The specific matter of paying a price for adoptions is yet another aspect of a more general problem on the limits to freedom of contract when the object of the contract involves behaviour which is debatable from the point of view of social ethics. Adoption with payment would thus be morally unacceptable, as would a contract for surrogate mothers – to be studied later in this chapter – or prostitution, because in all cases the trade would be in human beings which would be treated as mere commodities.[14]

The most serious problem for this type of argument is, however, the ethical legitimacy of the prohibition of a contract which in principle favours those who are party to it. Is there any sense, for example, in prohibiting prostitution because it is degrading for prostitutes if it is precisely they who would be damaged by such a prohibition? Or let us suppose – and the supposition seems more than reasonable – that to allow a mother to receive a price for her child would mean that some mothers would not resort to abortion but allow their pregnancy to continue to term. In this case it would be difficult to maintain that the child is more degraded if it is exchanged for money than if it is not allowed to be born because the pregnancy is terminated.

Moreover, economists have not expressed themselves properly on the subject of the proposal for adoption payments. When in 1978 Landes and Posner published their now classic article on 'The economics of baby shortage' and spoke of sale and purchase and the price of babies, they were using the wrong terminology and this was acknowledged some time later by Posner himself.[15]

This is not a matter of buying or selling people, but of buying and selling limited rights with respect to some persons. In order to sell a baby, in the literal sense of the term, the parents would have to have full right of ownership over their child, which is not the case. What parents have are only some specific rights to the custody and control of their children which they may lose if they do not behave properly towards them. So it would in fact be these rights and not the children themselves that would be covered by the contract. (And it should not be forgotten that in practice these rights are often argued over and informally transferred in exchange for monetary consideration in cases of divorce.)

In addition to this general critical approach to agreements in which the object of the contract are human beings, two other specific arguments are often mentioned against adoptions involving payment to the natural mother: that the payment does not guarantee the welfare of the adopted children, and that it is discriminating because it benefits the rich who can thus obtain the 'best' children.

According to the first of the two arguments, adoptions for a price could mean that children would be given in adoption to people intending to exploit them, either economically or sexually. Although the idea at first sight seems of interest, there is in fact little substance to it. Firstly, because what is being sold, as already stated, is not the child itself but the rights the parents have over the child. And these rights are limited by law. And, secondly, because exploitation of children, especially sexual exploitation in the western world, is relatively frequent within families where the children have blood ties and, even more so, in the case of second marriages or informal relationships on the part of the mother. There are no data to indicate that such abuse is more frequent amongst adoptive parents. What happens in actual fact is that there is often excessive tolerance towards natural parents and great mistrust of adoptive parents which, in the light of reality, is not justified. Some economists[16] think that damage could really be caused in the special case of the children of poor families who are handed over to rich families against the wishes of the children themselves. This criticism, however, is debatable and the problem could be easily solved by requiring the authorization of the child as soon as he or she is of sufficient age to decide.[17]

The argument that this proposal would benefit the rich against the interests of less well-off families reflects the widespread lack of faith in the market allocation mechanisms. It is true that it is only possible to choose in the market if one has a certain economic capacity. But the comparison should not be between a real market situation in which incomes are unequal and an ideal, fair market in which children are given in adoption according to criteria of perfect justice and equity. What we have is a system in which there is a large black market and in which influence peddling is not unusual in cases of adoption. A more open market could bring down the costs for those people who are today forced to adopt on the black market, which is often international, and this would benefit people with a more limited economic capacity. In addition, if we consider that the degree of influence of a specific person is usually closely linked to his economic capacity, anything that will limit the discretional nature of a public administration that is subject to this type of pressure will amount to an advantage for those who are not well-off.

But even if there were no black markets or influence-peddling, the sale of adoption rights would be more efficient than the type of administrative allocation that exists at present because the interest of the adoptive parents in each type of child would be evaluated better. Administrative allocation, based on supposedly objective criteria, would find it difficult to resolve this efficiently, whereas a market would have no difficulty in finding a solution.

In spite of these drawbacks, whether real or imagined, the proposed sale of parents' rights would have important advantages. All the parties involved – natural mothers, adoptive parents and children – would receive the benefit of better allocation which would bring down the number of abortions as the natural mothers would receive monetary compensation. The sale of rights would not involve the disappearance of public control which would have to be exercised equally for both natural and adoptive parents.

8   ECONOMIC ANALYSIS OF THE ADOPTION MARKET

8.1   Market equilibrium

Since there is a supply and demand for adoptions the problem of allocation can be studied in market analysis terms. In this specific case, this is a strictly controlled and segmented market in which, on the one hand, the public sector leaves little room for private initiative to balance supply and demand and in which, on the other, the rights in question refer to children of widely differing characteristics.

In order to simplify our analysis we shall assume, for the time being, that there is only one type of children for adoption – healthy newborns – and that any other characteristics (race, beauty and so on) are immaterial to the adoptive parents. Figure 5.5 shows the situation of this adoption market. The supply curve is inelastic because, since mothers are not allowed to receive any payment whatsoever, the number of children for adoption depends on other circumstances apart from price. Demand, on the other hand, is elastic to price because the children are considered as consumer goods.

The number of children for adoption, irrespective of price, depends on other variables – on the one hand, the extension of contraception, sex education or the cost of abortion and, on the other, the willingness of unmarried mothers to keep their children. Changes in these variables over recent decades have pushed the supply curve to the left to S_2 and S_3.

Demand is not only affected by the price but also by other factors acting in opposing directions. Because of greater social acceptance of adoption, the curve can be expected to shift to the right. But the advances in medical techniques to counter infertility allow many couples who, in other circumstances, would have tried to adopt to have their own children and this shifts the demand curve towards the left.

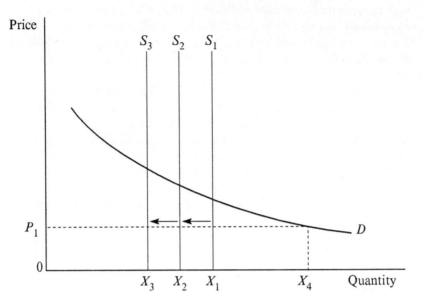

Figure 5.5   The market for adoption with no payment

Since this market is controlled by the government, which does not permit adoption payments, there is a clear surplus demand. Let us assume that the government fixes a symbolic price to be paid by adoptive parents (P_1) which is much lower than that which would exist in a free market. At this price, a very high demand for adoptions can be expected, $0X_4$. If the supply curve is S_1, we would have a surplus demand of $X_1 X_4$. If, because of the above circumstances, the supply curve moves gradually towards the left, we would expect increasing surplus demand ($X_2 X_4$ and $X_3 X_4$). As long as the government refuses to accept a market price, the allocation of an increasingly small number of children would be done by rationing and waiting-lists, according to the criteria established by the administrative authorities. Some adoptive parents, if unable to adopt a child on the legal market, would resort to the black market and pay a much higher price.

Let us now imagine a different institutional framework in which prospective adoptive parents and the natural parents of the prospective adopted children are allowed to reach agreements in which one of the most important elements is the payment of a price that is freely agreed by the parties involved. The supply curve would not then be completely inelastic and the supply of children would rise with the price as shown in Figure 5.6. This figure is based on specific social preferences which means that, if there is no price, the supply curve is S_3 and the surplus demand $X_3 X_4$ as in Figure 5.5.

The fact that the natural parents receive a price means that they are prepared to increase their offer of children for adoption so the new curve of supply moves to S_4. At the new point of equilibrium, the number of children given for adoption increases from $0X_3$ to $0X_5$, and the price for adoptive parents is now P_2. The surplus demand has disappeared.

Even though $P_2 > P_1$, this does not mean that for *all* adoptive parents there will be an increase in the adoption price. For those who, under the conditions given in Figure

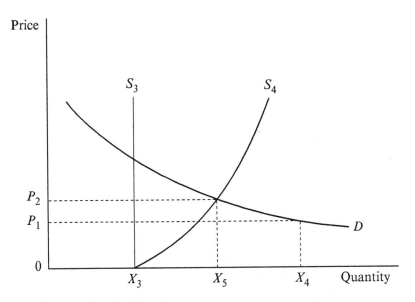

Figure 5.6   The market for adoption with payment

5.5, were prepared to resort to the black market, the price may be lower because the supply has increased and the risk premium they had to pay for entering into an illegal contract has disappeared.

8.2   Different Preferences of Adoptive Parents

An additional advantage that would be gained from the setting of prices in the adoption market is more efficient allocation amongst adoptive parents, expressing different preferences for certain characteristics of the children to be adopted. Let us now forget the assumption that all children are equal and admit that they are of different age, race or health. In order to simplify the analysis, let us take just one of these differentiating characteristics – age – although the analysis is also valid for the others.

Let us take a childless couple (C_1) who are keen to adopt a newborn child and who are not at all interested in adopting a child over two years of age. Then let us take a second couple (C_2) who also prefer to adopt a newborn child but will accept, with only a slightly lower degree of preference, an older child but with an age limit of five. Administrative allocation would hardly be likely to take into consideration this difference in the degree of intensity of the preferences which may, however, be considered in a market.

Figure 5.7 represents the utility obtained in terms of the child's age and the prices that each of the couples would be prepared to pay to adopt.

According to these functions, in the case of a one-year-old child, the utility obtained is the same for both couples who will both be prepared to pay the same price P_1. But if the child is under one year of age, the market will allocate it to couple C_1, who will be

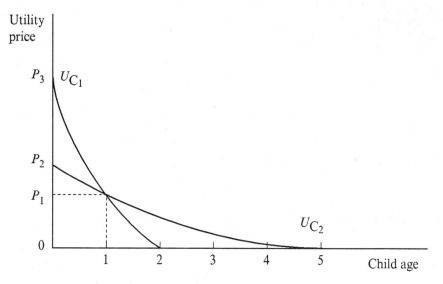

Figure 5.7   Utility and allocation of children for adoption in the case of two couples with different preferences

prepared to pay a higher price for it than C_2. However if the child is older than one but under five, it will be adopted by C_2 because they will be prepared to pay a higher price than C_1 who would not be competing with C_2 for the child because they would receive no utility from the adoption.

9   OTHER WAYS OF HAVING CHILDREN (II): SURROGATE MOTHERHOOD

Technological development has made possible a new way of creating the rights to custody and care of children – the artificial fertilization of a woman who accepts to carry the foetus and hand over the newborn child to the biological father and his wife. This is the most common case for the phenomenon known as 'surrogate motherhood'. In these cases the biological mother gives up her legal rights to the child she has given birth to, normally in exchange for monetary compensation.

The problems that arise from the existence of surrogate mothers and the possibility of regulating this type of contract became apparent throughout the world with the *Baby M* case in the Supreme Court of the North American State of New Jersey in 1988. Here a biological mother, who had signed an agreement such as that described in the above paragraph, appealed against a decision from a lower court which considered the contract valid and granted custody of the child to the biological father and his wife. The biological mother, who had changed her mind after giving birth and now wanted to keep the baby, managed to have the contract considered null and void by the Supreme Court and, although she did not obtain custody of her child, which was given to the natural father, did have her rights acknowledged and was granted the right to visit the child regularly.[18]

The arguments given by the Court to justify its decision do not seem very sound if analysed in the light of economic logic. On the one hand, the Court referred to the general regulations covering adoption which prohibited a contract of this type because it included payment of a price. On the other, it stressed the disadvantages of a contract like this for the child because, instead of coming into the world in an environment of peace and tranquillity it would find itself in the middle of a conflict between its father and mother. And, finally, it pointed out that the rights of the mother would disappear because she had given them up before the child was born, although with insufficient information and advice.

Criticism of adoption for a price and its possible effects on the child's future have already been discussed in a previous section. With respect to the rights of the mother, it must be pointed out that in adoption too the mother gives up her rights. In the case of a surrogate mother, she consciously gives up her rights before the pregnancy begins and the pregnancy would not take place at all unless the surrogacy contract has first been signed. The basic problem of the mother's rights seems therefore to be that in adoptions she has to receive competent advice whereas in surrogate motherhood this does not arise, and this seems to reflect an exaggerated faith in the importance of advice, irrespective of whether the matter also has an easy legal solution.

Finally the matter of the damage caused to the child by the dispute between its parents is merely the consequence of the legal uncertainty surrounding these contracts, which the decision from the New Jersey Supreme Court only accentuated.

In spite of the majority opinion against this type of agreement, surrogate motherhood contracts could be defended as efficient agreements, which could help to reduce the present imbalance between the supply and demand of children for adoption. Children born of surrogate mothers would have the advantage of entering families in which one of the parents is its natural parent and this would increase the level of satisfaction of those taking charge of them.

The agreement would thus be beneficial for all the parties involved. A child is born who, had there been no contract, simply would not have been born. The parents fulfil their desire for a child and the biological mother receives economic compensation for the physical and material costs of bearing it.

If surrogate motherhood contracts are considered null and void this is not likely to mean they will disappear altogether although there will be few of them because of the uncertainty created for the contracting parties. The father's situation will be weakened because only at the last minute can he be sure the mother will really give up her rights and not adopt a strategy of upping her price after the birth in exchange for transferring her rights and not fighting for custody. This risk will be enough to put off most potential fathers, so that many potential biological mothers who could have benefited from this type of agreement will be at a disadvantage.

NOTES

1. Posner, R. (1992b), pp. 270–72.
2. Some econometric studies show that each abortion reduces the population by a number much lower than 1. S.P. Coelen and R.J. McIntyre, for example, have calculated that 1.83 abortions are needed to reduce the population by one person. Coelen, S.P. and McIntyre, R.J. (1978).
3. Butz, W.P. and Ward, M.P. (1979).
4. Winegarden, C.R. (1984).
5. According to G. Becker, historical studies on the subject seem to indicate that, prior to the nineteenth century, rich men tended to have more children than poor ones, in both monogamous and polygamous societies. The same can be said of rural societies even in the nineteenth century. But already at that time negative correlations can be found between both variables in urban families. In the present century, the statistics available in advanced countries show both positive and negative correlations although, at relatively low income levels, the correlation is mainly negative and, at higher income levels, both variables appear to be independent or positively correlated. The statistics, however, do not allow us to reach definitive conclusions. Becker, G. (1991), p. 144.
6. See, for example, the following text from the Bible on the costs of redeeming one's votes to the Lord: 'And thy estimation shall be of the male from twenty years old even unto sixty years old, even thy estimation shall be fifty shekels of silver . . . .. And if it be a female, then thy estimation shall be thirty shekels. And if it be from five years old even unto twenty years old, then thy estimation shall be of the male twenty shekels, and for the female ten shekels. And if it be from a month old even unto five years old, then thy estimation shall be of the male five shekels of silver, and for the female thy estimation shall be three shekels of silver. And if it be from sixty years old and above; if it be a male, then thy estimation shall be fifteen shekels, and for the female ten shekels.'
7. Although this idea is in keeping with the basic principles of economics, it is not accepted by everyone; it is often not even taken into consideration when determining compensation for deaths in car accidents, since the rate table used currently in many countries does not take this problem into account.
8. For example, it appears that in France in the seventeenth and eighteenth centuries, for every 1000 children born alive, 720 survived the first year, 574 survived the first five years, and 525 lived ten years. During the first year of life, then, 25 per cent died. Some of these deaths were due to the custom of handing the newborn child to a wetnurse who looked after the child in her home together with many other children. Those mothers who kept their children and fed them themselves reduced the risk of them dying by half. It should be pointed out that the use of a wetnurse was by no means exclusive to the upper classes. Moreover, it was very frequent, also, for the child to be abandoned in the first few months of its life. Between 1773 and 1790, for example, an average of 5800 children were abandoned every year in Paris. Although it is true that people came from other towns to abandon them in the capital, the number is still high, since between 20 000 and 25 000 children were born in Paris each year. See Badinter, E. (1980), Ch. 3. Adam Smith states in *The Wealth of Nations* that the infant mortality rate was even higher in the middle of the eighteenth century in the poorer, colder region of the Upper Highlands

of Scotland, where there were cases of mothers who gave birth to 20 children and only one or two survived. Smith, A. (1776) (1976), I, p. 97.

9.   To quote just one case, see what a Spanish nurse declared regarding the civil war that devastated Burundi in 1995: 'Hardly any importance was paid to the newborn; for the inhabitants of the city of Kaburantwa, it was a waste of time to try to save a baby when in their country people were being killed who were very much alive.' *El Mundo*, 2 April 1995.

10.   Leibowitz, A. (1974), p. 438.

11.   Whithead, B.D. (1993).

12.   For example, in the United States, in 1990 over 13 000 children were offered for adoption and left unadopted, most of them coloured or having special problems. See Trebilcok, M.J. (1993), p. 278.

13.   The pioneering work along these lines is the article by E.M. Landes and R. Posner (1978). Also see Lemennicier (1988), Ch. 6.

14.   The term *commodification* has become fairly widespread in American literature to describe this type of contract. A characteristic work from this approach, which specifically refers to some of the matters covered in this chapter, is Radin, M.J. (1987). An overview of the problem can be found in Trebilcock , M.J. (1993), Ch. 2.

15.   Landes, E.M. and Posner, R. (1978); and Posner, R. (1992b), p. 410.

16.   Such as G.S. Becker and K.M. Murphy (1988).

17.   See Posner, R. (1992b), pp. 415–16.

18.   See the main points of the opinion of the Court in Pyle, R.C. (1994), pp. 427–8.

6. The intergenerational pact

1 MUTUAL ASSISTANCE BETWEEN PARENTS AND CHILDREN

The whole of society is organized for the protection of its youngest members. Care is normally undertaken by families and it is the parents who see to the maintenance and welfare of their children until they are able to look after themselves. This is the principal provision of the tacit agreement amongst the generations that has always been the basis of human society.

But there are some parents who cannot, or do not want to, care for their children, because they lack the necessary resources. Their personal circumstances prevent them from bearing such a responsibility or, quite simply, they are not interested in their children. Although obviously not the general rule, this does occur with relative frequency. The law establishes some minimum obligations, which would be unnecessary if all the members of society were altruistic towards their descendants and which, if not fulfilled, may lead to the loss of the parents' rights over their children. In the same way, the law also fixes certain obligations for children with respect to their parents if the latter are unable to look after themselves.

Legal regulation of the links between parents and children has resulted from a long historical process that has been manifest in customs and religious precepts as much as in civil legislation. The specific conditions set down in each society or culture have varied, with age, heritage or sex being used as criteria to establish a variety of obligations.[1] But all societies have set up patterns of intergenerational mutual assistance as a guarantee of survival.

The survival of a social group, however, does not involve care for each and every one of its members as we would understand this today. In many societies, care for children or parents depended on the specific situation of the family at a specific time, so the lives of children or the elderly often had very little value. It was not considered reasonable to devote efforts to protecting children who were unlikely to survive or who had serious health problems; and the abandonment of the elderly when their physical condition no longer enabled them to follow the group has been a frequent practice amongst nomadic peoples.[2] In the Christian era, it was generally the authors of catechisms and religious works who first insisted on the parents' obligations of maintaining and educating their children. State legislation only gained strength in this area as a result of the disinterest shown by parents in their small children in the eighteenth century, especially in the large cities, which was doubtless one of the causes of the high child mortality at that time. The legal reforms of the nineteenth century laid down these obligations in the civil codes that have been handed down to us with just slight modifications. Over recent decades there has been a great increase in State intervention enforcing the fulfilment of parents' obligations towards their children.

2   AN INTERGENERATIONAL PACT

As mentioned in earlier chapters an economic approach to the analysis of links between the generations does not exclude the existence of affection and altruism in relations between parents and their children. However, it does place the emphasis on the existence of tacit and explicit compensation between the two groups which, especially in traditional societies, is one of the foundations for the existence of the family.

One of the matters that has been of most interest in recent years to economists specializing in the study of the family and of social security is how to find the balance between the benefits exchanged between the various generations. That is, how to determine whether, as is often stated, people who are now at retirement age are currently obtaining returns at a level that does not correspond to the investment made at the time, or if it is true that some countries are today spending too much on their elderly and too little on their children.

With this in mind, it is interesting to analyse what benefits are involved as these have not always been the same over the years. In the first place, let us look at the services provided by the various generations of a farming family in a traditional agricultural society. In such cases, the family stands for practically everything throughout the life of its members. It is the school while they are children, the company for which they work as adults and the place they retire to when they become old. In this limited environment, it is easy to see what services are provided by each family member towards the others. Children are cared for by adults until they reach an age at which they become productive and can live from their own work. But when the parents can no longer work or be useful in some other way, it is the children who have to maintain them, thus reversing the roles. It is not difficult to see that here there is a tacit agreement amongst the members of the family. If the parents, when young, had not been sure their children would take care of them in their old age, their behaviour would have been different. If they had not expected to be cared for, they would have devoted less time and fewer resources to their children and would have tried to save up for their old age. For the younger generation, the former solution is preferable because it means they receive help when they most need it – while children – in exchange for supplying it when they can – as mature people. It is also preferable for the parents because they reach old age confident that they will not be abandoned by their own family. To use a very graphic expression from the American economist, Theodore W. Schultz, we could say that children are the capital of the poor in backward countries. So this tacit agreement suits both groups.

To use more precise economic language we could say that, in a family such as the one described, when the parents devote resources to bringing up their children, what they are really doing is acquiring certain property rights over the returns of the children's work once the latter reach the age when they become productive. The fact that the law provides for and is able to enforce these rights in the courts is irrelevant for such a family group because custom enforces the traditional practice and society punishes any behaviour that does not toe the line.

In modern industrialized societies this tacit pact does not disappear but undergoes significant depersonalization. As we have just seen, the traditional family was a much more complex entity than today's family because it offered, practically exclusively, a number of services which today are provided by both private institutions and the State. Two of these have been mentioned above – education and care for the elderly. Today these services can be obtained from both the private and the public sector. In fact one of the main causes of the so-called crisis of the modern family stems from the fact that the family has partially lost its *raison d'être*, although its social usefulness has increased in other aspects, formerly considered of secondary importance, such as affection towards the children or love for the spouse.

Since other institutions have taken on some of the activities that used to be carried out by the family group, it is now through the financing of these institutions, for example, schools or social security pension schemes, that we have to understand the agreement between the generations.

In addition, in the western world, most of the costs of education and assistance for young people are paid through taxation. But those paying and those receiving the benefits of such expenditure belong to different generations, so a service is being provided in the same way as it used to be by the traditional family. The difference is that it is no longer the parent devoting time and money to the education of his own child, but a whole generation of taxpayers that pay to provide a service for the younger generation. With time, those who were children will become productive workers and will pay taxes not just to educate their own children but also so that payments in the form of pensions will be made to the previous generation who, having reached retirement, receive no income from their own work.

We could thus analyse most of the costs financed by taxpayers to see how these intergenerational income transfers are made. Some of them are addressed directly towards a specific generation. Education benefits the young, pensions benefit the elderly. Others are less clear. Medical assistance, for example, involves expenditure which benefits society as a whole, although apparently it is the elderly who are the main beneficiaries.[3]

Figure 6.1 shows how, during his lifetime, a person passes through the stages of beneficiary, contributor, then beneficiary once again, with respect to his position within society. The key moments are at points *A* and *B*, which are the point of entry of a person into the labour market and the time of retirement respectively. Between these two points the person is a taxpayer, to the extent shown by the section with vertical lines. To the left of *A* and the right of *B*, he is a beneficiary to the extent shown by the sections with horizontal lines.

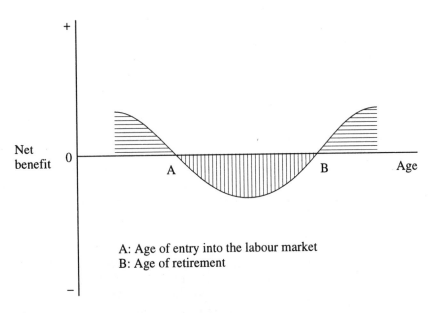

A: Age of entry into the labour market
B: Age of retirement

Figure 6.1   The pact amongst the generations

It is precisely the steep growth of expenditure by the social security on pensions and services to the elderly that has led some people to believe that the resources devoted to the elderly are excessive, if compared to the amount spent on the younger groups. In some countries, this belief is leading to a controversy, which practically amounts to a battle amongst the generations to get a larger slice of the limited public resources. And many people are calling for changes to the structure of public expenditure.

However the situation is much more complex than is apparent from the data on annual public expenditure. In countries in which the pension scheme is not based on capitalization of the contributions but on a distribution pattern in which there is no precise link between the amount contributed and the pension received, calculations cannot be accurate because it is difficult to determine the present value of the amounts paid through contributions over the years. And the situation is similar with the payment of taxes for financing public services, such as health or assistance for the elderly, and the utilization of such services in that the payments made when the person was working took place long before that person became a beneficiary, so it is not possible to make a simple comparison of the payments made with the payments in kind received later on.

It is wrong to compare in absolute terms the amount spent on young people and the elderly because while young people receive first and pay their contributions later, the elderly receive the benefit of their contributions many years after making their first payment. With this simple financial criterion, the results are very different from those obtained from just looking at the gross figures. It is no longer so clear that the elderly, taken as a whole, receive excessive benefits. Some of the people who, while working, did not pay taxes or social security contributions but today receive pensions or allowances could be considered beneficiaries of the current system of public expenditure. But it would be difficult to make such a statement for a whole generation.

This same criterion can be used to focus attention on another interesting circumstance – the varying social profitability of investments on groups of different ages. Let us suppose that what concerns us now is not so much the interests of specific people as the sum of benefits that all the inhabitants of a specific country expect to obtain from its social policy, which we can call the social benefit. The problem posed is precisely how to achieve, with limited economic resources, the maximum social benefit. Should any one group receive benefits at the expense of the others?

The answer to this question in economic terms goes against the interests of the elderly: investments in young people are more profitable than investments in retired people. There are two main reasons for this. The first is the greater number of years during which the resources invested will bring returns. Here we can think again of expenditure on education for children and young people. In economic terms, this expenditure is considered an investment in human capital, that is, as something that will improve the qualifications and productivity of those receiving it. Obviously this investment will, on average, give returns for many more years than expenditure on people during the last stage of their lives.

The second reason is the application of the general principle of decreasing marginal productivity of a factor of production, according to which the smaller the quantity of a factor – for example, the capital in a specific industry – the greater its productivity. Since the provision of human capital is scarce amongst the young, investment on them will be the most productive.

This greater profitability of investment on the young helps to explain why the State spends high levels of resources on education and why the law compels parents to care for their children and invest in them. It would be a mistake, however, to believe that it is up to the State to force the transfer of income from one generation to another only to achieve greater efficiency. The economic policy of a modern State is the result of a complex system of interests, many of which are in conflict. For a society to function, constant compromises are required and the strict criterion of short-term efficiency does not justify State intervention if it affects people's individual rights. If this were so, to talk of a social pact amongst the generations would be senseless. All the parties to an agreement have to be aware that they will obtain some benefit from it.

Can it be said that both the young and the old benefit from this overall pact amongst the generations? The answer is basically the same as in the case of a traditional family in which the agreement was from person to person. It is useful for the younger generation to receive assistance from adults during the first part of their lives although later they have to pay to maintain a generation of elderly people because, with the transfers they receive, they can obtain returns which will allow them to assist the elderly and still have a surplus. The pact will function as long as both groups receive a benefit from it. If the advantages tip the balance towards one generation rather than the other, as sometimes occurs, a crisis in the system will be inevitable.

In spite of the similarities between the tacit agreements within a single family and what we have called the depersonalized intergenerational pact, there are still important differences. The most significant is the different degree of altruism of each of the persons involved and the attitude of cooperation with respect to the other party to the agreement. As stated in Chapter 1, cooperation depends to a great extent on whether there is a close, stable relationship with other people. There are circumstances and institutions which condition us to act in a cooperative way, whereas other institutions or circumstances do not. The problem, in our case, is that observation of the real situation seems to show that in the welfare state cooperative behaviour amongst citizens is not widespread. In fact, quite the opposite seems to be the case.

The welfare state creates clear incentives for non-cooperative behaviour on the part of citizens, for two reasons at least. Firstly, the great benefits which groups, or generations in this case, can obtain by using political power for their own purposes. Strategies for gaining income are inefficient for the whole of the country's economy, but they may be very profitable for those that apply them successfully. Secondly, the individual advantages that may be reaped at the expense of others by acting as a *free-rider*, that is, by taking the benefits offered by the system while avoiding its costs. To not pay taxes, to fraudulently receive unemployment benefit and so on, may be efficient from the point of view of the individual but is very inefficient for society as a whole. Strangely enough, society does not morally condemn this type of behaviour because the welfare state system is not governed by the principles and circumstances which would make such attitudes unsustainable within a family.

What is most surprising in this analysis is that the welfare state, which was created in order to further social cooperation, has eventually become a source of antisocial behaviour. The replacement of the functions of the traditional family with its incentives for cooperative behaviour by a welfare state, which creates no such incentives, has become problematical. Although it is true that we cannot give back to families the functions they seem to have lost for ever, we cannot forget the problems that arise when these same functions are carried out by the welfare state.

3   THE INTERGENERATIONAL PACT AND FINANCING EXPENDITURE WITH PUBLIC DEBT

So far we have assumed that any expenditure paid for at a given time by a generation of taxpayers is financed with taxes collected at the same time as the actual expenditure. But this is not necessarily so, as some expenses may be paid by borrowing which will have to be paid for at a later date. This section aims to reflect on the possible effects of such borrowing on the pact amongst the generations.

In the case of the family pact, borrowing by the parents will be a burden which will eventually have to be paid for by the children and may cause a reduction in the estate passed on to them. But such borrowing will not necessarily make the children poorer. Whether or not this is the case will depend on the use of the resources obtained with the loan. If the debt has been used to improve the family farm, there will be a simultaneous increase in the assets and liabilities of the joint property and the net result will depend on the efficiency of the investment. If it has been spent on developing the human capital of the children, the value of the material estate will have decreased but the stock of human capital will have increased, facilitating the obtention of greater levels of income with a given physical capital stock. The net result for the family estate will depend on the relative productivity of the new human capital in comparison with the lost physical capital. Expenditure on consumption of the resources obtained with the loan will, however, lead to a decrease in the family estate. Parents will only finance their consumption in this way if their altruism towards their children is so limited that the utility of consuming these resources is greater than the loss of utility involved in the fact that their children will have to pay back the debt, or if they calculate that the money to be saved by their children in order to pay back the debt will only slightly reduce their own level of wellbeing after they have retired.

If we now go on to the overall pact between the generations, the problems are basically the same but with one clear difference. Any decisions on borrowing, investment or consumption are no longer taken by individuals but by a whole generation. The effects of any decision taken will be felt by each family individually, and parents will take whatever decisions they feel are right depending on the estate they hope to leave their children and their degree of altruism.

In the debate on the effects of public debt on future generations, over the last two decades an essential role has been played by the Ricardian equivalence theorem, according to which the financing of a specific item of public expenditure by taxes or borrowing will affect neither family consumption nor capital formation in an economy. This is because, on the one hand, financing from taxes will reduce the available income of taxpayers and therefore private consumption but, on the other, if financing of the expenditure comes from public borrowing, taxpayers will know that in future taxes will have to increase in order to pay off the debt, so they will take this effect into account by increasing saving and reducing consumption.

If taxpayers are alive at the time of the expenditure and maturity of the loan, the equivalence theorem presents no further difficulties. But the problem arises when we include two different generations in the model, with the first one deciding on the expenditure and the second one paying off the debt to the holders of the bonds. In this case the theorem will also be valid provided we accept that parents do not only maximize their own consumption but are altruistic and include within their own utility functions any consumption by their children. If this condition is fulfilled and we accept the assumption that all generations are altruistic towards their children, for the purposes of consumption or capital formation, which of the generations pays the taxes is not relevant. If expenditure is financed by borrowing and the taxes are paid by the children's generation, the parents will first have increased their rate of saving and this will have increased the estate they pass on.[4]

Few economists, however, doubt that the theorem of equivalence is based on fairly restrictive assumptions which include not just altruism but also the fact that this altruism involves uniform attitudes towards inheritance on the part of parents (exclusion of negative inheritance, for example), as well as lack of uncertainty and efficient capital markets. And the facts do not seem to confirm that the theorem is being fulfilled in practice because the great growth in public borrowing over the 1980s and 1990s in many countries has not brought with it the growth in the rates of private saving that the theorem predicts.

4 FAMILY, PENSIONS AND RETIREMENT

Men and women go through a number of stages during their lifetimes with respect to expenditure and income. In their early years, unless they have received goods through donations or inheritance they have zero income. It is during their maturity that they obtain higher levels of income. And generally, unless very wealthy, their income drops after retirement.

Figures 6.2 (a), 6.2 (b) and 6.2 (c) show the trends for income and wealth of a representative person throughout his lifetime. The subject is an employed worker who receives no donations or inheritance but who saves, thus forming some capital. It is also assumed that the payment of contributions to obtain a pension is completely voluntary.

Figure 6.2 (a) shows the worker's income if he spends all his revenue, saving nothing and making no pension contributions. His income will be zero until the

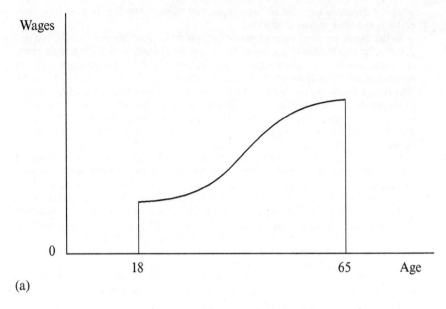

Figure 6.2a   Total wages for a worker throughout his life

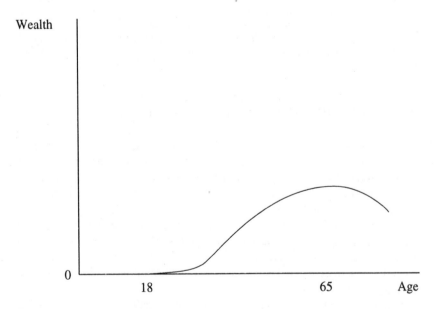

Figure 6.2b   Total wealth for a worker throughout his life

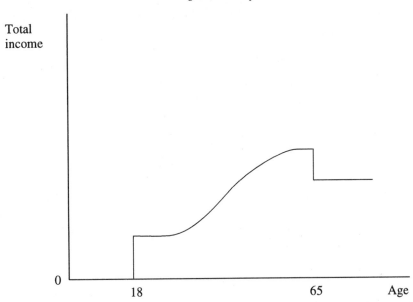

Figure 6.2c   Total income for a worker throughout his life

age of 18 when we assume he starts to work, and will be zero again as from 65 when he retires.

However this behaviour would not be very rational in a person concerned with his own wellbeing throughout his life. While it is reasonable for him to obtain no income and live with his parents until the age of 18, it would be normal during his working life for him to take some type of measure to ensure he will continue receiving some income after his retirement. Any such measure will involve some method of saving, with this term being understood as the allocation of a given part of revenue to activities apart from consumption with a view to increasing the estate. There are three main methods of saving:

1. The constitution of wealth in the form of real estate (houses, land and so on) and personal property (shares, bank deposits and so on) which, with varying degrees of liquidity and profitability, will offer the possibility of obtaining income in the future.
2. Periodic contributions to a public body or private company to ensure a pension at a specific age or at retirement.
3. Investment in children or other members of the next generation with a view to the retired person being cared for by them once he has stopped receiving an income.

The latter solution is that of the traditional family based on an implicit contract between parents and their children. In a modern society, however, the choice lies basically between options 1 and 2.

Economic theory has explained this fact by the so-called 'old age security hypothesis' whereby the demand for children tends to drop to the extent that economic progress creates more opportunities for saving by developing the capital markets. These markets allow the worker to save part of his current income for use at retirement without having to invest in his children which was the method of old age insurance used in the traditional agricultural society. Today this type of insurance is practically non-existent as can be seen, amongst other things, in the fact that the data seem to show that the decision to save for retirement is not affected by the circumstance of having had children or not.[5]

The formation of capital and trends over time are shown in Figure 6.2 (b). According to our hypothesis, which excludes donations and inheritance, capital formation starts at the age when work starts. When retirement age is reached, capital growth usually stops and normally, since income decreases, wealth also decreases as a result of excess consumption from this income. This gives rise to negative savings to an amount that depends both on the needs for expenditure and possible income and on altruism towards the descendants.[6]

Figure 6.2 (c) finally shows the total income curve for this representative worker. The main difference between Figures 6.2 (a) and 6.2 (c) is the income received by the worker after retirement. This comes from the revenue generated by the wealth that has been accumulated in either of the above ways. What is important is that the income which was zero in the first of the figures becomes positive in the third one although it is generally lower than the income obtained before retirement because of the loss of income in the form of wages. Rational conduct by a person aiming to maximize his welfare in the long term therefore requires saving throughout his active life so that it is the curve in Figure 6.2 (c) and not the one in 6.2 (a) that indicates his income.

Having established this principle, it needs to be determined which of these forms of saving are preferred to the others. In practice, the great majority of people try to ensure future income through option 2, that is, by receiving a retirement pension. This option means that, throughout his productive life, the worker receives lower net wages than he would obtain if he paid no contributions to a pension fund, in exchange for a pension when he stops working.

Preference for this option over option 1 is largely due to the fact that it is preferred, if not imposed, by the public administration. But even in a hypothetical situation of neutrality on the part of the State, most people would still prefer a pension to other types of saving partly because many people would find managing capital either difficult or disagreeable and partly because the risk of losing private capital may be greater than that of devaluation of a larger fund in which the variety of the assets will lead to greater diversification of the risk involved.

State intervention is, however, a factor of great importance and takes two forms. The first is through compulsory contributions to the social security scheme which is more economically rational in the case of contributions to obtain a minimum pension than in the case of contributions for larger pensions. This is because, in the former case, there is a problem of a moral hazard which may lead to inefficient results. By moral hazard we refer to the changing probability of a specific event taking place as a result of the existence of an insurance covering such a risk. In the case of pensions, non-compulsory contributions could lead to these inefficient effects as a result of the reduction in individual precautionary measures. In advanced societies today the trend is to guarantee that everyone receives a minimum welfare pension, even when no contributions at all have been paid. So unless it is obligatory to make minimum payments to the social security, this amounts to a clear incentive to avoid paying contributions. For example, if the guaranteed welfare pension amounts to 300 dollars and the pension obtained by the worker after paying minimum contributions is 400 dollars, then instead of receiving the latter figure in exchange for his contributions he would receive only 100 dollars because he would have received the rest all the same. This is why, if minimum pensions are guaranteed for everyone, the trend is to make contributions obligatory, at least for the lowest pensions.

Another way in which state regulation favours pensions as against other methods of saving is through special tax benefits for any funds spent by the worker on retirement plans, pension funds or other similar assets. In this way the public sector encourages private individuals to save to avoid the economic problems that may arise after retirement which might also incur costs for the State. However this preference for retirement plans and pension funds has been criticized with the argument that there are no economic reasons for it. If a person prefers to save on the stock market or in real estate and live on income from these investments after retirement, there is no reason why he should be penalized with respect to those who choose to pay into a pension fund. Because of the problem of moral hazard mentioned above, it is reasonable for the State to require everybody to make a minimum investment in a public system or in guaranteed private funds. But, with this exception, there is no reason why the State should not be neutral with respect to the various methods of saving and the way in which each individual organizes his retirement.[7]

Pension schemes in the modern welfare state, with their blurred distinction between contributions and benefits, have had unexpected effects on the behaviour of the insured parties and these have altered the links between generations. The first of these effects is the depersonalization mentioned above in the tacit agreement between parents and children who now form part of a much wider intergenerational pact. Children now fulfil their financial obligations towards their parents by paying taxes and contributions. And parents do not recover the investment made in their children through a direct link with them but through the payments they receive from the State in the form of monetary benefits or services.

An old age pension can also affect the decisions of parents concerning the number of children they wish to have and the size of the investment they are prepared to make in them. This works in two ways. Firstly, as already stated, the demand for children may drop when a person has other resources – in this case, a pension – guaranteeing a basic income in old age. But at the same time the investment in children may be greater if the parents know they will start to receive a pension as soon as they retire, because they will require fewer savings and can therefore spend a larger proportion of their income on their children.

But this is not necessarily the case. It is also possible they will just spend the money that in other circumstances they would have saved for their old age on a holiday, a car or whatever. One of the main effects of this is a reduction in national levels of saving as the social security acts as a substitute for private savings. It will be the degree of altruism of the parents that will determine the use of such resources. If the expected utility of expenditure on personal consumption is greater than that to be expected by the parents from improving the situation of the child, then these resources will be spent on consumption. But if the degree of altruism is greater and, in the parents' utility function, the increased utility of the child holds greater weight than their own consumption, then the funds will be devoted to the child.

5   RETIREMENT AGE AND PENSIONS AS PROBLEMS FOR DISTRIBUTION AMONGST THE GENERATIONS

In the pact amongst the generations described here, a person's retirement is a key stage in his life, because it marks the change from taxpayer to beneficiary. Retirement brings with it both advantages and costs. The advantages include the possibility of obtaining income without having to work, which makes it possible to enjoy the leisure which in the utility functions of most people, but not all, is a luxury commodity that now becomes more accessible. But the costs may be high. Income after retirement is usually lower – sometimes much lower – than that obtained while working. Expenses tend to be lower too but, for some, the drop in income may be a serious drawback. And many people face psychological problems on retirement which may be serious but are difficult to quantify economically.

If individuals could choose a time for retirement, the choice would depend on their own utility function in which the above-mentioned commodities (free time and money) are the most important elements. But when the time of retirement is not determined by the preferences or physical condition of each individual but is the same across the board, many people find that it does not necessarily bring maximum wellbeing. It is therefore not surprising that there is much disagreement over retirement being set at a specific age.[8]

In view of such opposition to the State's fixing the age for retirement and, given the high cost of forcing retirement on a pay-as-you-go pension system, it seems strange that most countries maintain compulsory retirement. A number of arguments are used to justify this practice. Setting aside problems of productivity or adaptation to technology which should be resolved by employees and employers without State intervention, we shall concentrate on two aspects that directly affect the unwritten pact amongst the generations that we have just been studying.

Firstly, justification for compulsory retirement is usually based on social justice. It is argued that people who have worked for a certain number of years have already made their contribution to society and are now entitled to be maintained by it. The argument continues that the earlier the revenue obtained from paid work can be replaced by a pension, the better the situation for people reaching a certain age. From the point of view of the pact amongst the generations, retirement is therefore presented as a benefit which the young generations offer to the older generations. If there is to be any objection within society, this should come from the people that are currently working who, after all, are the ones that have to pay. But what surprises those who use the social justice argument is that the data show it is not the young but the retired workers themselves, who supposedly are the beneficiaries, that are most against compulsory retirement, so the argument loses its validity.[9] The second aspect concerning the pact amongst the generations refers to the extensive unemployment in many countries and especially to the difficulties young people face in finding work. In countries with a high rate of unemployment, jobs are seen as one of the scarce goods that the different generations need to share out.

Economists argue that the problem is being approached from the wrong angle, that it is wrong to consider the volume of employment as fixed, that there is no set number of jobs to be shared out amongst the population of a country, or that data show that in the most advanced countries growth in the working population has led not to more unemployment but rather to greater wealth and greater employment. But even if the idea is wrong, if it is socially accepted, mechanisms of collective choice will be set in movement which may affect government decisions concerning retirement. And it may even turn out that long-standing pressure by groups of young workers will be strong enough to prevail over the interests of their elders. However this argument explains the reason for any decisions taken but not the actual decision. If we abandon the belief, for example, that there is a limited number of jobs to go round, the younger generation would benefit not from bringing forward the age of retirement but from putting it off because this measure would reduce the tax burden on employed workers.

In western political systems, political competition amongst the generations to get the State to act in their favour and against the interests of the others takes the form of pressure on the parties to orientate their programmes in the desired direction. Politicians, being in turn maximizers of a utility function in which the main argument is the conservation or obtention of power, will take their decisions on intergenerational distribution according to the costs and benefits expected in terms of votes and electoral support for each of the economic policy measures they adopt. The problem is therefore very complex and the result difficult to predict. On the one hand, it will depend on the capacity of the various groups to organize themselves and exert pressure. A protest by unemployed young people, for example, may have a much greater electoral cost than complaints by a large number of pensioners. But, on the other hand, the structure of the population pyramid is also relevant. In a society with a large proportion of elderly people, it will be very difficult for any politician who hopes to win elections to ignore their influence. And given the trends in the population pyramid in most western countries, which show sustained growth in the proportion of those above 65 with respect to total population, it is reasonable to assume that the weight of the elderly will continue to increase.

NOTES

1. The different roles played by sons and daughters in the care of the elderly is of special interest here. In most traditional cultures it was the responsibility of the son, especially if he had inherited the family property, to care for his parents, because the daughters, as long as they had not remained unmarried, had joined another family and were expected to care for their husband's parents. See an interesting economic analysis of the traditional Chinese family in which this custom prevailed, in Frey B.S. (1992), pp. 87–101. However, in some traditional cultures this task fell entirely on the women. Herodotus, for example, stated that amongst the ancient Egyptians, if the sons did not want to maintain their parents they were under no obligation to do so, whereas the daughters were. Minois, G. (1987), Ch. 1.
2. On the problem of the elderly and ethnography, see Beauvoir, S. de (1970), Ch. 2.
3. It has been calculated that in Spain, for example, approximately 35 per cent of hospital beds are occupied by patients aged over 65 who, moreover, tend to stay in hospital much longer. And the population aged over 65, which in Spain represents about 15 per cent of the whole population, consumes 65 per cent of the country's medication. Cabrillo, F. and Cachafeiro, M.L. (1990), p. 75.
4. The pioneering work in this field which has become the basis of today's debate on the theorem of equivalence is Barro, R.J. (1974).
5. Although of limited value, we have some data showing that in 1993 the percentage of retired men who had saved for their old age was practically the same for unmarried and married men. However, there is a substantial difference in saving amongst married and unmarried women, with the latter probably relying for their old age on the savings made by their husbands. De Miguel, A. (1995), p. 774.

6. Note that altruism is most relevant in this case because, since the welfare of the children is included in the utility function of the retired person, the problem of maximization changes in that the aim is also the utility of people who are going to live longer than the person taking the decisions on expenditure. The next chapter of this book analyses this matter in greater detail.

7. A more thorough argument in favour of freedom of choice in savings for retirement is given in Morgan, E.V. (1984).

8. In 1968 Marjorie Bremner carried out a study for the London Institute of Economic Affairs into the attitudes of the British people towards State control of certain situations that directly affected their lives. One of the matters analysed was public opinion on whether or not the State should establish the age for retirement or whether it should be left to the individual. The result was a surprise to some people, with 59 per cent of those surveyed coming out in favour of the latter method and only 36 per cent preferring regulation by the State. Bremner, M. (1968).

9. In the above-mentioned study by M. Bremner, the answers to the question mentioned in the above note are broken down according to age group. The results are interesting. Whereas only 46 per cent of young people between 16 and 24 years of age supported free choice of the age of retirement, with 50 per cent preferring it to be established by the State, the preferences amongst workers aged between 45 and 64 were 65 and 32 per cent respectively for each of these options. That is, the nearer they were to the age of compulsory retirement, the less they were in favour of it. Bremner, M. (1968), p. 32.

7. Inheritance

1 WHY INHERITANCE?

Family links have economic implications even after the death of a member of the family because estates are normally transferred from one generation to another when a person dies. Inheritance is therefore of great economic importance not just because it allows for the transfer of the estate but also because it may determine the behaviour of the testator and heirs before the death of the former.

Why do people accumulate a greater amount of assets than they can use while alive and leave them as inheritance to other people, usually their closest relations? There is a wide range of answers to this question.[1] Some people find such accumulation satisfying in itself; others because it protects them against future risks. Let us take the case of a person who finds no satisfaction in setting aside capital nor has any interest whatsoever in transferring his fortune to others. Under ideal conditions in which this person knows with absolute certainty what his flow of income and date of death will be as well as the exact amount of any extra costs arising – illness, hospitalization and so on – he will gain maximum satisfaction from distributing his expenditure during his lifetime in the most convenient way and will leave zero assets, or less, at the time of his death. But, if he lives under conditions of uncertainty with no information on many of these aspects, he will prefer to have set aside some capital to which he can resort to if necessary and probably, at the time of his death, his net assets will be positive.

There is a third reason for setting aside capital: the desire to transfer it to one's descendants after death. Alfred Marshall, for example, considered that the greatest motivation for a person to work and save was precisely this desire to leave assets to his children and that, if this possibility did not exist, people would buy a lifelong income with their capital and would work and save less.[2] According to the ideas expressed in Chapter 1 of this book, this argument means that the members of one generation act in an altruistic way with respect to the members of the following generation because in their own utility functions they are using the utility function of their descendants as their argument. In this case, the process of maximizing the utility function will not be limited by the life of the testator but the latter will obtain maximum satisfaction from using his assets both for his own consumption and for leaving an inheritance for his descendants.

The transmission of property at death may also follow other motivations. It is possible that a non-altruistic person for whom the heirs' utility functions mean nothing at all will still transfer his estate to his heirs for his own personal interest. His reason may be to pay for the services rendered to him by them during the last years of his life. The testator may consider it useful to not reduce his capital or lose control of it during his life but to leave it at death to those who cared for him. It may also be acceptable for the heirs to receive no payment at all for the care given – or to accept a lower payment than would be demanded if they were not heirs – and to receive the testator's estate on his death.

The agreement may therefore be beneficial for both parties, even where there is no altruism. However, an important problem arises in this type of agreement: that of control by the heir of the testator's provisions. Inheritance law establishes as a general rule that a person may rectify his will as often as he likes. And the fact that it is practically impossible for the alleged heir to know for sure whether or not he will receive the testator's estate at his death makes it difficult to establish the sort of agreements just described. What generally happens in the relations of an elderly person with his descendants is that there is a certain degree of altruism on both sides and this facilitates and gives strength to the tacit agreement. The old person wishes to be cared for by his descendants, but at the same time feels some degree of satisfaction at leaving them his estate. The latter in turn consider it their duty to care for the old person and that receiving his goods at his death will constitute sufficient payment for their efforts. In many countries the law restricts testamentary freedom in order to reduce the cost of control by the descendants, although this creates serious problems of efficiency as shown in the next section.

2   THE REGULATION OF INHERITANCE

When studying the relations between the members of a family in terms of costs and benefits, it must be remembered that the regulations that govern contracts and services of all types between them are not always the same as those that govern such arrangements where there are no family links. The market does not offer, for example, perfect services to replace the family care that an old person needs, not only because of the special links existing within the family but also because of the restrictions established by law. It must also be pointed out that the investments made over the years by parents in their children are not completely free; and that many legal systems maintain the legitimate share for the children who, by law, receive part of their parents' estate on their death, which limits the possibility of negotiating future bequests.

But the law does not only limit the rights of the testator when determining who should be the heirs; it also sets considerable fiscal incentives for individuals to leave all or most of their property to their closest relations and penalizes them if this is not done by taking away a significant proportion of the estate in the form of higher rates of taxation.

Such special civil legislation and tax rules for family inheritance are undoubtedly based on the consideration of the family as something more than just a group of related persons, who establish agreements involving the provision of services in line with the general principle of freedom of contract. It can even be stated that some of the characteristic institutions of family law in some countries – such as the legitimate share mentioned above – are based on the existence of a certain type of community of assets within the family which does not only affect the two or three generations that usually live together but reaches into the past and towards the future to include previous and subsequent generations. According to this traditional vision of the family, the person who at a specific time owns property – most of which has probably been received in the form of inheritance – does not own it in the full sense of the term but rather just holds and administers the family property and must eventually pass it on to the following generation. The case of entailed estates governed by the right of primogeniture in which the majority of the family property – especially real estate – is inherited by the eldest child to prevent it from being split up is probably the most significant example. But it is not the only case. In addition to physical assets, the family also owns a name which is transmitted from one generation to another and which in a traditional society is of great economic value because it reduces the cost of information with respect to whoever holds it and to some extent plays a similar role to that of a brand of a consumer good or the goodwill of a company. So in a traditional society, if one member of a family leads a disreputable life this will affect the whole family because he is lowering the value of a property – the surname – which is owned by all the family members.

The great social changes that have taken place in western society in recent decades have resulted in the disappearance of many of the characteristic institutions of the traditional family. But legislation in some countries still governs inheritance as if the family community were more important than it really is. Let us return to the case of the legitimate share mentioned above.

In many former societies the property of a dead person passed automatically to the descendants. In primitive Germanic law, for example, freedom to make a will was very restricted because it was considered that children had an inalienable right to their parent's estate. Economic life at the time offers a good explanation for this custom. In a society in which land constituted the main source of wealth and in which farming was carried out on a family basis, the death of the patriarch really only amounted to a change in the head of the family. In addition, in feudal society, lands were transferred to a person and his family group rather than to a separate individual. In such a situation in which the individual right to property as we understand it today was not yet fully developed, there was not much reason for the free disposal of an estate.

In some European agricultural societies such as the farms in ancient Sweden, transmission of the family estate normally took place before the death of the parents and irrespective of the right to inherit. The procedure was as follows. At a certain age, the owners of a farm transmitted it to their grown-up children and retired to a nearby home. In exchange, the children entered a commitment, often in written form, to provide them with clothing, food and money. There was therefore no inheritance in the strict sense of the term, and transmission of the estate entailed the obligation to care for the elderly parents.[3]

Over time, concern for keeping the family property together gave rise to institutions such as primogeniture and ultimogeniture which governed the passing of the real estate property – the family farm – to the oldest or youngest of the children, with the other children receiving a payment in cash or in goods not including the main farm.

The institution of primogeniture had great economic importance because it not only determined the structure of production but also population trends in that it forced those who owned no land to remain celibate. The heir, on the other hand, was tied to the farm. 'The first-born belongs to the land. The latter inherits him', stated K. Marx on the subject of hereditary succession in traditional families.

A subject that has not been much studied by economists is why in most cases it was the eldest son who inherited while in some areas it was the youngest. The most plausible reason is that primogeniture aimed to involve the heir in agricultural production for a long period of time, before the disappearance of the father and entrepreneur. Ultimogeniture aimed to delay the transmission of the management functions as long as possible while guaranteeing that the farm would be taken over by a young person on the father's retirement.[4]

In the late Middle Ages another institution which restricted the free disposal of an estate by the testator became established in some European countries – entailment. This, in addition to passing the inheritance to only one of the children – usually the eldest – compelled this child to eventually do the same with his own estate. This situation initially arose in some cases as a royal privilege, aiming to reinforce the social position of the nobility, but later it was established for all the land-owning classes.[5] In other countries this institution developed later. The English strict settlement, for example, only appeared in the seventeenth century. But in all cases it served as a legal instrument to strengthen the position of the heir with regard to his siblings. It has also been argued that in England it implied an attack on women's rights as women benefited more from the succession system of medieval common law than from an institution which in practice basically transmitted property along the male line.[6]

Anyway this institution had a high social cost not just because of the implicit loss of wellbeing because a person was not able to freely dispose of his property, but also because it created serious difficulties for the existence of an efficient market for farming properties which would have led to better land utilization. This fact undoubtedly contributed significantly to the disappearance of the right of primogeniture in the first third of the nineteenth century.

It was in this century that many European countries introduced the institution of the legitimate share which is still a basic feature of many inheritance systems. Although its origin goes far back in time, the legitimate share of the estate in the modern sense of the term, namely the obligation to set aside part of the estate for the heir by necessity of the deceased person with the testator being entitled to freely dispose of another part of it – a larger or smaller part depending on the individual situation – was actually institutionalized in the legal reforms of the nineteenth century. But it was not generally well received. As soon as the succession laws were changed to abolish the right of primogeniture, the new system based on the existence of heirs by necessity who were to receive most of the parents' estate, received great criticism in some countries. There were complaints that the new system tended to break up the family estate and, above all, that by limiting people's capacity to dispose of their property and destroying the possibility of maintaining farms as a single unit, the role of parents became less important. Thus, for example, in 1869 the economic and social reformer F. Le Play insisted that the legitimate share system resulted in the destruction of the parents' authority in peasant societies.[7] The obligation to equally distribute a substantial proportion of the inheritance effectively put paid to a system that had lasted for centuries through which inheritance by necessity involved much more than just sharing out property and was actually the basis for the transmission of the family property as a single unit.

The legitimate share can be understood as an attempt to equalize the position of the children who had previously been treated in a discriminatory fashion by favouring the first-born. But the idea behind them is still the existence of a family community within which the property must necessarily be transmitted. However, traditional families also imposed duties and patterns of behaviour. One of these and perhaps the most important was the acceptance by the family members of a hierarchical structure headed by the old patriarch who administered the property.

Today this hierarchical structure has disappeared because it is incompatible with a modern economy and modern society. And in most cases the different generations do not even live under the same roof. The elderly have lost their authority within the family but, surprisingly, they have not lost their obligation to leave most of the property to their children over whom they no longer have any authority.

One of the results of this type of regulation for succession is the substantial reduction of the possibilities of an old person to agree with other persons or institutions on the care he may need in old age in exchange for a future inheritance. Or, to put it in more general terms, this type of regulation seriously limits a person's property rights because it restricts his ability to freely agree on its transmission to a person who can offer him the specific service he requires. It can be argued that it is possible for a person to freely dispose of his property during his lifetime and that this can be done by an old person aiming to organize the last years of his life without relying on his children. But this is only partially true because, while it is true that a person's expenditure is not limited by law, his rights to freely make gifts is limited because an important legal principle establishes that nobody may give or receive in the form of a donation more than he may give or receive through bequest. And this objection does not affect the essence of our argument, namely, the fact that there is a limitation on the transmission of property through inheritance, based on the idea of a family community – in which each member has certain rights and obligations – which is in fact non-existent.

This idea has had such strength over the centuries that any actions by parents aiming to reduce their children's inheritance has been socially condemned on numerous occasions and the courts have often come out in favour of the interests of the children and against the will of the deceased person. This is a very long-standing tradition. For example, in ancient Rome the so-called tribunal of the *centumviri* existed to resolve the legal problems arising on matters of inheritance; and this tribunal usually deemed that any testators who did not leave a significant proportion of their property to their closest relations was clearly not mentally fit and, at the request of the relations, the will was cancelled in view of the alleged insanity of the deceased testator.[8] Another interesting case can be found in English legal tradition. Even though the lawful share of the inheritance does not exist as an institution in English law, custom and social pressure meant that the interests of the closest relations for a long time prevailed over the will of the deceased. In 1852 John Stuart Mill wrote that anyone with close relations should leave as little property as possible to people outside the family circle because otherwise they would run the risk of being declared insane by a jury after their death and of having part of their property sold to pay the high costs of the process of cancelling the will.[9]

These ideas are still at the basis of inheritance law in continental Europe. There is no doubt that, even if there were complete testamentary freedom, most people would still leave their estate to their children and descendants. This is logical for the reasons of altruism and close contact mentioned above. But it is one thing to freely appoint one's children as heirs and another to be legally compelled to do so. Really what these laws do is to reduce, with little justification, the property rights of people who may wish to fully exert these rights during their old age while at the same time placing excessive importance on the rights of children with respect to their real filial obligations. It would be absurd to try to maintain the principles on which the traditional family was based in a society which is very different to that in which such families existed. Nor is there much sense in conserving a system of heirs by necessity that was conceived for a type of family that disappeared many years ago.

3   INHERITANCE, RENT-SEEKING AND ALTRUISM

From the point of view of efficiency there are also arguments in favour of regulations restricting the free will of the testator. The most important of these is the consideration that the prior, definite determination as to who is going to inherit reduces expenditure for any possible heirs on improving their position in the distribution of the estate. In economic theory terms, there would be a reduction in 'rent-seeking' activities.[10]

The term 'rent-seeking' indicates socially unproductive activities carried out by economic agents with a view to obtaining special advantages such as a monopoly position for the sale of a product, or a customs tariff making competition by foreign companies more difficult and so on. Although the theory of rent-seeking has centred on those cases in which a specific legal requirement or a political decision may lead to privileges for certain persons or companies, it can be extended to all cases in which the income to be transferred is such that it becomes efficient for those who would benefit to devote resources to obtaining the income in question. If the expected earnings from the transfer – or inheritance in this case – amount to, say, 10 000 dollars, a possible heir will be prepared to invest resources to the point at which, at the most, the cost will equal the expected earnings.[11]

If there are no regulations determining exactly who is to receive the inheritance, each of the possible heirs will think their likelihood of obtaining it will increase in direct proportion to the amount spent on rent seeking. But, since this activity will not increase the total amount of the inheritance, its net value for the heirs (the total amount minus the cost of obtaining it) will decrease in proportion to the amount of resources spent on it.

However, the problem becomes more complex if a detailed analysis is made of the specific actions that may be taken to obtain better results in the distribution of the inheritance and if a distinction is made between the possible attitudes – either altruistic or non-altruistic – of those taking them. Conduct tending to improve the possible position of an heir in the distribution may certainly lead to social wastage and may fit perfectly into the usual concept of rent-seeking (the expense of predisposing the testator against another heir, for example). But in most cases the activities will aim to convince the testator of the person's worth by providing greater care and so on. This expenditure will reduce the net value to be received by all the heirs together, but will not necessarily lead to a loss of social welfare. This is because the testator's wellbeing will increase during the period before his death but with the special characteristic that, in the case of altruistic heirs, these activities will also increase the wellbeing of those carrying them out.

In order to analyse the effects on wellbeing of these types of conduct, let us suppose that a testator has two possible heirs, Ch_1 and Ch_2, whose share in the estate to be bequeathed has not yet been determined and may be altered at any time by the testator. If neither of the possible heirs is altruistic, then here we have the typical game situation in which the non-cooperative attitude (in this case, rent-seeking) will prevail as long as there is no agreement between the parties. This is the situation shown in Figure 7.1 in which, if Ch_1 and Ch_2 do not negotiate successfully, they will both choose the rent-seeking strategy (R), and the net value obtained by each of them will be that shown in the upper

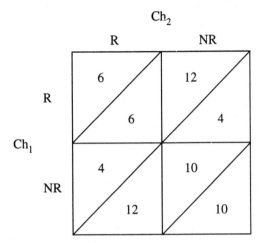

Figure 7.1   Non-altruistic heirs and rent-seeking

left box (6). If, however, they were to negotiate and reach an agreement, they would both choose the non-rent-seeking strategy (NR) and would obtain values of 10.

The situation is different, however, if we assume that the two potential heirs are altruistic with regard to the testator (but not with regard to the other heir). In this case the activities of caring for the testator do not benefit the latter alone, because in themselves they increase the wellbeing of the heirs for whom the wellbeing of the testator is one of the arguments of their own utility functions. This is the situation shown in Figure 7.2. Both the altruistic attitude of each of the heirs and the attempt to improve their relative positions in the distribution of the estate make them both choose strategy C (caring for

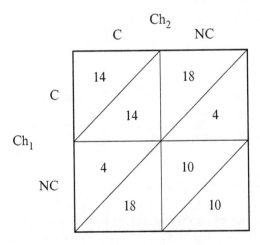

Figure 7.2   The strategies of altruistic heirs

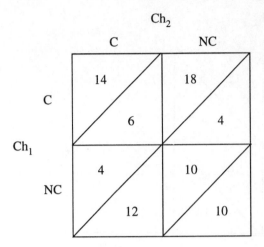

Figure 7.3   The strategies when only one of the heirs is altruistic

the testator) and equilibrium is reached in the upper left box, with values of 14 for each of them.

It is not difficult to see from our example that the same box will be reached if only one of the potential heirs is altruistic. Figure 7.3 shows the case in which Ch_1 is altruistic towards the testator but Ch_2 is not. The values for Ch_1 are therefore the same as those in Figure 7.2, but those that Ch_2 is able to obtain from strategy C are lower (the same as those in Figure 7.1), because for this heir the only utility obtained from caring for the testator is the increased percentage of the estate received. In this case the altruistic heir will follow the same strategy C as in the previous case. But the non-altruistic heir will do likewise because he would expect lower benefits from strategy NC (not caring for the testator). Note that, even if equilibrium is reached with the same strategies as in the case of the altruistic heirs, the benefit obtained by Ch_1 is higher than that obtained by Ch_2.

In short, the strategy for improving the individual's position in the distribution of the inheritance may be socially desirable if the heirs are altruistic with regard to the testator even if they are not altruistic with regard to the other heirs. But even if rent-seeking were socially unproductive, it could not be concluded that a rigid inheritance law is preferable to a law allowing greater freedom for the testator. In order to determine the efficiency of testamentary freedom it would be necessary to compare the costs of the socially unproductive rent-seeking activities with those caused by legal restrictions on the testator which may be much more relevant than the former.

4   CONDITIONED INHERITANCE

A very different matter is that of the limitations the testator himself establishes with respect to the use of the goods received. Let us suppose that the testator leaves a flat to his children with the proviso that they are not to sell it or use it for a specific activity, or he leaves his wife the ownership of certain goods with the proviso that she does not remarry.

The economic problem that arises with this type of provision is basically one of conflicting interests. If such conditions are valid, the testator's level of wellbeing increases because he obviously set them because they represented a benefit for himself; but they reduce the wellbeing of the heir because they constitute a limitation on his right of ownership of the goods received. The final effect of such provisions on social welfare is therefore indeterminate and each case would have to be studied separately to analyse their efficiency.

Inheritance law usually accepts conditions in testamentary provisions but establishes important limitations: basically it considers null and void any conditions that are impossible or illegal. These restrictions to the conditions that may be established by a testator give rise to serious problems, the most obvious being how to keep abreast of any changes in both customs and law. Let us take the example of a person who on his death left his property to a foundation giving grants to male law graduates allowing them to study for the profession of notary and stipulated that, if this condition was not met, the property would pass to his descendants. When the condition was set, women were not permitted to become notaries so it complied with both law and customs at the time. But let us suppose that the foundation begins to give grants to women and the testator's descendants claim the return of the capital because of non-compliance with the conditions. It would be unlikely for a court in Continental Europe to find in favour of the claimants and it would be doubtful that the testator's wellbeing would have decreased because he could have expected that some day there would be women notaries. But in other countries there are cases in which the courts have applied conditions of this type so the subject is clearly more complex than it seems at first sight.[12]

An economic analysis of the problem of conditions in wills requires the consideration of any possible benefits and costs for both testators and potential heirs. The following section gives an analysis of this from the point of view of welfare economics.

5   CONDITIONED INHERITANCE AND SOCIAL WELFARE

If we accept the premise that a person obtains maximum satisfaction from his property when he can use it and dispose of it at will, then clearly for a testator the best possible inheritance law is that which allows him to establish whatever conditions he wants and whatever period he considers most appropriate for these to be fulfilled. However, for the heir these conditions entail limitations on his rights of ownership of the property received, and these may lead to a reduction in his level of wellbeing with respect to the level that could be reached if the property could be used with no limitation. In addition, here we have the special characteristic that this reduction in welfare takes place for the benefit of a deceased person.

So the interests of the testator and the heir are in conflict over the degree of limitation – both qualitative and over time – involved in entailments on inheritance. This in turn leads to the problem of the social efficiency of entailed inheritance. On the one hand, limitation of the right to establish conditions for inheritance may create negative incentives towards inheritance in the conduct of people wishing to leave entailed property to their successors and, on the other, the conditions may restrict the optimal allocation of resources by a specific society. If one of the main aims of inheritance law is to promote efficiency, a solution should be found leading to the best possible allocation of resources from the social point of view.

The problem can therefore be shown as

$$\text{Max } (SB - SC)$$

where *SB* and *SC* represent the social benefit and social cost generated by entailed inheritance. If the degree of restriction – qualitative or over time – of the entailed inheritance is named *g*,

$$SB = SB\,(g)$$

$$SC = SC\,(g)$$

$$\text{with } \frac{dSB}{dg} < 0 \ \text{ and } \ \frac{dSC}{dg} > 0$$

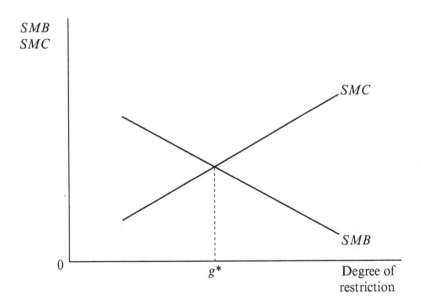

Figure 7.4   Costs and benefits of entailed inheritance

Therefore, stricter or longer-lasting entailments on inheritance involve increasing marginal costs and decreasing marginal benefits.

Maximization requires that

$$\frac{dSB}{dg} - \frac{dSC}{dg} = MSB - MSC = 0$$

that is, equality between the social marginal benefit and the social marginal cost: *SMB = SMC*.

Figure 7.4 shows how this point of equilibrium is determined. The curve for *SMB* decreases whereas the curve for *SMC* increases with respect to g, as shown above. And the optimum degree of regulation will be determined by point g^*.

While in theory it is easy to determine this point, in practice to determine the optimum degree of conditionality is extremely complex. It cannot even be stated that the social costs and benefits of restrictions are the same for all possible entailments, so it is very difficult, from the point of view of an economic analysis, to make general recommendations on the extent to which the law should allow or limit such entailments.

6   THE STATE AND CONVEYANCE OF THE FAMILY ESTATE: INHERITANCE TAX

The role of the State in the transfer of property within a family does not only involve setting limits to free disposal by the testator or regulating the conditions set by the testator on the usage to be made by the heirs of the property inherited. It also plays a very important role as tax collector by appropriating part of the property transferred, the amount not being a fixed proportion of the sum donated or bequeathed but varying depending on the sums involved and the personal circumstances of each of the beneficiaries.

One of the arguments frequently used in favour of this type of tax is the limitation that society can establish on the right of people to freely dispose of their property at the time of their death.[13] Although the State would be using a different method for regulating inheritance the objective would be similar. The State claims part of the inheritance but at the same time creates incentives for the closest relations to be the heirs because the tax rates increase inversely to the relationship between the deceased and the heir.

The most important argument to justify these taxes, however, is based on the fact that they constitute an important tool for redistributing income because they help to create equality. To take the old argument used by J.S. Mill, people are entitled to transfer their property when they die because, if this were not possible, the right to ownership would not exist in the full sense of the word, but this does not mean that society cannot limit the amount received by each heir[14] in order to eliminate the large fortunes that are useless for society and, in Mill's opinion, can only be spent on ostentation and on buying up power.

Reduction of inequality of wealth is usually presented as an important objective because the data show that wealth is distributed in all countries in a less equal way than income.[15] And it is thought that this distribution might distort competition based on the talent and hard work of the individual. There is no agreement on the validity of this argument – it is accepted or rejected depending on whether greater equality in the distribution of wealth is accepted as a value in itself. But it is interesting to point out that this objective may be in contradiction with the incentives that the State itself sets for the transfer of inheritance to the closest relations. Restrictions on testamentary freedom, and the tax benefits granted to the close relations but not to more distant relations or other people, tend to mean that the property remains within the family and therefore is not actually distributed, so achieving the opposite effect to what is desired.[16]

A less important argument is the revenue that can be obtained from this tax for the public sector. In addition, the revenue is obtained at a relatively low social cost as the sacrifice that has to be made by the taxpayer is not so great as with other taxes because it is just a question of taking away some of the money or assets that the taxpayer is anyway receiving gratuitously.[17] Practice in all countries shows that, in spite of this advantage, the actual amounts collected are not particularly great so the main reason for the existence of inheritance tax is more likely to be found in the ideas expressed initially.

But however commendable its aims, inheritance tax involves such large costs that many economists recommend its abolition. The most relevant of these costs is that it constitutes a negative stimulus for saving and capital formation on the part of the testator.[18] As stated at the start of this chapter, if people do not plan their consumption during their lifetimes so that, while keeping enough for any possible unexpected risk, when they die their estate will be worth approximately zero. This is mostly because the older generation wants to pass its property on to younger people, mainly their children. Since we started with the hypothesis that parents are altruistic with regard to their children, this means that people who bequeath property obtain greater utility from the fact that their children receive their estate than from other possible alternatives (such as lavish expenditure).

However, it is difficult to believe that people would feel any satisfaction from the State's keeping part of their estate on their death. If this were the case, all testators would have to do would be to transfer part of their unentailed property to the State – a rare occurrence. As a result, the greater the share of the State in the inheritance – that is, the higher the inheritance tax rate – the fewer incentives there will be for saving and capital formation, and this will be prejudicial not just for the children but also for the national economy as a whole.

The altruism of the person donating or bequeathing property gives rise to another inefficiency factor in inheritance tax. This is the argument we could call double utility or wealth creation through inheritance.[19] The idea is simple. When a donation or bequest is made, there is an increase in utility for the person making it because otherwise, as seen above, it would not take place. But this increase in utility is obviously not limited to the donor or testator. The person who receives the property is doubtless the main beneficiary. If for the former the increase in utility is based, owing to his altruism, on the fact that he obtains greater satisfaction from the donation than from spending the property personally, for the latter it represents a gratuitous revenue involving no cost at all. As a result, from the point of view of welfare economics, there is a dual benefit which the tax reduces to a larger extent than it actually increases social welfare through the revenue collected. If the transfer of property from the heir to the public treasury had no other effect than this redistribution of income, it could be argued that the loss of welfare for the heir would be compensated for by the social benefit generated from the public expenditure made possible by this estate. But in this case, as stated above, the benefit for the donor is zero because he obtains no satisfaction whatsoever from donating to the State. And the final consequence of the tax is therefore a net loss for society.

7 INHERITANCE TAX AND LOSS OF WELFARE

Any transaction in an economy comprises the exchange of a specific good (J), for another good (Z), which in most cases is money. If the transaction is made freely, both parties will benefit, because the utility for the person passing the good J in exchange for Z will be greater than before the transaction, and the same can be said for the person passing over Z in exchange for J. The condition for the transaction to take place is therefore that, as a result of it

$$U_1' > U_1 \text{ and}$$

$$U_2' > U_2$$

where U and U' represent the utilities before and after the transaction and the subscripts 1 and 2 represent each of the parties. In order for this condition to be met it is necessary that, for each of the interchanged units of Z and J,

$$\frac{\partial U_1}{\partial Z} > \frac{\partial U_1}{\partial J} \quad \text{and} \quad \frac{\partial U_2}{\partial J} > \frac{\partial U_2}{\partial Z}$$

So here we have a simultaneous increase and decrease in utility as a result of the transaction and the final result should be a net benefit for each of the two parties.

A donation, however, gives rise to a different problem because here there is an element of altruism in one of the parties which did not exist in the previous transaction.

Let us assume that a parent (P) makes a donation for his child (Ch) of a specific amount of money (Z). The utility functions for P and Ch, before and after the donation, will be:

$$U_P = U_P(x_1, x_2 \ldots x_n, Z_P, U_{Ch})$$
$$U_P' = U_P'(x_1, x_2 \ldots x_n, Z_P', U_{Ch}')$$
$$U_{ch} = U_{Ch}(x_1, x_2 \ldots x_n, Z_{Ch})$$
$$U_{Ch}' = U_{Ch}'(x_1, x_2 \ldots x_n, Z_{Ch}')$$

where $Z_P > Z_P'$ and $Z_{Ch} < Z_{Ch}'$

In this case the following will also be true:

$$U_P' > U_P \text{ and}$$
$$U_{Ch}' > U_{Ch}$$

In the case of the child, the reason is clear because, *ceteris paribus*, utility will increase because he has a larger sum of money:

$$\frac{\partial U_{Ch}}{\partial Z} > 0$$

For the parent the increased utility will come from his altruism, because in his own utility function he gives greater value to the increased wellbeing of his child than to his own satisfaction from continuing to have this same amount of money.

As in the first case, there is a net increase in utility for both parties. But now what is being compared is not the utility provided by the exchanged goods because, in the case of the child, there has been no loss of utility from giving up a good as consideration and, in the case of the parent, what is being compared is his increased utility – because of the increased satisfaction for his child – and the loss of utility involved in giving up a certain amount of money.

If a tax is established to reduce the amount received by the donee (in this case, the child), this will be detrimental for both the donor and the donee – for the latter because he receives a smaller amount of money and for the former because, even if he relinquishes the same amount of Z, his wellbeing will decrease to the same extent as his child's utility increases his own utility.

NOTES

1. There is extensive literature on the social usefulness of the institution of inheritance, and an analysis of the subject usually accompanies most studies on inheritance tax. To mention just a few works on the subject, see Tullock, G. (1971). Two years later the same journal published a debate on Tullock's article. See Greene, K.V. (1973), Ireland, Th. (1973), Koller, R.H. (1973) and Tullock, G. (1973).
2. Marshall, A. (1925), p. 228.
3. Gaunt, L. and Gaunt, D. (1986). See especially p. 491.
4. On inheritance in Europe in the late Middle Ages and the Renaissance, see Bresc, H. (1986).
5. This was the case in Castile. See Sempere and Guarinos, J. (1847).
6. This theory is maintained by Spring, E. (1995).

7. It seems that Le Play, in addition to criticizing the way in which the lawful share of inheritance was regulated, tried to convince Napoleon III that he should reform the French Civil Code to allow the transmission of the family property to just one of the children. Gide, C. and Rist, C. (1927), pp. 719–25. In Spain the attempt to widely impose the Castilian regime for the legitimate share was seriously opposed in some regions when the draft Civil Code of 1851 was drawn up.
8. Espín, D. (1970), Vol. V, p. 406.
9. Mill, J.S. [1848] (1909), p. 229.
10. For the application of the theory of rent-seeking to inheritance law, see Buchanan, J. (1983).
11. Under certain conditions this investment could be even greater than the net income to be obtained. See Tullock, G. (1980).
12. A good example can be found in the North American case *Evans* v. *Abney* (396 U.S. 435, 1970). For an analysis of this case see Posner, R. (1992a), pp. 508–9.
13. For a conventional justification of inheritance tax, see Musgrave, R. and Musgrave, P. (1989), Ch. 25.
14. Mill, J.S. [1848] (1909), p. 228.
15. This greater inequality in the distribution of income as opposed to the distribution of wealth is undoubtedly true. But there are some serious errors in the calculations because they do not take into account one of the basic elements of the wealth of most people – the real value of the flow of returns expected from their rights to receive a retirement pension.
16. An exception are the tax exemptions on donations made to foundations and associations which the State considers of public interest and which usually aim to carry out activities leading to more equitable distribution of income.
17. However, there are exceptions to this smaller effort for the taxpayer because, if what is being transferred are properties such as a home or a small working family business, payment of the tax may make it necessary to sell the home or to borrow to keep the business in operation.
18. Note that it could be argued to the contrary that this tax, since it reduces the amount the heirs expect to receive, encourages them to save more and set aside greater capital. This idea is implicit in Mill's argument mentioned above in favour of reducing the amount a specific person may inherit.
19. This is the term used in the full coverage of this argument given by Bracewell-Milnes, B. (1989).

8.   Family protection and pro-natalist policies

1   FAMILY PROTECTION AND INCENTIVATION OF MOTHERHOOD: A HISTORICAL CONSTANT

Governments have practically always regulated family life and have used the fiscal system to set incentives for certain types of behaviour, especially with respect to growth in the birth rate. There have been many societies which, at various times, were concerned to increase their population. In some cases the aim was to defend certain special characteristics that were under threat from other cultures and, in others, it was to meet the need to populate large deserted areas in countries undergoing colonization. But the most usual motivation was undoubtedly the idea that there is a direct link between the power of a nation and the number of its inhabitants.

And from Roman times to the twentieth century a tradition can be detected in the history of political and economic thinking that directly links the variables of population and power. Some general characteristics can be mentioned. In all cases, there were certain group values that the authorities considered of more importance than individual values. It was also accepted that the instruments of power – laws, public office or taxation – could be used to attain the objectives set. And, of most interest to us, although it is women who give birth and care for children, most of the measures for increasing the birth rate were addressed not to women but to men. It was men who were punished by higher taxation or the withdrawal of their public offices if they had no children, or who were rewarded if they had a large family. Women, meanwhile, had no direct relationship with authority.

Almost all societies and cultures have insisted on the importance of children. But it is usually considered that the first systematic laws in the western world aiming to increase the birth rate – the so-called Julia and Papia-Poppaea laws – were passed in the Roman Empire by Augustus. These laws established discriminatory treatment for unmarried men and for married men without children, such as limited access to public office or limited capacity to receive inheritance, and they set time limits for widows or divorced women to remarry. Although these measures do not seem to have been particularly efficient, the argument behind them is significant: the need for more children to guarantee the survival of the State.[1]

There was to be no such determined pro-natalist policy again until the mercantilist period that was characterized by the constitution of new States between the sixteenth and eighteenth centuries. This ties up with the hypothesis of linking national policies for expansion with pro-natalist policies. The new States created permanent armies which involved huge costs and, more importantly for our purposes, the need for a large population. A wide variety of policies was drawn up in order to achieve this objective. And in the case of countries with large colonial territories the advisability of restricting emigration was often mentioned.

Much legislation of a fiscal nature was promulgated with a view to implementing a family policy that would be in line with the interests of the State. There are many examples. In seventeenth-century England there was a capitation tax on unmarried men and widowers. In France at the same time there were tax exemptions for people marrying before the age of 20 and annuities were offered to families with more than 10 children. Spain also had similar laws offering tax exemptions to those with large families. The pro-natalist policies that were addressed specifically to women basically involved relaxing or eliminating the regulations that imposed severe sanctions on unmarried mothers and trying to reduce the number of abortions and infanticides that were very common throughout pre-industrial Europe.[2]

Although in the nineteenth century, especially in some countries such as Great Britain where the influence of Malthus was significant, this concern for increasing the birth rate decreased and in some cases even took the opposite direction, the idea of the advisability of a high birth rate did not disappear from Europe. The most outstanding case was in France, especially in the decades following the Franco–Prussian war when the link between the birth rate and national power once again became an issue. After the defeat, many people in France feared their country would face tremendous difficulties in the face of an expansive Germany which had much higher birth rates.

Nor has this idea been unknown in the twentieth century. The authoritarian regimes that arose in Europe between the two world wars placed great importance on increasing their populations in order to fulfil their plans for expansion. In National Socialist Germany this went together with the philosophy that the supposedly superior races should dominate. And the political philosophy of Franco's Spain incorporated many of the principles of the Falangist movement that had been established during the 1930s, including those relating to the family and the birth rate. Growth in the population is still today an openly declared objective in certain countries in a situation of conflict. One such is the State of Israel which constantly analyses the comparative birth rates of the Arab and Jewish communities and encourages immigration by Jews from other countries.

From the economic point of view, implicit in all these policies is the belief that an increase in population amounts to a public asset which can justify income transfer from certain groups to others in consideration for the services that are offered to the community by those with large families. Chapter 9 covers in greater detail the possible justification for tax exemptions and grants to those producing children and human capital.

2   THE EFFICIENCY OF FAMILY POLICY: REGULATION VERSUS FISCAL POLICY

State intervention in the decision taken by a couple on the number of children they wish to have has basically taken place in two ways – legal regulation on the one hand and public expenditure and tax policies on the other.

Legal regulation is usually understood from an economic viewpoint as creating incentives or disincentives for certain types of conduct. Laws are a society's way of showing its preferences and how it expects its members to behave. In the specific case of family law, both legal rules and custom have marked the concern of many societies to raise their birth rates and to maintain certain types of relationship amongst the different members of the family group.

In addition, legal rules may enforce income transfers from certain social groups to others. For example, a labour law introducing compulsory early retirement could lead to relative impoverishment of a specific sector of the population. And regulations on the family economy or those establishing obligations between parents and their children may give rise to a redistribution of income that is not necessarily welcome for all the parties concerned.

The main objective of fiscal policy is not to mould individual behaviour but to finance, as efficiently as possible, certain expenses that it has been agreed should be made by the public sector. But this is not its only function. There may be at least two other objectives behind fiscal laws – to transfer income amongst certain social groups, and to create incentives leading to improved social allocation of resources.

So on these last two objectives there may be certain points in common between legal rules and fiscal policy, and a society may aim to achieve a single objective using one or the other. One of the basic subjects in the final chapters of this book may serve to explain this situation. If we think of the above-mentioned objective of increasing the birth rate, according to the results achieved in Chapter 5, we know that a basic variable in the determination of the birth rate in any society is the cost of having children, and the most important component of this is the opportunity cost of the time devoted to bringing them up and educating them. A pro-natalist policy would therefore have to set as one of its main objectives a reduction in this opportunity cost. Such a reduction can be achieved in two ways – by reducing the price obtained by women in their market activities, or by increasing payment for the activities of bringing up and educating children. The first method involves simply excluding women, by means of formal restrictions or custom, from all or most highly paid activities in the labour market. The second method is based on subsidizing or offering tax deductions to women – or to the family – according to the number of children in the household.

Both methods have been used with the former being the most common in most societies until recently. The latter has imposed itself at times when the sharp increase in public expenditure has come in parallel with a change in public opinion whereby the exclusion of women from a large number of labour activities is considered unacceptable in the modern world. When these matters are studied, it has practically always been considered that the analysis of public expenditure should clearly be left to economists while the study of the legal regulations governing family life has mostly been the concern of jurists, politicians and moralists. However, there are also obvious economic implications in the discrimination created by family law or labour law. The idea that legal regulations may have distorting effects on a couple's decision whether to have children or not fits perfectly into modern economic theory of the family. And texts can even be quoted to show that this was perceived by earlier economists. For example, Robert Malthus, being concerned about the excessive growth in the population, studied several formulas for reducing the birth rate which he explained in the second edition of his *Essay on the Principle of Population.* And one which he specially recommended was the reduction of the great incentives for women to marry if they wanted to improve their social position. In his opinion, this objective could be achieved by showing greater respect towards unmarried women and granting them greater personal freedom in order 'to place them nearer upon a level with married women'.[3]

Both formulas have therefore served over the years to achieve the same purpose – to allow the state to influence the birth rate. But their collateral effects are very different. If we look first at the strictly microeconomic effects, it can be stated that the main effect of both legislation, which discriminates against women in the labour market, and a fiscal policy offering financial aid to women with children, will be to reduce the opportunity cost of having children and therefore to create an incentive for bigger families. But there is one important difference in the results obtained depending on the method used. Whereas with the first method women will feel their wellbeing has decreased and the reduction in the opportunity cost of having children is due to a drop in their potential earnings on the market, in the case of subsidies, their wellbeing increases.

However the shift in the emphasis of pro-natalist policies from legal regulation to fiscal policy seems to be based not only on reasons of equity or justice but also on reasons of economic efficiency. For an economic system, the existence of discrimination, whether imposed by regulations or custom, is inefficient to the extent that it does not allow the market to show the comparative advantages of the agents involved in it and the division of labour is not based on these advantages. There is therefore a loss of income for the community in which such discrimination is practised.[4]

In the case of racial discrimination, the activities carried out by those who discriminate and those who are discriminated against are, in principle, interchangeable because there is no reason why anybody with sufficient intelligence and training cannot occupy a specific post. With sexual discrimination, however, there is a basic element involved which makes a difference. There is no symmetry whereby all activities can be carried out indistinctly by one or another group, because men do not give birth to children. There are certain biological conditions that prevent men from being paid for giving birth to children, if such payment were ever to exist. However this obviously does not mean that it would be efficient for all women to devote themselves to producing children. There are a number of differences within the group of women with respect to their opportunity cost of maternity, not to mention their preferences because children are also a consumer good, which make the optimum volume of resources allocated to bringing up children different in each case, ranging from a large number of children to zero.

Restrictive legal regulation tends to produce a uniformly inefficient result. When access by women to well-paid jobs is prevented, the opportunity cost of the time devoted to bringing up and educating children is reduced. But this reduction is not the same in all cases. For some women, whose human capital for the purpose of market activities would not have allowed them to opt for such jobs, the effect of the discrimination is relatively unimportant, but for others who could have aspired to such positions, the cost is much greater. So discriminatory legislation creates an equal incentive to produce children for people with very different comparative advantages, which is very inefficient.

Fiscal policy, on the other hand, makes it possible to create incentives so that, within the group of women, the principle of labour division based on the comparative advantage of the economic agents is still valid. And it means that women can specialize in market activities or domestic work depending on the shadow price of the time spent at home. This notion will be explained in a subsequent chapter in connection with the problem of monetary aid as opposed to free services as optimum tools for family aid policy.

3 EFFECTS ON WELLBEING OF TWO WAYS OF RAISING THE BIRTH RATE

As shown in the previous section, policies based either on legal restrictions or on subsidies may serve to achieve the same goal of raising the birth rate. But their side effects as regards women's wellbeing are very different. A basic of utility maximization analysis can explain this more accurately.

Let us define a utility function for women as we have done in previous chapters using, for the sake of simplification, only two arguments – children and the goods (X) that can be bought with the income obtained on the labour market:

$$U = U(Ch, X)$$

This function is subject to the usual budget constraint:

$$Y = X P_x + Ch\pi_{Ch}$$

Figure 8.1 represents the effects on women's wellbeing of the traditional policy of legally restricting access by women to the labour market, whereas Figure 8.2 represents the effects on wellbeing of a policy granting subsidies for children. The starting-point in both graphs is the indifference curve I_1, together with the price lines ChX_1 in Figure 8.1 and Ch_1X in Figure 8.2.

With free market access, equilibrium is reached at point A, which represents the maximum wellbeing that a woman can reach. The price lines ChX_2 and ChX_3 show the relative price changes that would result from increasing the exclusion of women from

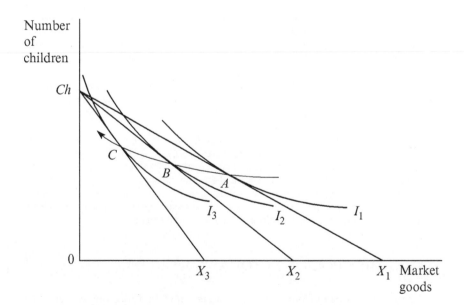

Figure 8.1   Effects of restricting access to the labour market for women

Number of
children

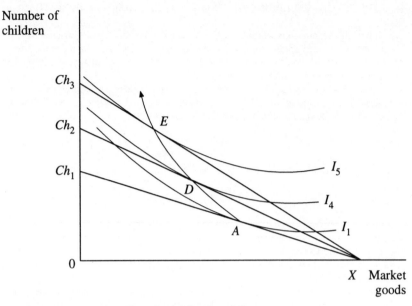

Figure 8.2   Effects of a policy of subsidies for mothers

the labour market by legal restrictions. These relative price changes would reduce the opportunity cost of having children and would lead to a substitution effect which would move the equilibrium successively to *B* and *C*, and these points show a progressive decrease in involvement in the market and greater specialization in child rearing. The rise in the opportunity cost of obtaining income in the labour market would also result in a reduction in wellbeing represented by the equilibrium in the indifference curves I_2 and I_3, which lie to the left of the initial indifference curve.

Figure 8.2 shows, from the same point of equilibrium *A*, the successive points of equilibrium that would be reached by introducing a subsidy or tax exemption that increases with the number of children. Here too the new points of equilibrium, *D* and *E*, show greater specialization in child rearing and a decreasing involvement in market activities. In this case subsidies reduce the opportunity cost of having children and this change is reflected in the slope of the new price lines Ch_2X and Ch_3X. The substitution effect will then lead women to increase the number of children they have, and new points of equilibrium *D* and *E* will be reached. But there is an important difference in the results obtained in each case. In the first case, wellbeing decreases the more children a woman has and, in the second, wellbeing increases, as can be seen in the position of the new points of equilibrium in the I_4 and I_5 indifference curves to the right of I_1.

4   FAMILY POLICY IN TODAY'S WORLD

When the European Population Conference met in 1982, the conclusions established by the participants were that in order to mitigate, at least partially, the drop in the standard of living of parents caused by their obligations towards their children, it would be necessary to take a number of measures, of which the following were the most important:

1. Families should be offered tax benefits and subsidies to improve their economic situation and make up for the loss of income caused by the birth of the child and throughout the period during which the child is largely dependent on them.
2. One of the parents, either the mother or the father, should be allowed the possibility of taking a period of time off work without their career being affected.
3. Children should be offered any welfare services they need, including an environment that is considered safe from both the physical and social points of view.
4. Families with children should be helped to find housing that is suitable for their needs.[5]

Since then, while abiding by these principles, the family policy of the European Union (EU) has been extended to cover other objectives, the most important for our purposes being that of helping to remove obstacles to the practice of a professional activity on the part of parents by means of measures facilitating the combination of domestic and professional responsibilities.[6]

The application of such a family policy is costly. When studying the subject of pro-natalist policies and family subsidies it must be borne in mind that they can only be valid for countries that have reached a certain level of income, not only because it is in such countries that the birth rate tends to be lower but also because they are the only countries that have the sort of wealth and tax systems that make them affordable. Not even the most basic support for mothers in the form of medical care during pregnancy and labour is available worldwide. A report drawn up in 1985 by the World Health Organization indicated that, whereas in western Europe and the United States 100 per cent of mothers receive specialist care during pregnancy and labour, the percentages dropped to 64 per cent in Central and South America, 49 per cent in Asia and 34 per cent in Africa, even dropping below 30 per cent in many parts of Africa.[7]

NOTES

1. 'My only object is the perpetuity of the State . . .', stated Augustus, and for this purpose a man should 'take a wife and provide for children'. On the birth policy of Ancient Rome, see Stangeland, C.E. (1966), pp. 29–39.
2. Stangeland (1966), pp. 118–37.
3. Malthus, T.R. (1803) (1967), Vol. II, p. 210.

4. This does not mean that discriminatory behaviour on the part of specific people or companies is necessarily irrational. On the economic theory of discrimination, see Becker, G.S. (1971).
5. Council of Europe (1982).
6. Comisión de las Comunidades Europeas (1993), p. 111.
7. World Health Organization (1985), pp. 4–5.

APPENDIX

Public expenditure on family welfare in the countries of the EU

This appendix gives a simplified and schematic approach to the main programmes in the EU for family assistance policy. A brief description of its two most relevant aspects – maternity benefit, and financial assistance and tax benefits for families in 1995 (European Communities 1995)[1] is followed by an analysis of the importance of these policies in quantitative terms within the public expenditure of European countries.

All the member countries offer aid to mothers in the form of medical services and leave or paid time off. In order to obtain such aid, women usually have to be insured or to be the wives or relations of someone who is insured, although to be entitled to medical care it is often sufficient only to reside in the country in question, with no further requirements.

Most of the countries offer medical care throughout the pregnancy and during labour in state health institutions or in officially approved centres. In Germany and Italy it is possible to use private hospitals that can be freely chosen from amongst those that have official approval. In Greece and France there is also free choice and the beneficiary receives a sum of money to cover her hospital expenses.

On the matter of paid maternity leave, the differences are greater. Firstly, the maximum duration of such leave is extremely variable – from a maximum of 28 weeks in Denmark to a minimum of 90 days in Portugal. There is also a wide variation in the percentage of wages that is paid during leave. Some countries, such as The Netherlands or Germany, offer 100 per cent of the wage, although in some cases there is an upper limit and in others the amount actually received may even be above 100 per cent because it is taxed at a lower rate than the wage. In other countries the benefit is lower than the usual wage received by the mother by percentages which vary between 10 and 30 per cent. When compared with EU reports for previous years, the data show that in no case has the duration of paid maternity leave decreased, and in some countries there have even been slight increases. The possible effects of a policy extending such leave are discussed below.

Now let us comment on financial aid and tax benefits for families. Subsidies are paid to families with children in all the member States of the EU. In all cases except for one, the benefits are paid as from the first child. The exception is France, where aid is only received for the first child if aid is also received in compensation for a low family income.

Benefits are normally paid up to the ages of somewhere between 15 and 18 although the age can be raised to 27 if the child is still a student or remains at home. In addition, several member States of the Union establish no age limits for receiving aid in the case of children who are seriously ill.

Where there are marked differences is in the amounts paid for each child and this can be seen from the figures (given in ECU). Such a comparison can never be exact because the purchasing power of an ECU (European Currency Unit) is not the same in all the countries and because much of the expenditure on children goes towards goods that are not tradable internationally and for which the prices vary from country to country to a greater extent than the general price indices. But, even taking these factors into account, there are large differences. France is the European country offering the highest benefits with monthly payments of 102 ECU for the second child and 131 each for any further children. At the opposite extreme, the country offering the smallest benefits is Greece – only 4 ECU per month for the first child, 11 for the second and 17 for the third.

An initial quantitative criterion that is used by the EU to evaluate the size of family benefits is the percentage of the benefit with respect to the net average wage of the beneficiaries. Table A8.1 shows these data for families with one, two and three children.

Table A8.1   Family benefits as a percentage of the net wage of the beneficiaries (1991)

	One child	Two children	Three children
Belgium	7	20	38
Denmark	6	11	15
Germany	6	12	21
Greece	4	8	12
France	1	22	50
Ireland	2	4	6
Italy	3	6	11
Luxembourg	22	28	40
The Netherlands	4	10	16
Portugal	4	9	14
Spain	2	3	5
United Kingdom	5	9	13
EU average	6	12	20

Source: Eurostat

The big differences between the different countries are easy to see. Whereas in some cases (France or Luxembourg, for example), benefits for children may represent a significant proportion of the parents' income, in others (such as Spain or Ireland) subsidies are very low, even in the increasingly less frequent case of families with three children.

To complete this Appendix, it may be of interest to give some macroeconomic figures on public expenditure in the countries of the European Union under the headings of 'family' and 'maternity'. It must be emphasized that these figures are only an approximation to the measurement of public expenditure on family aid. There are many other items of public expenditure that are not included here, such as education, health care, housing grants and so on, that also involve income transfers. The beneficiaries are more likely to be families with children than unmarried people or childless couples, so can really be considered family aid or promotion of the birth rate according to the concept covered in the previous chapter. But, since it is impossible to make an accurate estimate of everything involved in subsidies for the family, we shall take the statistics for public expenditure on these two functions of family benefit as published by Eurostat.

These data from the EU statistics need to be clarified on at least two points. Firstly, when analysing time series it must be remembered that the ratio between social protection and gross domestic product (GDP) has not remained constant. In the case of some countries (such as Spain), this is most relevant because the ratio increased substantially during the decade so the reduction in the percentage of social expenditure on the family would be less marked if the figure to be calculated were expenditure on the family and maternity with respect to GDP. Table A8.3 shows these data for 1993.

Table A8.2   Expenditure on family and maternity benefits as a percentage of social welfare expenditure

	1980	1993
Belgium	11.3	7.5
Denmark	10.8	11.5
Germany (FR)	10.2	7.7
Greece	3.7	1.0
France	12.7	9.0
Ireland	11.0	12.1
Italy	7.5	3.5
Luxembourg	10.0	12.4
The Netherlands	9.6	5.1
Portugal	8.0	5.1
Spain	4.5	1.8
United Kingdom	13.1	10.9

Source: Eurostat.

Table A8.3   Percentage of public expenditure on social benefits and on the family/maternity function in terms of GDP for the countries of the EU in 1993

	Social expenditure/GDP	Family/maternity expenditure/GDP
Belgium	27.6	2.07
Denmark	33.2	3.82
Germany (FR)	27.6	2.12
Greece	16.3	1.63
France	30.9	2.78
Ireland	21.4	2.59
Italy	25.8	0.90
Luxembourg	24.9	3.01
The Netherlands	33.6	1.71
Portugal	18.3	0.93
Spain	24.0	0.43
United Kingdom	27.3	2.97

Source: Eurostat

There is, however, one further point. There is no doubt that part of the difference in the amount of the subsidies can be explained in terms of the different shapes of the population pyramids. A country with a very low number of minors, if the real level of aid is to be the same, would spend less than other countries with a wider based population pyramid. And the reduction in the birth rate that has taken place over recent decades in

European countries may help to explain why the figures given in Table 8.2 are generally lower for 1993 than for 1980. But this argument cannot be used to explain the low public expenditure on family and maternity benefits of countries such as Spain and Italy, which are currently the countries with the lowest birth rates in Europe but in which the decrease began later than in most European countries. The effect of this delay is that the percentage of population of an age giving entitlement to family benefits is higher in Spain and Italy than in the other countries. For instance, according to the Eurostat data, in 1991 the percentage of population in Spain aged below 20 (this being the age considered relevant in European statistics to explain the total amount of family benefits) was 27.8, and this figure was only exceeded in the EU by Ireland and Portugal. The population structure would therefore have required greater, not less, expenditure on family aid in comparison with other EU countries. The question arises, however, as to whether the low level of public expenditure on family protection is more a cause than an effect of the very low birth rates in these two countries.

NOTE

1. This publication follows the ILO classification system for social welfare programmes. There are 10 different headings covering the large number of social programmes of all types existing in the EU. Two of these are of special interest for our purposes – maternity and family benefits. In order to facilitate comparison of the situations in the various countries, the amounts are expressed in ECU, taking the exchange rates at the time of data compilation.

9. The economic foundations and effects of a policy for the family

1 PARENTS AS PRODUCERS OF EXTERNALITIES

One of the basic theorems of economic analysis is that equilibrium in a market with perfect competition amounts to a situation of social optimum.[1] However there are many cases in which this situation is not reached because one of the basic premises of market functioning fails. The clearest case is obvious, that of pure public goods. When providing such goods – for which the most representative example is the national defence – the market is not the most efficient institution because they do not meet the requirement of the existence of different levels of demand and it is not possible to prevent them from being utilized by those people who are not prepared to contribute to financing them. But there are also other cases which are very common in today's world and in which, although not governed by the same conditions as pure public goods, activities take place which affect the public sphere. In them, the economic agents either cannot appropriate all the profits their action has generated or they do not have to pay all the costs they have caused. These are the so-called external economies and diseconomies.

A classic example of the latter can be found in companies that contaminate the environment and which force many people who do not benefit at all from the activity of these companies to pay costs in the form of contaminated water or air. But for the purpose of the problem to be discussed below, it is the external economies that are most relevant. In order to understand the problem of the goods that generate this type of effect we should think of another typical case, that of the beekeeper whose bees pollinate the crops of the next-door farmer. In this case the beekeeper generates positive external effects because he produces for his neighbour a profit which he cannot appropriate for himself. As a result, the beekeeper's activity will be less than the social optimum because, since he cannot obtain for himself all the benefits he generates, he will set his level of production at a lower amount than he would reach if his externality were to affect the benefits received.

This model can be applied to any case in which certain persons or businesses generate profits for third parties without receiving consideration for them. If this happens, economic theory justifies the payment of subsidies to anyone generating externalities to such an amount that it compensates them for the difference between the social benefit generated and their own private benefit. The effect of such subsidies is, on the one hand, to improve the situation of those producing positive external benefits and, on the other, to raise the level of production of the goods generating them.

In order to find economic justification for the policy of family subsidies based on criteria of efficiency, we need to set aside criteria of fair income distribution and resort to reasoning of this type.[2] In our case we are analysing whether it is efficient for a part of society – the part formed by childless people – to have to transfer income to those who have children. The reason for this efficiency may be that parents generate externalities benefiting those who have not had children and that, unless income transfers are required from the latter towards the former, the birth rate would fall below the level considered appropriate for a specific society. This is why the question we should ask is whether the fact that a couple have children and educate them can in any way affect people that have nothing to do with the two generations of a family.

Life in society makes it inevitable that both external economies and diseconomies will arise. The case of a criminal is a good example of how the behaviour of such a person represents a cost for society, irrespective of his relationship with his parents. In many other cases, social interaction will on its own create external economies. The cases mentioned in the previous chapter of societies whose objective is to increase population is a good example of the latter.

For our purpose it is therefore very important to determine whether this interest in increasing the birth rate actually exists today or not and what are the reasons for it. In many European countries the most common argument for a higher birth rate is the problem of financing social security so that it can meet the needs of an increasing number of pensioners. More specifically, the ratio between the number of workers and the number of pensioners has become a widely used criterion to explain the crisis in today's pensions systems. But really this argument has little economic sense because for workers to pay the pensions of retired workers is not a necessary feature of all pensions systems. It is rather the result of a pay-as-you-go system. With a funding system, the members of a specific generation would not have to pay the costs of the pensions of their elders, because they would be completely financed by the accumulated contributions paid by each worker and the corresponding returns. It therefore does not seem reasonable to blame the population pyramid when what is directly responsible is the current social security system.

There may be sounder economic arguments in favour of the idea that the production of children generates positive externality. For example, in countries with a very low population density, an increase in the number of young people could lead to more efficient utilization of the natural resources or better division of labour. And the opposite would be the case in nations with a very high population in proportion to their size or natural resources.

But there are other important reasons. We have already seen how parents obtain non-monetary benefits from their children. And this may also occur with childless people who may obtain benefits that are not strictly of a monetary nature, but are more psychological or cultural, from the existence of a larger number of children. And, since these benefits are desired by the people living in a country, they affect their behaviour. A large proportion of the European population wants to live in a society in which the number of children is not very small even though as individuals they are not interested in looking after them. Other people think that, if the population drops too far, immigration will be inevitable, bringing in young people from other countries whose lifestyle, religion or culture they dislike. So in these cases too the production of children would generate external economies for these people.

If such effects existed, there would be two theoretically possible solutions to the problem of a birth rate that is lower than the optimum from the social point of view. Firstly, the property rights of parents over their children would be strengthened, as would the returns from their investments in human capital. Secondly, there would be subsidies allowing parents to appropriate to a greater extent the social benefit they produce.

The first of the solutions would eliminate the externality as it would allow for more correct functioning of the market. In fact, all externality is due to an imprecise definition of property rights and theoretically it can be corrected by clarification and reinforcement of these rights.[3] But in practice, it is often impossible to apply such a measure, as in our case in which parents can only exert their rights – if they exist – with respect to the rest of society by means of public expenditure. The payment of a subsidy to parents would be the only real solution to the problem created by the external economy.

The problem of the generation of external economies by parents has not yet been fully studied, and there is no general agreement on the subject. An argument which goes against the theory upheld here is based on the altruism of parents and on their rational conduct to maximize their utility functions. If we accept that parents are altruistic and seek the wellbeing of their children, it can be concluded that the former will internalize all the externality when reaching a decision on the number of children to have. As a result, there will only be externality if there are estates to be inherited and the children marry, as this would extend the benefits of their action outside the framework of the initial family.[4]

Other arguments insist that it is impossible to justify family benefits from the point of view of efficiency, pointing out that both the number of children and family structure are individual decisions and that public intervention, far from increasing efficiency, will only create distortion in each person's choice.[5] Along the same lines, some economists defend the idea that family benefits should be limited to people who need State protection because of their low income level, and they conclude that families with sufficient income to maintain their children with their own resources should not receive public benefits at all.[6]

These approaches are undoubtedly fairly reasonable but they do not seem to affect the essence of the argument followed here. In the above case, the problem does not involve so much the relationship between parents and their children as the relationship between people who have children and others who, while childless, through a process of collective choice, express their preference for a society with a large number of its 'own' children, that is, children having the cultural and social characteristics of their country. So these are the benefits that third parties can obtain from the behaviour of people with children.

If we accept the conclusion that, in the sort of economic and social circumstances that exist in Europe today, parents produce external economies, then the economic problem changes to become one of how to distribute the cost of the subsidies to be received by those who have children and bring them up. It is difficult to base this distribution on criteria of individual preference, because we do not know everybody's preferences in this respect, and the maximizing conduct of each taxpayer would lead him to manifest an absolute lack of interest in increasing the number of children. Such an attitude would give rise to the well-known problem of free-riders. The solution for this is to establish coercive payments which, in our case, would take the form of taxes on the beneficiaries of the externality.

So the conclusion is that the decision to grant subsidies should be approved by society by means of a procedure for collective choice, as with the provision of national defence or other goods of a public nature; and the distribution of the cost amongst taxpayers should take into account the general principles of sharing out the tax burden. As with any subsidy for external economies, such payments would have two results. On the one hand, there would be compensation for the external benefits being generated which, without subsidies, would constitute transfers from producers to non-producers; and, on the other, an incentive would be created to increase the number of children.

But clarification is required. Who is it that we are calling *producers* of children? Obviously it is parents, but it is important to remember that, although the father and mother act together in the generation of the child, they do not take on the costs in the same proportion. In line with the pattern established in this book, if it is the woman who gives birth to the children and who devotes many more hours to their upbringing, it is she who generates most of the external economy and it should therefore be the woman who should directly receive the subsidies.

This may seem unimportant and in most cases it is because, in practice, State aid is granted to the so-called family units, that is, to fathers and mothers jointly. But, in some situations it may have very significant effects with respect to the quality of life of women and children. This could occur when family benefits are received by the man and used for the purchase of goods that bring no benefit whatsoever to his wife and children. It has been seen how, in some countries of the Third World, improved income per capita has gone together with greater malnutrition in children because, since the income is received by the men, they have increased their expenditure on products such as motorcycles or radios which they prefer to the traditional family expenses.[7] Such a situation is unlikely to arise in Europe. But, even in advanced countries, there are often cases where parents show a great lack of concern for the needs of their children and, although this is not widespread conduct, it exists to a greater extent amongst fathers than amongst mothers. And in these cases, family benefits should be handed directly to whichever of the parents actually cares for the children.

Moreover, in our western world, it is not unusual to find cases of battered women who, after trying to leave their homes, end up returning because they are unable to earn a living for themselves and their children. Subsidies to mothers could represent very useful aid under such circumstances. This could be expected to lead to an increase in the rate of separations and divorces because the opportunity cost of separation would be lower for women. Although such a rise in the divorce rate is usually considered a negative social marker, in our case it would not be because it would not create incentives to break up families which could work well but would make it possible to achieve a second optimum, because divorce would be preferable to a situation of continuous harsh treatment.

2   EXTERNALITIES AND MARKET EQUILIBRIUM

In order to fulfil the first basic theorem of the economics of welfare, according to which competitive markets allocate production resources efficiently in the Paretian sense, it is necessary for the condition to prevail whereby the marginal benefit of producing a specific good must be equal to its marginal cost:

$$MB = MC$$

The reason for this is that, given the increasing MC and decreasing MB, if *MB* is greater than *MC*, social welfare will increase if a larger quantity of the good is produced; whereas if *MC* is greater than *MB* it would be in the interests of society to reduce production to the point at which both magnitudes are equal.

In the case of children, however, the existence of external economies makes it necessary to reformulate the above equality because now it is necessary to distinguish between two different concepts of *MB*: the private marginal benefit (*PMB*) and the social marginal benefit (*SMB*), being:

$$SMB = PMB + E$$

where *E* represents the value of the externality.

The problem arises when, if producers equalize the marginal cost and their private marginal benefit, as a consequence of E it turns out that

$$MC = PMB < SMB$$

According to the above, this situation is not a social optimum because it would involve a level of production of the good under consideration – in this case, children – that would be lower than the optimal level. This situation, based on the principle that parents generate external economies, is shown in Figure 9.1. If the externality is not taken into consideration, parents will equalize the MC with their PMB and will have a number of children equivalent to $0Ch_1$. Since, for $0Ch_1$, $MC < SMB$, the number of children is lower than the social optimum.

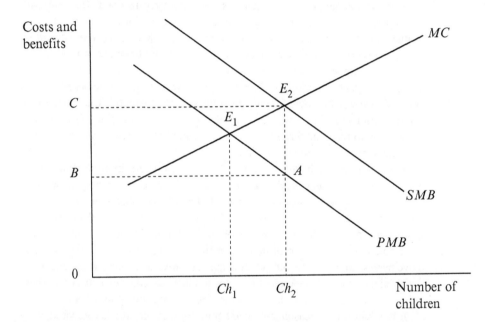

Figure 9.1   Parents as generators of external economies

In order to reach this optimum, if a policy reinforcing parents' rights of ownership cannot be applied, it will be necessary to subsidize parents so that the PMB curve moves to the right until it meets the SMB curve.[8] If this is done, the point of equilibrium would move from E_1 to E_2 and the number of children would become $0Ch_2$, which is the social optimum because for this quantity

$$MC = SMB$$

The subsidy per child in this case would be AE_2 and the total subsidies paid by the public sector would be determined by the rectangle BAE_2C. The externality disappears because society pays the parents an amount equal to the value for society of this externality.

3   THE FAMILY AND PUBLIC FINANCING OF EDUCATION

For a very long time the public sector has been allotted the task of creating human capital in many ways. The State has not only tried to ensure that children are educated but has also spent huge sums of money on maintaining teaching centres of all types. What is the reason for this expenditure? It seems clear that education is not, strictly speaking, a public good. Consumers have different preferences for education, the principle of exclusion can be easily applied to those not paying the costs and there has always been a private supply of educational services in exchange for payment, as with any private good. But there are several explanations as to why public funds are spent on education. The first is that education creates external economies. When a person receives education, that person is the main beneficiary because as a result he or she will be able to command a higher income in the future and will obtain greater satisfaction from the money spent on consumption. But, together with these private benefits, there are also some public benefits, the most important of which is the existence of a more efficient and less troublesome society. A society made up of people who know how to read and write is likely to function better and be generally better integrated than an illiterate society.

Moreover since education is one of the factors determining income levels, widespread education will allow for less unequal income distribution and in many societies this in itself is considered a good. It can be said that, if education offers monetary returns, the possibility will exist – in a free capital market – of borrowing money during the years of study and returning the loan when the investment starts to be profitable. But the peculiarities of this type of loan have been seen to be a serious obstacle that has prevented banks from developing an efficient financial market in this sector and this has led, even in the case where education is financed by loans, to a large presence of the public sector.

But, whatever the reason, and whether or not these arguments are valid, what is relevant from our point of view is the fact that in practice the public sector is financing a large proportion of education costs in most countries. And the question that arises immediately is why does it only finance that part of education that takes place within public or private schools? If this type of education is subsidized there is no reason at all why there should not also be subsidies for the education given at home which can thus be said to be discriminated against.

If the justification for public subsidies to schools is the existence of external economies then this argument is reinforced. In fact economists tend to accept the conclusion that, although all types of education generate private and public benefits, the ratio between private benefit and public benefit increases as we go to higher levels within the educational system. This is the reason why many economists who defend free primary education[9] are in favour of paying the costs and financing on credit, if necessary, the costs of higher education. That is, the education offered in the family is the education that contributes most to the creation of the social harmony that was mentioned above as an argument for justifying public expenditure on education. And, following this reasoning, there should therefore be no discrimination against home education when awarding public subsidies.[10]

4   EFFECTS OF FAMILY PROTECTION POLICY ON THE BIRTH RATE

The effects of policies for family protection are a subject of much debate both because of their complexity and because, when studying them, we need to determine not only whether the objectives of each of the programmes applied have been met but also if there have been any negative effects. And there certainly have been many negative effects, some with important consequences, as we shall show below. But often such undesirable effects are not due to the mere existence of a policy of family protection but to the specific ways in which such a policy is applied.

The first point to be covered is the influence of policies for family protection on changes in European birth rates. How have these policies affected decisions on the number of children to have? There is no easy answer. On the one hand, if we look at the trends in birth rates in European countries over recent years it seems clear that the results have not been exactly remarkable. But, on the other hand, we do not know what would have happened if these family protection policies had not existed; that is, to what extent birth rates would be lower than current rates if there had not been any State support for mothers and children.

The data given in the previous chapter indicate that these policies have been applied very tentatively and experience in some countries has shown clearly how family aid has been one of the areas suffering the greatest cutbacks in public expenditure programmes at times of economic crisis and budget deficits. In view of the current situation of public finance in most European countries, this trend can be expected to continue, at least in the short term.

If we return to microeconomic analysis, it must be stated that one of the most important economic problems arising from pro-natalist policies is the link between increased income and changes in the birth rate. If what fiscal policies do to promote childbirth is increase the disposable income for those with children, it can be argued that the success of such policies will depend to a great extent on the behaviour of the birth rate when disposable income changes. In

Chapter 5 we rejected the idea that the inverse relationship between the number of children per couple and the income level could be taken as proof that children are inferior goods. This is an important point because, if they were inferior goods, an increase in a family's disposable income would result in a reduction, not an increase, in the number of children.

The question of quality as opposed to quantity in decisions on the number of children to have and the human capital investment to be made in each of them is a different matter. Family economics support the hypothesis that there is a strong negative correlation between the two variables. And data seem to confirm this hypothesis.

This trend to replace quantity by quality makes it difficult to estimate the real influence of pro-natalist policies on the number of children. What economics predicts is that, given the utility maximization model in which children are considered consumer goods, as explained in Chapter 5, the mere existence of a subsidy for children, *ceteris paribus,* will have positive effects on the birth rate. And this will be the case even if there is a reduction in the birth rate resulting from the long-term trend towards a preference for quality rather than quantity. In short, it cannot be stated that a drop in the birth rate at a time when a policy of fiscal incentives for childbirth is being applied means that the latter is inefficient. It could simply mean that the long-term trend towards a lower birth rate and the substitution of quantity by quality of children has not been completely countered by these fiscal stimuli.

It is also difficult to judge whether or not a family policy has been successful with respect to a specific objective such as raising the birth rate when the objectives of such a policy have hardly ever been precisely defined. Most family policies have not been set up with the aim of improving the birth rate but of improving the standard of living of families with children. Such measures doubtless also result in a higher birth rate but they cannot be considered a failure if this does not occur.

The literature on the effects of family protection policies on birth rates has given extensive coverage to the case of France because this country has adopted the most determined pro-natalist policy. The results of such studies show that, although the French policy is relatively efficient in comparison with those of other European countries, its effects have been limited. The conclusion of the best known of these empirical studies is that reached by G. Calot and J. Hecht,[11] namely that the French pro-natalist policy is responsible for only 10 per cent of the French fertility rate. These estimates have been criticized because they are based on comparisons between the birth rates of France and neighbouring countries, a rather debatable method.[12] What is clear is that, if there is specific concern to substantially raise the birth rate, measures such as those adopted so far in Europe would be insufficient.

5 FAMILY POLICY AND SUPPLY OF LABOUR

Any measure of economic policy may give rise to undesired effects and fiscal policy in relation to the birth rate is no exception. As stated above, it is generally very difficult to distinguish between strictly pro-natalist policies and those aiming to protect the family in that a family's wellbeing directly affects the birth rate. This means that the undesired effects of pro-natalist policies are usually of the same type as the undesired effects of other social security and welfare state programmes.

Much has been written on the effects of taxation on the supply of labour. Here we shall focus not so much on the effects of taxation on the behaviour in the labour market of the average family as on the reaction to the policy for taxation and subsidies of those social groups who are most dependent on social security programmes. The specific problem to be studied is the situation which arises with policies that make it more attractive for certain social groups to live off subsidies than to work; that is, the policies that have given rise in some countries to the existence of a poor, marginalized class who live off social security and have no incentive to change their lifestyle. This is usually called the 'poverty trap'.

The objective of welfare state programmes is to offer everybody the basic services and consumer goods that some people would be unable to obtain alone. It is widely accepted that modern developed societies have attained sufficient wealth to be able to guarantee for all their members certain minimum standards of health, education, nutrition, housing and so on. And it is also accepted that in such societies there is a sufficiently widespread social consensus for the State to be able to adopt policies for income redistribution by means of compulsory transfers – generally by means of taxation – from higher-income groups to lower-income groups.

This all seems perfectly fair but two problems arise. The first is that often the decision as to which groups should be on the receiving end and which on the giving end of such transfers is not always based on strict criteria of real income differences but on the actual lobbying strength of the groups and on how the government assesses the political costs and benefits of such charges and transfers.

The second problem is the reaction of the people involved and their economic behaviour. This is the moral hazard problem that was mentioned in Chapter 6 when studying the problem of the disincentives that welfare pensions may create for savings in the form of pension contributions. The concept is applied here to the fact that many people, if they know they can benefit from social security programmes and that their basic needs will always be met by the welfare state, will make less effort to earn the minimum amount of money they require to subsist than if such social aid did not exist. This means that, in addition to those people who for reasons such as illness, age, lack of intelligence or just plain bad luck need to resort to programmes of social aid, there will also be many others whose incentive to work to meet their own needs will be reduced by the mere existence of such aid.

It is in behaviour in the labour market where these effects are clearest. In the case of well-qualified workers who can earn a high salary, social aid will not be very significant. But for an unskilled person, social aid may represent a very significant percentage of his potential income and therefore will be an important incentive to leave the labour market.

The more complex the social security system, the easier it is for someone to be eligible for several programmes and to reach an income level that acts as a complete disincentive to work. In some advanced countries, a significant number of people have made living off social security a veritable way of life. And in those nations where tax pressure is very high and social subsidies are generous, the combination of aid and taxes that are even levied on very low wages means that there are some people who are better off living on subsidies than working.

So to what extent do pro-natalist subsidies and family aid affect these situations? To a very great extent because, in some countries, aid has reached such high levels that, although it may not substantially affect reproduction rates, it certainly may affect the behaviour of the beneficiaries. The problem is illustrated in Figures 9.2 and 9.3. The former shows what would normally be considered a desirable situation, one in which greater effort is awarded with an improved standard of living for the family. In this model the State guarantees a minimum income 0A so that a family can meet its basic needs. Public aid is so structured that an increase in the gross income from work will never give rise to a reduction in net income so parents always have an incentive to join the labour market and devote a greater number of hours to work. Figure 9.3, however, shows the effects of a model in which the joint action of family aid and the tax system may lead to a reduction in net income resulting from an increase in the gross income from work. This occurs when the granting of family aid depends on income being below a minimum level and when wages are subject to an income tax that offers no special advantages to parents with children. The result as shown in this second graph is to create a clear disincentive to work for people whose gross income from work is below 0C, as they will obtain no net benefit at all – and between points B and C will obtain losses – from their work.

This represents the situation in some parts of Europe.[13] In countries in which the scope of family protection is still low, the problem of creating disincentives to work at these income levels is not relevant although it is with respect to unemployment benefit. So it would seem that the problem is one of quantity rather than quality and could become relevant if the social security programmes in such countries follow in the near future a similar path to the programmes existing in

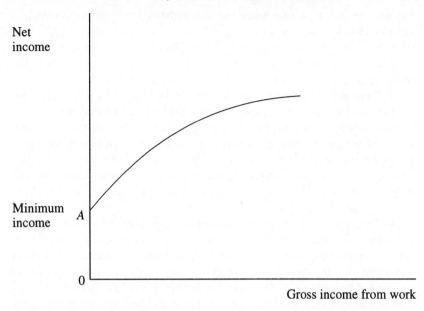

Figure 9.2   Net income and gross income from work: the ideal model

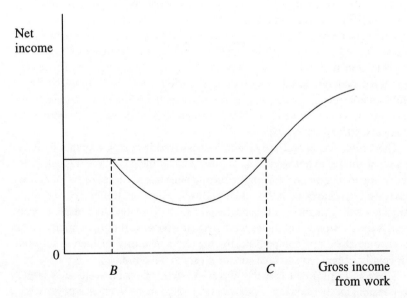

Figure 9.3   Net income and gross income from work: the distorted model

countries follow in the near future a similar path to the programmes existing in other countries.

An especially interesting case for studying the effects of child benefit on the attitude of women towards the labour market and their level of wellbeing is that of women who, in some social security systems, receive subsidies because they are mothers and often survive on these alone. In the United States they are called 'welfare mothers'. Most of these women have very little education and non-existent training. However, they seem very skilled in obtaining funds from the social security, from several programmes at a time, even though legally they may be incompatible. The aid system has led some of them to become real professionals in the art of obtaining subsidies. Many are unmarried or divorced mothers who have no interest in getting married as this would prevent them from receiving social security aid.

On the matter of deciding how many children to have, their behaviour does not seem to follow any pattern. There are cases in which they have children to receive benefits but, generally speaking, these are women with such a low cultural and social level that they have made no attempt whatsoever to plan their future nor have they made any decision on the number of children they want.[14]

If we use the family economics term 'quality of children' to describe the human capital children receive in the form of time and resources devoted to them by their parents, the children of 'welfare mothers' can be said to be of very poor quality. Such mothers tend to be indifferent towards their children or to have no authority over them and, as is only to be expected, there is often a high percentage of criminals and drug addicts amongst them.

There are great differences in the amount of time that such women live on social security benefits. Widows and divorced women eventually find some sort of work and therefore do not depend totally on receiving aid. Those who become dependent on subsidies for longer periods tend to be women who have children at a very early age. The majority of such women in the United States are Afro-American, generally never marry and fall into a poverty trap from which is is very difficult to escape.

The United States welfare system is structured in such a way that it creates many incentives to not work. The amount paid by the government is calculated according to income so paid employment entails a lower level of social aid. We have seen that mothers in this situation usually have no training or very little. Any wages they might receive tend therefore to be very low. As a result, in many cases they are simply not interested in working because the slight improvement in income does not compensate for the drop in utility of having to work, especially if they have to take care of a very small child.

There is little doubt that the current system of social welfare is largely responsible for this situation which not only keeps many women at poverty level but also creates behavioural habits that, especially in the case of very young women, may exclude them from the labour market for the rest of their lives. This amounts to a strong argument against income-based welfare systems which create a disincentive to work and in favour of distinguishing between child benefits and poverty subsidies.

6   EFFECTS ON THE DEMAND FOR LABOUR

Another important effect on the labour market of family protection policies is that exerted by maternity benefit on the demand for labour. Such measures which aim to help women with children may have a negative effect on their labour situation in that their potential earnings may drop and the probability of their becoming unemployed may increase.

As shown in the previous chapter, in all EU countries mothers are entitled to leave for childbirth – usually between 14 and 18 weeks. And it is also usually possible for mothers to request longer periods of leave at a lower salary, sometimes with a guarantee that the job is kept for them, so that they can care for their small children.

In some countries, the main financial weight of such periods of leave is taken by the companies themselves whereas in others it is taken by the social security system. But companies consider they are affected not just because they have to finance the social security but also because of the problems created by the absence of an employee. Replacing an employee generally requires a period of adaptation and has a certain cost. This is because any worker needs to have not just human capital of a general type which will be of use in any job but also specific human capital to allow him to adapt to the organization and functioning of a specific company. If a worker is to be replaced, this specific human capital has to be passed on to the new worker and this inevitably involves costs.

In other words, women who become mothers give rise to extra costs for the companies employing them. We have seen, in line with the model explained here, that all members of society – especially if the birth rate is low – may be considered to benefit from the birth of a child and therefore it seems logical for the burden of such subsidies to be shared by the whole of society. But there is no reason why the specific company employing the expectant mother should have to take on these extra costs.

For the company, a woman with children is more expensive to employ than a childless woman or a man competing for the same job. It is no surprise, therefore, that when choosing from a number of candidates, companies tend to put women whom they see as potential mothers, *ceteris paribus*, at the end of the list. It is perfectly reasonable for companies to segment the labour market according to this criterion and, as a result, the unemployment rate for women with the characteristic of potential mothers tends to be greater than that for groups of men or women who are not potential mothers.

It could be argued that the legal reforms that are being introduced in some countries allowing fathers to take some of the maternity leave may be at least a partial solution to the problem. But we need to be cautious in evaluating the results of such measures. Firstly, because it is inevitable that part of the leave period has to be taken by the mother for obvious biological reasons and, secondly, since today's salaries are higher on average for men than for women, it is to be expected that the worker with the lowest income in the family – normally the woman – is most likely to use the leave period because the opportunity cost of her domestic work is lower. And finally, because customs are changing, child care is still essentially a female task in most countries.

There is therefore no simple solution because it is difficult for a mother to take advantage of the benefits offered by social security when she has a child and simultaneously to meet the requirements of a job. This gives a new turn to the widely accepted idea that longer maternity leave is advantageous for women as a group because, while this is undoubtedly true in some ways, at the same time it can be expected to damage their position in the labour market. Two alternatives can be considered. The first fits in with the externalities described above. If some companies cover a cost as a result of which the whole of society obtains a benefit, the way of internalizing such externalities would be to make some sort of compensation to the companies. It would be technically difficult to determine how to evaluate such payments because, for the reasons given above, they should not be limited to the cost of the worker's wage and social security. But the reasoning behind the conclusion seems clear.

A second solution would be to reduce maternity leave and offer a service substituting the mother's care in the form of nurseries specializing in the care of newborn babies. These could be run by the work centres, the public sector or private companies but they would under all circumstances be financed by social security which would have recourse to the funds that were released by the reduction in leave periods. This solution would not eliminate the cost for a company of an employee having a child but at least it would reduce it and would encourage employers to show less sex discrimination when taking on staff.

The objective of both proposals would basically be the same – that women who want to continue in the labour market should suffer the least possible damage. They might therefore encourage an increase in the birth rate by reducing one of the most important costs of motherhood today for women, namely the deterioration of their labour situation.

7   ECONOMIC ANALYSIS OF THE EFFECTS OF MATERNITY LEAVE

In order to analyse the effects of maternity leave on wages and demand for female employees, the starting-point will be an economy in which there is no sex discrimination in wages and in which men and women are equally productive. Let us suppose that in

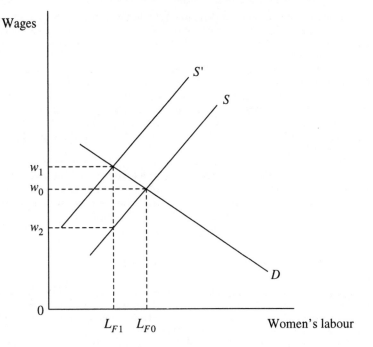

Figure 9.4   Effects of maternity leave

this situation of equality we introduce a single differentiating factor of maternity leave and that such leave can only be taken by women.

Let us call the initial salary paid to all workers w_0 and the average cost per worker for the company of having to allow such periods of leave C. Figure 9.4 shows the effects on the labour market for women of introducing such obligatory leave periods. The cost C affects companies in a similar way to a tax on the employment of women. Therefore the supply curve of women's labour (S) moves upwards (to S'), to an extent that is equivalent to C. The total cost now for a company to employ a woman rises to w_1. But women will only really receive a monetary wage of w_2. And the number of women employed will drop from L_{F0} to L_{F1}.

The cost C will not therefore be taken on as a whole by the company because part will be paid by the women themselves in the form of a reduction in their wages. According to a well-known result in economic theory, the degree to which this distribution of the cost takes place will depend on the elasticity of the demand and supply functions of women's labour, with greater costs for companies the lower the elasticity of their demand.

This elasticity in the demand for work by women will be determined in our case, under *ceteris paribus* conditions, by the elasticity of substitution of female labour by male labour. In some sectors, this substitution of women for men will take place smoothly. In other cases, it will be absolutely impossible (models or actresses, for examples). In general, the greater the value of the elasticity of substitution, the more women will be damaged by the effects of an increase in the costs of maternity leave because it will be easier for companies to reduce the demand for female labour.

Since in most cases it will not be difficult to substitute a woman worker with a man worker, the conclusion is that, under the conditions defined above, maternity leave will mean that fewer women will be employed and, at the same time, that women will take on a substantial part of the cost of maternity leave.

If we modify the basic premise that all workers initially receive the same wage and we now assume that there is some sex discrimination in the wages received by men and women, the introduction of maternity leave may have fewer effects on the employment of women, at least as long as wages paid to men exceed the sum of wages paid to women and costs *C*. The conclusion is therefore that, the greater the equality of wages and the lower the initial extent of discrimination for reasons of sex, the greater the losses of jobs for women that are caused by maternity leave.

Finally, if labour regulations were to prohibit any sort of discrimination against women and were to prevent their wages from falling below those of men, the loss of jobs for women as a result of maternity leave would be even greater because we would then have a situation of higher wage costs for women under conditions of equal productivity and this would lead companies to reduce their female staff in most sectors.

NOTES

1. More specifically, a Pareto optimum situation – that is, one in which the production and distribution structure cannot be reorganized without reducing the wellbeing of some people – is achieved in the case of perfect competition when the producers and consumers fulfil certain conditions in their maximizing behaviour and there are no externalities.
2. This basically follows the argument in Cabrillo, F. (1990), pp. 31–8.
3. This idea is the basis of the Coase theorem which establishes that externality would not exist in an economic system in which property rights are clearly defined and can be negotiated without transaction costs. The basic result of the theorem is that the initial attribution of property rights is not relevant for the purpose of efficient allocation of production resources, provided that such rights can be negotiated by the parties involved. See Coase, R. (1960).
4. See, for example, Nerlove, M., Razin, A., and Sadka, E. (1987a and b).
5. Papps, I. (1983).
6. Papps, I. (1984).
7. See, for example, Hoskins, M. (1980).
8. In the graph the externality per product unit appears as a constant and this allows the PMB and SMB curves to be parallel but this simplification does not affect the basic conclusions.
9. There are many reasons why the State has subsidized elementary education over history. No mention has been made in the text, for example, of the role played by primary schools in countries with high levels of immigration in helping to create national awareness amongst very different ethnic and cultural groups. But it is not difficult to see in this and in other cases that there is an important element of public good in this expenditure.
10. There is no doubt that subsidies for family education may give rise to serious problems if they were applied, the most important of which would be the quality control of the service offered to the child which is much easier to carry out within a school. But these practical difficulties do not affect the basic principle of the argument.
11. Calot, G. and Hecht, J. (1978).
12. See Demeny, P. (1987).
13. See, for example, the cases studied by Morgan, P. (1995).
14. See Kamerman, B. and Kahn, A. (1988).

10. Technical problems involved in an economic policy for family protection

Having looked at the family support measures existing within the EU and the basis for and possible effects of these policies, we shall now go into some of the most important matters to be considered when drawing up a specific family support and pro-natalist policy.

1 AID FOR MOTHERS AND INCOME LEVEL

A much debated matter in connection with fiscal policy for families is whether or not to link the amount of subsidies and deductions to the beneficiaries' income. The programmes for aid in the EU countries adopt varying approaches. In some, child benefit is not related to income and, in others, it is linked from the start with the family income. And in a third group the income level leads to increases or decreases in the basic fixed amounts.

What needs to be determined is whether in these cases two types of subsidy that are based on two very different concepts should be taken together. On the one hand, in a welfare state, grants are given to those people or families that do not have what are considered by society to be minimum income levels. On the other hand, aid is offered to women or families which, according to the pattern described above, produce a good for which there is social demand, namely children, irrespective of their income. Although for the first type income should be the basic criteria for determining the amount of aid provided, there is no apparent reason why the benefit or tax deduction for children should be affected by the income level.

The way in which the objective of family aid is seen will influence the decision taken. If it is not considered advisable to apply a policy supporting families with children because it is not accepted that a higher birth rate would benefit society as a whole, then it is reasonable to conclude that family benefits should depend on the family income and that, above a certain level, there should be no subsidies for families whether or not they have children. If, however, the aid is seen as compensation for the social benefit generated, then all parents, whatever their income level, should be subsidized.

If we accept the latter approach, there is a further matter that needs to be studied. Should a single amount be paid to all mothers irrespective of their incomes, or, if we accept that any families generating externalities should be subsidized, should there be some differentiation in the actual amount paid? It could be argued that, although the external benefit obtained by society is the same in the case of poor or rich children, the costs paid by the family are different because, given the principle of the decreasing marginal utility of income, the costs are higher in terms of utility for poor families than for rich families. This statement not only poses yet again the insoluble problem of how to compare utility for different people but it forgets the effects that act in the opposite direction. The first of these is that, since rich families spend more on the creation of human capital than poor families – for example, by paying for private schooling – the external economies they generate are greater for society. And the second is that, if we accept the decreasing marginal utility of income, the utility offered to poor families by a specific sum of money is greater than that obtained by rich families. So analysis in strict terms of utility gives an unclear result.

If we then add the possibility that other grants may be based exclusively on criteria of insufficient income, then it would seem that subsidies based on the generation of externalities should not be linked to the income level of the mother or family receiving them.

2   THE AMOUNT OF SUBSIDIES AND THE THEORY OF EQUIVALENT INCOME

Let us now analyse the problem of how to determine the amount of the benefits that are paid only for bringing up children, irrespective of income supplements. One of the most widely used criteria in the specialist literature on social security for determining the optimal amount of such benefits is the so-called criterion of *equivalent income*. This is understood as the amount of income required by a family A to maintain a similar standard of living to that of another family B that is made up differently. For example, it could be said that the income of a family comprising a couple with one child is equivalent to twice that of a family comprising a single person if this proportion of two to one allows both families to reach a similar standard of living.[1] Based on this idea, the optimal amount of a child benefit has been considered as that which would allow a specific family to maintain an equivalent income after having children to the income it had before.

The problem of comparing the standards of living of different families of different sizes is extremely complex, even if we just measure the levels of consumption of goods offered on the market. Solutions are usually based on the need to increase family consumption in line with the increased size of the family. The best-known formula is probably the 'Oxford Scale' which defines the units of consumption of the various family members as follows:

- first adult: 1 unit of consumption (UC)
- second adult: 0.7 UC
- child aged under 6 months: 0.3 UC
- child aged between 6 months and 10 years: 0.5 UC
- child aged between 10 and 14 years: 0.7 UC
- child aged above 15 years: 1 UC

Other patterns have been drawn up varying slightly the above estimates of consumption. For example, the INSEE pattern used in France allocates 1 UC to the first adult, 0.7 to the second adult and each of the children aged over 15 years, and 0.5 UC to each child aged under 15.

The most serious problem is not, however, how to estimate the volume of consumption for each member of the family unit but that this model excludes from the pattern any goods that, while not purchased in the market, provide satisfaction to the family, the most important of which is obviously the children themselves. It is therefore unreasonable to try to establish equal levels of satisfaction. Such a premise would imply that children only represent costs for their parents and that the latter gain no utility whatsoever from their offspring. The starting-point for modern economics of the family is, quite the contrary, that children offer not just costs but also satisfaction for the parents which constitutes one of the arguments of their utility functions. And this must be taken into account when comparing standards of living.

Since it is not possible to make interpersonal comparisons of utility, the equivalent income argument takes us nowhere. There is no point in establishing an amount for an optimal subsidy if it is based on levels of wellbeing which are determined according to subjective factors that cannot be objectively measured or compared.

3   EQUIVALENT INCOME AND WELLBEING

Figure 10.1 shows the effects of child benefits on the level of wellbeing of parents for whom their children take the role of consumer goods. The indifference curves in this graph represent utility functions

$$U = U (X, Ch)$$

in which, as on other occasions, X represents the market goods that the parents can purchase with a given income and Ch the number of their children. The income restriction is also determined here by a series of budget lines defined by the equation

$$Y = X P_X + Ch\pi_{Ch}$$

Let us suppose that, given a specific monetary income, a set of prices P_X and an opportunity cost π_{Ch}, the initial income is defined by the budget line B_1. In this case, the parents will reach their point of equilibrium at point A, where this budget line is at a tangent to the indifference curve I_1; they will have Ch_1 children and will consume X_1 market goods. The subsidies that make it possible to maintain an equivalent level of consumption when the number of children increases are reflected on the budget lines located to the right of the initial straight line (B_2, B_3 and so on). At the new points of equilibrium C, D and so on, we can assume that the principle is fulfilled that consumption of market goods does not vary and, therefore, that the level of X is constant. The result is a growth in the parents' level of satisfaction which is represented by the new indifference curves I_2 and I_3. Equivalence in the level of consumption of market goods cannot therefore be taken as the criterion for determining the optimal amount of family benefits.

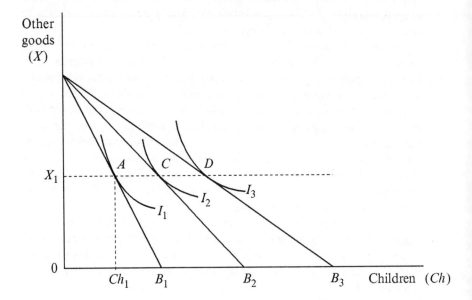

Figure 10.1   Equivalent income and effects of family aid on parents' utility functions

We have now seen how the consideration of children as consumer goods questions the very basis of the equivalent income model. But children do not only imply monetary costs and non-monetary benefits. They also imply opportunity costs which are difficult to estimate by the market when they do not refer to the reduction of the parents' productive activities but to the reduction in leisure activities (theatre visits, travel and so forth). If the levels of wellbeing are to be taken as constants, these costs should also be taken into account when determining the optimal amount of benefits.

In a world of subjective, non-comparable utility functions, it is impossible to put this into practice. The alternative option is to determine the amount of the subsidies according to parameters that are simpler to measure and to handle on the part of those making decisions on family policy. Such parameters would include: (a) the objectives that the public sector hopes to achieve through them; (b) the behaviour of families with regard to the number of children desired; and (c) the price and income elasticity of the demand for children with respect to variations in price caused by the public policy of subsidies. This approach would not only seem to be more accurate and realistic, but would also make it possible to differentiate the subsidies according to the number of children, as shown in the next section.

4 SUBSIDIES AND DEDUCTIONS FOR EACH CHILD

The various social security systems in the EU countries do not give a single answer to the question whether all children should receive the same treatment for the purpose of family benefits. Here we need to consider three matters separately. Firstly, should subsidies be offered as from the first child? Secondly, should the amounts paid per child be the same or should they vary? And, thirdly, should the age of the children affect the amount of the benefits?

The answer to the first question is the same in practically all the European countries. The subsidy is paid as from the first child. But this was not always the case. In Great Britain, in the original project by Beverage, which was later to serve as a model for the organization of social security in many countries, the theory was that family benefit should be paid for each of the children, except for the first. The reason given was that the salary of an employed person should be sufficient to meet the needs of the parents and of at least one child but that larger families might face serious problems if they did not receive aid.[2]

Today the only country in the EU which does not offer a subsidy for the first child in all cases is France where aid is paid for the first child only when the family does not reach a minimum income level and only while the child is under the age of three. According to the approach taken in this book, the exclusion of the first child from child benefit – it would be different in the case of aid to raise the family income level – could only be justified if the marginal social benefit from the first child were no greater than the marginal private benefit. In this case, there would be no external economies and the subsidy would not be justified. But it is obviously not easy to know if such external economies exist or not for the first child. The data show that, in most people's opinion, the difference between the private and social marginal benefit increases with the increase in the number of children per family. But they do not determine whether the difference exists and to what extent in the specific case of the first child.

The second question is whether the amount of aid should be the same for each child. The comparison of private and social benefits allows us to answer this. The private marginal benefit obtained by a family from the production of children decreases as the number of children increases and may quickly reach negative values. From the social point of view, however, the marginal benefit curve is different. Since the number of children that a single family can have is an infinitesimal share of the total number of children in a single country, the marginal social benefit should be considered as constant because the behaviour of a single family cannot have any significant effect on the country's child population as a whole. That is, the function of marginal social benefit should be represented as a straight line parallel to the axis indicating the number of children within a specific family.

Figure 10.2 shows the marginal benefit of having children for a family, before receiving any benefit, and for society. The function of private marginal benefit has been defined on the assumptions that there are external economies as from the first child and that a family obtains a marginal benefit that is positive for the first and second child and negative as from the third. These hypotheses reflect the preferences of the majority of European families. Note

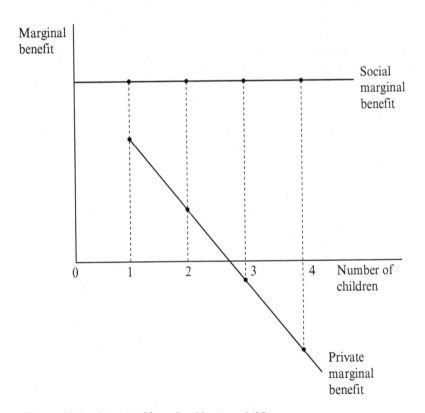

Figure 10.2   Marginal benefit of having children

that, for the purpose of this discussion, the exact point at which the function of private marginal benefit begins to give negative values is not particularly relevant. What matters is the increasing difference between one sort of benefit and the other.

The implications of this analysis are clear. If subsidies and tax deductions are justified by the difference existing between the social and private marginal benefit, we have to conclude that the difference will increase as the number of children increases so aid should therefore also increase. This shows the reasoning behind the French policy drawn up during the 1970s that placed a premium on the birth of the third child.

So far we have only considered the problem of the number of children. But we also need to look at the problem of quality, defined as human capital created by devoting time and resources which, as stated in Chapter 5, is inversely related to quantity in that an increase in the number of children tends to mean that the investment in human capital on each of them is reduced. If this is so, subsidies that increase with the number of children tend to value quantity over quality. The solution, from the point of view of efficiency, would be a policy that maximizes both variables together. But this is not easy to put into practice. Measures such as those applied in France, Belgium or Germany, which aim to slow down the increase in aid as from the third or fourth child, could be interpreted in this way.

The last of the matters mentioned at the start of this section is whether or not the amount of aid should vary according to the age of the children. In most of the EU countries there is no such differentiation but in some (namely, Austria, Belgium, France, The Netherlands and Luxembourg) supplements have been established as from a certain age (depending on the country). But these differences are difficult to justify for reasons of economic efficiency. They could be explained by the greater expense involved for parents with children of these ages. But this difference in monetary expense might be more than compensated for by the increased non-monetary expenses – that is, by the opportunity costs of giving up activities for which free time is necessary – that small children require in comparison with older children. And the latter receive subsidies – mainly in the form of educational services – that are greater than those for smaller children. There do not therefore seem to be any differences in the value of the externalities generated that can justify greater subsidies as from a certain age.

5   TAX DEDUCTIONS AND DIRECT PAYMENTS OR SUBSIDIZED SERVICES

A matter that always arouses controversy in the planning of welfare and social security programmes is whether the beneficiaries should receive money or free or reduced price services. These are sometimes called demand and supply programmes. The latter, which is the most frequent formula, involves the provision free of charge for the user, or at subsidized prices, of services in the area of health, education, transport and so on. The main problems involved are therefore limited options for users and public sector inefficiency.

By way of an alternative, proposals have been made for tax deductions and monetary payments which would allow greater freedom of choice for the beneficiary and would avoid the costs and inefficiency of state-run services. The main objection to this type of payment is that it should not serve to increase the income available for any activity – drugs or alcohol could be given as examples of socially undesirable consumption – but rather to promote the consumption of 'necessary' goods, such as medical treatment or education. Those against tax deductions and monetary payments argue that the restriction of an individual's freedom by determining where his money can be spent is more of an advantage than a disadvantage of the system of subsidized services.

In his book *The Economics of Welfare*, Professor Pigou stated that he was in favour of subsidies in kind and not in cash because 'many people are unable, through lack of knowledge, to invest resources in themselves or their children in the best way'. And, surprisingly, he considered that 'the art of spending money, not merely among the poor, but among all classes, is very much less developed than the art of making it'.[3] As a result, resources might be badly used so the national income would be lower than it might be under optimal conditions. And the earnings obtained by the poor might be lower than the loss resulting from withdrawing resources from wherever they might have been allocated if the transfer had not existed. He concluded that monetary transfers would be more efficient if some method of control were established over the activity of the person receiving them.

This approach by Pigou gives the key elements of what we could call the 'accepted thinking' on this matter. But there are two important problems. Firstly, it assumes that the authorities know people's needs better than they do themselves. And, secondly, by denying people's capacity to use the aid received as they think best is to deny the very essence of democracy. If a person is not able to decide what would be best on matters that concern him directly, how can he be expected to decide correctly on public affairs and on choosing the right people to represent him politically?

But there is a middle way between monetary payments and free or subsidized services which links payments to the consumption of certain goods but at the same time sidesteps public sector inefficiency and gives freedom of choice to beneficiaries. This is the voucher system. By giving education or health vouchers, the person receiving the subsidy is forced to spend the money on 'necessary' goods such as education or health but at the same time he can choose the public or private company that will provide them.

These general considerations are relevant for the specific case of family benefit. Here too there are sound arguments for stating that cash payments offer important advantages over free or subsidized services. The main one is that such payments do not only allow greater choice but also lead to more efficient allocation of the human resources of each beneficiary. Cash payments allow the mother receiving them to specialize in market activities or in the direct care of her children. If she chooses to work in the market, the aid allows her to obtain from the market any necessary substitution services such as those offered by nurseries and the like. If she chooses to care for her children herself, the loss of income from the market is compensated for, at least partially, by the monetary aid received. So she will make her decision according to her capacity for earning money in the market and her personal preferences.

It would be a mistake for state policies not to take into account the great range of situations of the women receiving benefits and to try to force them to adopt uniform, inefficient behaviour. If a woman has an interesting, well-paid job, child benefits are unlikely to encourage her to give it up and specialize in caring for her children. But another woman with a poorly paid, unpleasant job or one who works in domestic activities, carrying out for another person the same tasks she also has to do in her own home, might consider that leaving her job and caring for her own children would be the most efficient solution. Some criticisms of this freedom of choice, which are based on the idea that a policy of monetary aid would reduce the presence of women in the labour market, might, in effect, conceal a paternalist policy which seeks women's wellbeing in accordance with certain predetermined values by putting very different situations on the same basis and not allowing women to make their own decisions.

It cannot be denied that tax deductions and monetary subsidies also give rise to many problems, the most important of which is probably that incentives for having children may exert most influence on groups with low social integration and very poor cultural levels. This could in turn result in a reduction in the quality of children. An example of the harmful effects of some social security programmes would be the 'welfare mothers' mentioned above. But the problem involved in these social security programmes does not concern the form they take so much as the disincentive to work they create. The undesired effects are mostly due to the fact that these programmes take income as the criterion for determining the amount of aid. There is therefore a pressing need for establishing a clear distinction between programmes of aid for people with low income levels and those for mothers or families in their capacity as producers and carers of children. And the latter should not be linked to income or withdrawal from the labour market.

Another possible drawback is the need to control the behaviour of the mothers receiving cash benefits. Since children cannot assert their own rights, it should be up to the State to ensure that any subsidies paid out actually reach the children. It could be stated, and most economists would agree, that such policies for state control would be costly and inefficient. This is undoubtedly true but it would not change matters. Today, with or without subsidies, the law imposes certain obligations on parents for the care of their children which, if not fulfilled, may lead to the parents losing custody of their children. And it is the State that today has authority for watching over parents' behaviour. So there would not be much difference with respect to the current public system of protection. It could even be argued that reception of benefits could constitute an incentive for improved child care because of the risk of having custody withdrawn if they do not comply with their legal duties.

Returning to the subject of schools that receive public subsidies, there too there is public control which tries to guarantee certain minimum conditions of organization and functioning. And the costs of such control are undoubtedly lower than the costs of the loss of efficiency that usually arises when the services are offered by the State. Moroever the need to compete in the market would force any private institutions offering services to families to adopt quality criteria that would attract any potential demand.

As yet there is not much experience of programmes for the partial privatization of family aid policy. One of the most interesting cases is the American experience of the 1980s, when the objective was to replace a large proportion of the free and subsidized services offered by the public sector by direct aid to families, especially in the form of tax deductions.[4] The aim of this reform was, firstly, to give parents greater freedom in choosing the institution that would care for their children and, secondly, by transferring to the private sector many of the services previously offered by the public sector, that market competition would lead to greater efficiency and a lower social cost for the provision of such services.[5]

The debate that arose out of this reform is valid outside the United States because if any project of this type were proposed in Europe it would lead to similar reactions. Advocates of privatization stress the beneficial effects of offering parents greater variety for child care. This greater variety should have two consequences; firstly, sharp growth in the private companies working in the sphere of child care and, secondly, improved quality of the services offered as a result of increased competition.

But the most serious criticism of a policy of this type is usually formulated not in terms of efficiency but in terms of income distribution. For example, in the American case, even the most hardline critics of the project acknowledged that middle-class families in general benefited from the freedom of choice and range of services made possible by the new system. But they claimed that the poorest sectors of society suffered because they were unable to take advantage of the benefits offered to the middle classes through income tax deductions. The American data indicate that, for people in the lower income bracket and those living in one way or another on other social security programmes, this is a real problem. And if a similar plan were presented in a European country a solution would have to be found for lower-income families unable to receive the benefit of tax deductions.

In more general terms, if it is decided that at least part of the state aid for children should not adopt the form of free or subsidized services, but rather of monetary transfers, then the technical problem of how to put these into effect would have to be faced. There are two possible methods – direct payments and tax deductions. In the EU countries both solutions exist and arguments can be given to support both. The main advantage of tax deductions is that they are simple to administer and therefore less costly for the State. And the main disadvantage is the above-mentioned problem that they are impossible to apply in the case of low-income people who either cannot attain the minimum level required for making an income tax declaration or whose tax rate is not high enough for the appropriate deductions to be made.

It is, however, possible to find mixed procedures to solve this problem. One of the most interesting is the proposed 'negative tax on children' which would function in a similar way to Milton Friedman's idea of establishing a negative income tax.[6] According to this proposal, parents with sufficient income would receive the aid in the form of a tax deduction and those not reaching it would receive cash payments. The advantages of such a solution are, firstly, that it is fairer because the aid programme is thus applied to all parents whatever their income level and, secondly, that its cost would be lower because administration would be through the tax declaration.

6   COMPATIBILITY BETWEEN WORK AND SUBSIDIES: A WAGE FOR HOUSEWIVES

In spite of criticism from many international organizations, including the EU itself, that family benefits are payable subject to the mother not being in paid employment, it is widely thought that in order for women to receive certain types of family aid they should not be receiving a salary. Where aid is subject to such conditions, this is basically only a reflection of the general principle whereby paid activity in the market is considered incompatible with the reception of monetary transfers from the public sector, whether these take the form of child benefit, pensions or any other similar payment.

In the case of aid for mothers with children we need to distinguish between two different situations. The first is that of direct incompatibility, that is, where a law prohibits the granting of child benefit to mothers receiving an income from work. The second is incompatibility which, although not formally established by law, exists in practice when aid can only be granted if the minimum income level is not reached.

There does not seem to be any reasonable basis for either of these types of incompatibility, even though they are widely supported. As stated above, the labour and domestic situations of mothers vary so it should be they who adopt decisions concerning their lives. The only legal condition for receiving public aid should be that they fulfil their obligations towards their children as established by law. The rest should be up to them. As also stated above, one of the undesirable effects of programmes, which either directly or indirectly only grant aid if the mother does not work, is that the beneficiaries may end up isolated and even become social security 'professionals'. These situations are sometimes very difficult to escape from and should be avoided whenever possible.

The possible economic justification, as presented in this book, for a policy of public expenditure and taxes that would transfer income to mothers bringing up children, therefore, has nothing to do with proposals for a wage for housewives, that is, the transfer of income to those women who remain at home for the simple reason that they do just this. The purpose of a wage paid by the State to housewives would be to pay for domestic work through transfers from the tax system. For such transfers to be justified from the point of view of efficiency, it would be necessary for net taxpayers, that is, men – whether married or unmarried – and women, who are not housewives, to obtain some benefit from the activity of those receiving this wage.

These external benefits may arise, as we have already seen, where there are children and in the generation of human capital through their education. And they may also exist if women carry out activities such as the care of the elderly or sick as these tasks would otherwise have to be covered by the budget of public institutions. But the activity of the housewife in itself – apart from motherhood and related functions – only produces benefits for herself and her partner, who should be the person paying for this activity, either in the form of periodic payments or by passing on to her part of the property acquired during the marriage or by any other system. There seems to be no reason why society as a whole should pay for a benefit that is received only by the husband or partner.

What would happen if a wage were established for housewives? The answer seems clear. Subsidies or tax deductions as a rule aim to orientate behaviour by offering incentives. If society pays for women to be housewives, a larger number of women would prefer to do just this. That is, the wage for housewives would not only involve income transfers that would be difficult to justify but would create incentives for women to stay at home. And this in the current situation would be unlikely to benefit either women or the European economies.

NOTES

1. See McClements, L.D. (1977).
2. *Reform of Social Security* (Green Paper), (1985), p. 28.
3. Pigou, A.C. (1938), p. 754.
4. In 1982 a document from the American Department of Labour explained this in relation to one of its most important family benefit programmes, that of day centres for small children. 'At present the Federal government is shifting away from giving direct support and subsidies to day care centers and toward an emphasis on tax credits for parents and tax incentives for employers. This trend is likely to continue.' Quoted in Kamerman, S.B. and Kahn, A.J. (1989), p. 235.
5. The method adopted by the North American government was a rapid transfer of funds from one programme to another so that the main weight of state assistance in this field was borne by tax deductions. The following example shows the comparative situation of child care programmes in 1980 and 1986, that is, before and after the Reagan reform:

	Expenditure in millions of dollars	
Programmes	*1980*	*1986*
Supply programmes	1616	1929
Demand programmes	1191	3555
Tax deductions	956	3410
Other demand programmes	235	145
Total expenditure	2807	5484

   Source: Table drawn up by the author based on data given in Kamerman S.B. and Kahn, A.H. (1987), p. 19.
6. This negative income tax basically entails setting a minimum income as from which taxpayers start to pay the tax; for lower incomes, the taxpayer not only does not pay taxes but actually receives from the State grants that increase inversely to the income. The application of this type of tax to family benefits is proposed by Hardie, A. (1986).

Glossary of economic terms

ceteris paribus   a condition which is often established in economics that requires the elimination of the influence of any variable – except for the one under study – from the results obtained.

comparative advantage (principle of)   in accordance with this principle, a person specializes in the production of those goods and services that he or she can make or provide at a relatively lower cost.

consumer goods   products which reach domestic consumers and provide utility.

demand function   mathematical relationship between the demand for a commodity and its price, the prices of other goods and the consumer's income and taste.

efficiency   a situation or practice which are considered efficient in economics when they achieve the greatest possible productivity or satisfaction through scarce resource utilization.

elasticity   measurement of the degree to which change in one variable affects another (for example, the degree to which an increase in price or in income affects the demand for a good).

externalities   costs that are external to a firm or a person, in the sense that they do not enter into the firm's or person's cost of production calculation (external diseconomies) or benefits that do not yield any revenue to the firm or person in question (external economies).

free rider   strategy whereby a person aims to enjoy the benefits that a given activity or investment provide without contributing to their financing.

game theory   branch of mathematics, with many applications in the field of economics, that studies strategies for behaviour in situations of conflict or cooperation.

human capital   a person's knowledge and occupational or professional training.

income effect   variation in the demand for a good as a result of the changes brought about in the purchasing capacity of a consumer by a change in the price of the good.

inferior goods   goods for which demand decreases with increased income. Inferior goods have negative income elasticities.

Kaldor–Hicks criterion   situation A is preferred to situation B, from the social point of view, if those people who benefit from moving from B to A could compensate the losers and still be in a better position than at B.

marginal cost   increment in total cost required to produce one more unit of output.

marginal utility   the extent to which a consumer's satisfaction would increase if he or she had one more unit of a good.

moral hazard   change in the probability of a certain fact taking place as a result of the existence of some type of insurance that reduces the value of the loss for the person affected.

Nash equilibrium   in game theory, a combination of strategies in which no player could obtain better results if he or she were to modify his or her own strategy, given the strategies chosen by the other players.

normal goods   goods for which the demand increases with increased income. These goods have positive income elasticities.

opportunity cost   value of the alternative use of a factor of production (or of time) which allows us to measure the cost of activities that have no market price (such as measuring the cost of housework in terms of the salary that is not obtained from the market).

Pareto criterion   situation A is preferred to situation B, from the social point of view, if and only if a member of society at least is better at A than at B and nobody is better at B than at A.

production function   mathematical relationship between inputs of factors of production and output of product.

production goods   goods made for the purpose of producing consumer goods and capital goods.

relative price   price of a good measured not in terms of money but in terms of another good.

satisficing strategy   strategy that aims not to achieve optimum utility but simply to achieve a certain satisfactory result.

shadow price   value attributed to resources that do not have a precise market price. Opportunity cost.

substitution effect   variation in the demand for a good as a result of a change in its relative price. A rise in price leads to a reduction in the demand for that good and growth in the demand of its substitutes.

utility function   mathematical relationship between the consumption of some given goods and the satisfaction that a person obtains from such consumption.

utility maximization   strategy that aims to obtain the greatest possible satisfaction from the consumption of goods of all types, with a budget constraint.

Bibliography

Allen D.W. (1992), 'Marriage and divorce: comment', *American Economic Review*, (82), 679–85.

Axelrod, R. (1984), *The Evolution of Cooperation*, New York: Basic Books.

Badinter, E. (1980), *L'amour en Plus. L'histoire de L'amour Maternel (XVIIe–XXe siècle)*, Paris: Flammarion.

Barro, R.J. (1974), 'Are government bonds net wealth?', *Journal of Political Economy,* (82), 1095–1107.

Beauvoir, S. de (1970), *La Vieillesse*, Paris: Gallimard.

Becker, G.S. (1971), *The Economics of Discrimination*, Chicago: University of Chicago Press.

Becker, G.S. (1991), *A Treatise on the Family*, Cambridge, Mass.: Harvard University Press.

Becker, G.S. and Murphy, K.M. (1988), 'The family and the State', *Journal of Law and Economics*, (31), 1–18.

Becker, G., Landes, E. and Michael, R. (1977), 'An economic analysis of marital instability', *Journal of Political Economy*, (85), 1141–87.

Bernheim, B.B. and Stark, O. (1988), 'Altruism within the family reconsidered: do nice guys finish last?' *American Economic Review*, (78), 1034–45.

Boserup, E. (1987), 'Inequality between the sexes', *The New Palgrave. A Dictionary of Economics.* London: Macmillan, vol. II, pp. 824–27.

Boserup, E. (1989), *Women's Role in Economic Development*, London: Earthscan Publications.

Bozon, M. (1990), 'Les femmes et l'écart d'âge entre conjoints. Une domination consentie II', *Population* (3), 565–602.

Bracewell-Milnes, B. (1989), *The Wealth of Giving*, London: Institute of Economic Affairs.

Bremner, M. (1968), *Dependency and the Family*, London: Institute of Economic Affairs.

Bresc, H. (1986), 'L'Europe des villes et des campagnes (XIIIe–XVe siècle)', in Burguière, A. et al. (eds), *Histoire de la Famille,* I, Paris: Armand Colin pp. 385–419.

Bronfenbrenner, M. (1971), 'A note on the economics of the marriage market', *Journal of Political Economy* (79), 1424–25.

Buchanan, J. (1983), 'Rent seeking, noncompensated transfers and laws of succession', *Journal of Law and Economics* (26), 71–85.

Burguière, A., Klapisch-Zuber, C., Segales, M. and Zomabend, F. (eds) (1986), *Histoire de la Famille*. Paris: Armand Colin (2 vols).

Butz, W.P. and Ward, M.P. (1979), 'The emergence of countercyclical US fertility', *American Economic Review* (69), 318–28.

Cabrillo, F. (1990), 'Los hijos como bienes privados y como bienes públicos: un análisis económico de la maternidad', in *Mujer y Demografía*, Madrid: Ministerio de Asuntos Sociales (Instituto de la Mujer)-Universidad Complutense, pp. 31–8.

Cabrillo, F. (1995), 'La teoría económica de la hipergamia', in Corona, J. and Puy, P. (eds), *Economía en Broma y en Serio*, Madrid: Minerva Ediciones-Fundación A. Brañas, pp. 59–73.

Cabrillo, F. and Cachafeiro, M.L. (1990), *La Revolución Gris*. Barcelona: Ediciones del Drac.

Cabrillo, F. and Cachafeiro, M.L. (1993), 'Estrategias nupciales', in Garrido, L. and Gil Calvo, E. (eds), *Estrategias Familiares,* Madrid: Alianza Editorial, pp. 145–54.

Calot, G. and Hecht, J. (1978), 'The control of fertility trends', in *Population Decline in Europe: Implications of a Declining or Stationary Population*, London: Edward Arnold, pp. 178–96.

Coase, R. (1960), 'The problem of social cost', *Journal of Law and Economics* (3), 1–44.

Coelen, S.P. and McIntyre, R.J. (1978), 'An econometric model of pronatalist and abortion policies', *Journal of Political Economy* (86), 1077–1101.

Cohen, L. (1987), 'Marriage, divorce and quasi rents; or, 'I gave him the best years of my life', *Journal of Legal Studies* (XVI), 267–303.

Coleman, J.L. (1982), 'The economic analysis of law', *Ethics, Economics and the Law. Nomos XXIV*, 83–103.

Coleman, J.S (1986), 'Social theory, social research and a theory of action', *American Journal of Sociology* (91), 1309–35.

Collard, D. (1978), *Altruism and Economy*, New York: Oxford University Press.

Comisión de las Comunidades Europeas (1993), La protección social en Europa. Luxemburgo.

Cooter, R. and Ulen, Th. (1988), *Law and Economics*, Glenview, (Ill): Scott, Foresman and Co.

Council of Europe (1982), *European Population Conference: Conclusions*, Strasbourg.

Dawkins, R. (1989), *The Selfish Gene*, 2nd edn., Oxford: Oxford University Press.

Demeny, P. (1987), 'Pronatalist policies in low-fertility countries: patterns, performance and prospects', in Davies, K., Bernstam, M. and Campbell, R.

(eds), *Below-Replacement Fertility in Industrial Societies*, Cambridge: Cambridge University Press, pp. 335–58.

De Miguel, A. (1995), *La Sociedad Española 1994–1995. Informe Sociológico de la Universidad Complutense*, Madrid: Editorial Complutense.

Ellman, I.M. (1989), 'The theory of alimony', *California Law Review* (77), 3–81.

Espín, D. (1970), *Manual de Derecho Civil Español*, vol. V Madrid: Ed. Revista de Derecho Privado.

European Communities (1995), *La Protection Sociale dans les Etats Membres de la Communauté. Situation au 1er Juillet 1995 et Évolution*, Strasbourg.

Frey, B.S. (1992), *Economics as a Science of Human Behaviour*, Boston: Kluwer.

Gaunt, L. and D. (1986), 'Le modèle escandinave', in Burguière, A. et al. (eds), *Histoire de la Famille*, vol. II, pp. 471–95.

Gide, C. and Rist, C. (1920), *Histoire des Doctrines Économiques depuis les Physiocrates jusqu'à nos Jours*, 4th edn., Paris.

Goldberg, S. (1994), *Why Men Rule? A Theory of Male Dominance.* La Salle (Ill): Open Court.

Goody, J. (1976), 'Inheritance, property and women: some comparative considerations', in Goody, J., Thirsk, J. and Thompson, E.P. (eds), *Family and Inheritance*, Cambridge: Cambridge University Press, pp. 10–36.

Greene, K.V. (1973), 'Inheritance unjustified?', *Journal of Law and Economics* (16), 417–19.

Grossbard-Schechtman, S. (1993), *On the Economics of Marriage. A Theory of Marriage, Labor and Divorce*, Boulder, US: Westview Press.

Hardie, A. (1986), 'Negative child tax for economic efficiency', *Economic Affairs*, Aug. Sept., 17–19.

Harris, M. (1989), *Our Kind*, New York: Harper & Row.

Hoskins, M. (1980), *Income Generation Activities with Women's Participation*, Washington: USAID.

Iglesias Ussel, J. (1994), 'Familia', in *Informe Sociológico Sobre la Situación Social en España*, vol. I, Madrid: Fundación Foessa, pp. 415–547.

Ireland, Th. (1973), 'Inheritance justified: a comment', *Journal of Law and Economics* (16), 421–22.

Jacobsen, J.P. (1994), *The Economics of Gender*, Cambridge, US and Oxford, UK Blackwell.

Kamerman, S.B. and Kahn, A.J. (1987), *Child Care: Facing the Hard Choices*, Dover, MA: Auburn House.

Kamerman, S.B. and Kahn, A.J. (1988), *Mothers Alone. Strategies for a Time of Change*, Dover, MA: Auburn House.

Kamerman, S.B. and Kahn, A.J. (eds), (1989), 'Child care and privatization', in *Privatization and the Welfare State*, Princeton: University Press.

Koller, R.H. (1973), 'Inheritance justified: a comment', *Journal of Law and Economics* (16), 423–24.

Landes, E.M. (1978), 'Economics of alimony', *Journal of Legal Studies*, (7), 35–63.

Landes E.M. and Posner, R. (1978), 'The economics of baby shortage', *Journal of Legal Studies* (7), 322–48.

Lardinois, R. (1986), 'En Inde, la famille, l'État, la femme', in Burguière, A. et al. (eds.) *Histoire de la Famille*, vol. II, pp. 267–99.

Leibowitz, A. (1974), 'Home investment in children', in Schultz, Th.W. (eds), *Economics of the Family*, Chicago: University of Chicago Press.

Lemennicier, B. (1988), *Le Marché du Mariage et de la Famille*, Paris: Presses Universitaires de France.

Malthus, T.R. [1803] (1967), *Essay on the Principle of Population*, London: Dent, (two vols).

Marshall, A. (1925), *Principles of Economics,* London: Macmillan.

McClements, L.D. (1977), 'Equivalence scales for children', *Journal of Public Economics*, (8), 191–210.

Mill, J.S. [1848] (1909), *Principles of Political Economy* (ed. S.W. Ashley), London: Longmans.

Ministerio de Cultura-Instituto de la Mujer (1988), *La Mujer en Cifras*, Madrid: Ministerio de Culture-Instituto de la Mujer.

Minois, G. (1987), *Histoire de la Vieillesse. De l'Antiquité à la Renaissance*, Paris: Fayard.

Mirowski, P. (1994), 'Tit for tat: concepts of exchange, higgling and barter in two episodes in the history of economic anthropology', in De Marchi, N. and Morgan, M.S. (eds), *Higgling. Transactors and their Markets in the History of Economics*, Durham: Duke University Press, pp. 313–42.

Morgan, E.V. (1984), *Choice in Pensions. The Political Economy of Saving for Retirement*, London: Institute of Economic Affairs.

Morgan, P. (1995), *Farewell to the Family? Public Policy and Family Breakdown in Britain and the USA*, London: Institute of Economic Affairs.

Murdock, G.P. (1937), 'Comparative data on the division of labour by sex', *Social Forces*, 551–53.

Musgrave, P. and Musgrave, R. (1989), *Public Finance in Theory and Practice*, 5th edn., New York: McGraw-Hill.

Nerlove, M., Razin, A. and Sadka, E. (1987a), *Population Policy and Individual Choice: A Theoretical Investigation*, Washington, DC: International Food Policy Research Institute.

Nerlove, M., Razin, A. and Sadka, E. (1987b), *Welfare Economics of Endogenous Fertility*, New York: Academic Press.

OECD (1991), *Employment Outlook*, Paris: OECD.

Papps, I. (1980), *For Love or Money? A Preliminary Economic Analysis of Marriage and the Family*, London: Institute of Economic Affairs.

Papps, I. (1983), 'Do we need a policy for the family?', *Economic Affairs*, June, 252–55.

Papps, I. (1984), 'Benefits for poor children', *Economic Affairs*, October–December, 21–3.

Peters, H.E. (1986), 'Marriage and divorce: informational constraints and private contracting', *American Economic Review* (76), 437–54.

Peters, H.E. (1992), 'Marriage and divorce: reply', *American Economic Review* (82), 686–93.

Phillips, R. (1991), *Untying the Knot*, Cambridge: Cambridge University Press.

Pigou, A.C. (1938), *The Economics of Welfare*, London: Macmillan.

Posner, R. (1992a), *Economic Analysis of Law*, Boston: Little, Brown and Company.

Posner, R. (1992b), *Sex and Reason*, Cambridge, MA: Harvard University Press.

Pyle, R.C. (1994), *Family Law*, Albany: Delmar.

Radin, M.J. (1987), 'Market-inalienability', *Harvard Law Review* (100), 1849–1937.

Rathbone, E. (1917), 'The remuneration of women's services', *Economic Journal*, (27), 55–68.

Reform of Social Security (Green Paper), (1985), London.

Scitovsky, T. (1941), 'A note on welfare propositions in economics', *Review of Economic Studies* (9), 77–88.

Sempere and Guarinos, J. (1847), *Historia de los vínculos y mayorazgos*, Madrid.

Smith, A. [1776] (1976), *An Inquiry into the Nature and Causes of the Wealth of Nations*, Oxford: Oxford University Press (two vols).

Smith, A. (1978a), *Lectures on Jurisprudence*, Oxford: Oxford University Press.

Smith, A. [1759] (1978b), *The Theory of Moral Sentiments*, Oxford: Oxford University Press.

Spring, E. (1995), *Law, Land and Family. Aristocratic Inheritance in England, 1300 to 1800*, Chapel Hill: North Carolina University Press.

Stangeland, C.E. (1966), *Premalthusian Doctrines of Population: A Study in the History of Economic Theory*, New York: A.M. Kelley.

Stark, O. (1989), 'Altruism and the quality of life', *American Economic Review*, (79), Papers and Proceedings, pp. 86–90.

Stark, O. (1995), *Altruism and Beyond: an Economic Analysis of Transfers and Exchanges within Families and Groups*, Cambridge: Cambridge University Press.

Swedberg, R. (1990), *Economics and Sociology*, Princeton: Princeton University Press.

Trebilcock, M.J. (1993), *The Limits of Freedom of Contract,* Cambridge, MA: Harvard University Press.

Tullock, G. (1971), 'Inheritance justified', *Journal of Law and Economics* (14), 465–74.

Tullock, G. (1973), 'Inheritance rejustified', *Journal of Law and Economics* (16), 425–74.

Tullock, G. (1980), 'Efficient rent seeking', in Buchanan, J., Tollison, R. and Tullock, G. (eds), *Toward a Theory of Rent-Seeking Society*, College Station: Texas A and M University Press, pp. 91–112.

Whithead, B.D. (1993), 'Dan Quayle was right', *The Atlantic Monthly*, April, 47–84.

Williamson, O. (1986), *Economic Organization: Firms, Markets and Policy Control*, New York: Harvester Wheatsheaf.

Wilson, E.O. (1975), *Sociobiology: the New Synthesis*, Cambridge, MA: The Belknap Press of Harvard University Press.

Wilson, E.O. (1978), *On Human Nature*, Cambridge, MA: Harvard University Press.

Winegarden, C.R. (1984), 'Women's fertility, market work and marital status: a test of the new household economics with international data', *Economica* (51), 447–56.

Wolf, M. (1994), 'Marital economics', *Financial Times*, 21 Sept.

World Health Organization (1985), *Coverage of Maternity Care: a Tabulation of Available Information*, World Health Organization.

Index